THE CHEROKEE FREEDMEN

Recent Titles in
Contributions in Afro-American and African Studies
Series Adviser: *Hollis R. Lynch*

RED OVER BLACK: Black Slavery Among the Cherokee Indians
R. Halliburton, Jr.

NEW RULERS IN THE GHETTO: The Community Development
Corporation and Urban Poverty
Harry Edward Berndt

BLACK ETHOS: Northern Urban Life and Thought, 1890–1930
David Gordon Nielson

THE FLN IN ALGERIA: Party Development in a Revolutionary Society
Henry F. Jackson

OLD ROOTS IN NEW LANDS: Historical and Anthropological
Perspectives on Black Experiences in the Americas
Ann M. Pescatello, editor

AFRICANS AND SEMINOLES: From Removal to Emancipation
Daniel F. Littlefield, Jr.

AMERICAN SOCIALISM AND BLACK AMERICANS: From the Age
of Jackson to World War II
Philip S. Foner

BLACK ACADEMIC LIBRARIES AND RESEARCH COLLECTIONS:
An Historical Survey
Jessie Carney Smith

THE AMERICAN SLAVE: A Composite Autobiography, Supplementary
Series
George P. Rawick, editor

TRABELIN' ON: The Slave Journey to an Afro-Baptist Faith
Mechal Sobel

REVISITING BLASSINGAME'S *THE SLAVE COMMUNITY*:
The Scholars Respond
Al-Tony Gilmore, editor

THE "HINDERED HAND:" Cultural Implications of Early African-
American Fiction
Arlene A. Elder

THE
CHEROKEE
FREEDMEN

FROM EMANCIPATION TO AMERICAN CITIZENSHIP

DANIEL F. LITTLEFIELD, JR.

Contributions in Afro-American and African Studies, Number 40

Greenwood Press
Westport, Connecticut • London, England

Library of Congress Cataloging in Publication Data

Littlefield, Daniel F.
  The Cherokee freedmen.

  (Contributions in Afro-American and African
studies; no. 40 ISSN 0069-9624)
  Bibliography: p.
  Includes index.
  1. Cherokee Indians—Slaves, Ownership of.
2. Afro-Americans—Indian Territory—Relations with
Indians. 3. Indians of North America—Indian
Territory—Slaves, Ownership of. 4. Freedmen—
Indian Territory. I. Title. II. Series.
  E99.C5L5 301.45'19'7073 78-53659
  ISBN 0-313-20413-6

Library of Congress Catalog Card Number: 78-53659
ISBN: 0-313-20413-6
ISSN: 0069-9624

First published in 1978

Greenwood Press, Inc.
51 Riverside Avenue, Westport, Connecticut 06880

Printed in the United States of America

10 9 8 7 6 5 4 3 2 1

To MARY ANN

CONTENTS

ILLUSTRATIONS

PREFACE

From the end of the American Civil War until the citizenship
rolls of the Cherokee Nation were closed in 1907 and the Nation
was dissolved, people of African descent played a decisive role in
Cherokee history. Although the history of African slavery among
the Cherokees has been presented in R. Halliburton's *Red over
Black*, there has been no study of the Cherokee freedmen from
their emancipation to their admission to citizenship in the United
States.

This book represents such a study; it emphasizes the freedmen's
struggle to establish their rights to citizenship in the Cherokee
Nation and, as citizens, to the lands and tribal funds. It demonstrates
the ways in which the struggle helped lay the groundwork for
inroads upon Cherokee autonomy over internal affairs of the tribe
and how it contributed ultimately to the dissolution of the Cherokee
Nation and the opening of the Indian Territory to non-Indian
settlement.

I have tried to capture the drama, complexity, and—sometimes
—tedium of forty years of legal maneuvering by a people trying to
define their rights and, in some respects, to define themselves.
Although it was not my original intent, I have presented the history
of a people caught in the wheels of bureaucratic machinery that was
often as absurd, cold, and uncaring as any contrived by Americans
in the twentieth century.

Research for this project was done during my tenure as a Fellow
of the Institute of Southern History at the Johns Hopkins University
in 1973 and 1974. The research was supported by a Younger

Humanist Award from the National Endowment for the Humanities. My thanks go to the National Endowment and to the Johns Hopkins University for making the work possible. My thanks also go to the archivists of the Natural Resources Branch of the National Archives and to Martha Blaine, archivist in the Indian Archives Division of the Oklahoma Historical Society. They were most helpful in the research stages of the book but bear no responsibility for its content. My apologies go to all others who have helped shape this work in some way but whom I have not mentioned.

DANIEL F. LITTLEFIELD, JR.

THE
CHEROKEE
FREEDMEN

chapter 1   BACKGROUNDS

Between 1839, when removal of the great majority of Cherokee Indians to Indian Territory was completed, and the outbreak of the American Civil War, the Cherokees established the Western Cherokee Nation. Despite political strife during the early years, it was the time during which the Cherokees established the social and civil institutions that prevailed, though modified, during the post-Civil War years.[1] It was the time, too, in which were founded many of the divisive forces among the Cherokees, forces that contributed in great measure to the dissolution of the Cherokee Nation and to the extinguishment of its title to the tribal lands.

When the great body of Cherokees arrived in the West in 1839, there began several years of civil strife that often bordered on war and threatened to create an irreparable division of the Cherokee people. The Cherokees were split into three factions. The first was the Old Settler party, comprised of those who had voluntarily removed to the West before the signing of the removal treaty of 1835. Most of them had occupied lands in northwestern Arkansas until 1829 when, in consequence of a treaty during the previous year, they gave up those lands in exchange for lands in the northeastern part of present-day Oklahoma. The second faction was known as the Treaty or Ridge party, comprised of Cherokees led by John Ridge and his father, Major Ridge, who had encouraged and approved the removal treaty. Many of this group had voluntarily removed to the West and had joined the Old Settlers after the signing of the removal treaty but before the forced removal of 1838 and 1839. The Old Settler and Treaty party Cherokees numbered about six thousand in 1840. The emigrant Cherokees, who came over the "Trail of Tears," were known as the Ross party, for they had supported Chief John Ross in his opposition to the removal treaty. They numbered about sixteen thousand.

The civil conflict erupted over the system of laws that would prevail in the Cherokee country. The Old Settlers, who were supported by the Treaty party, insisted that since they had been in the West for two decades prior to the removal of the Ross Party and since they had a system of laws already in operation, their laws should prevail. The Old Settlers had written laws but no constitution. Their executive department consisted of three chiefs of equal rank, and the legislative department had a two-house council—the National Committee and Council—composed of members elected from each of four districts into which the country had been divided. Each district had a judge who heard civil and criminal cases, from whose court the convicted could appeal to the council. The laws of the Western Cherokees were enforced by a squad of mounted police, the National Light-Horse in each district.[2]

The Ross party Cherokees were not willing to accept the Old Settlers' system of government. They had brought with them from the East over a decade of experience in constitutional government, and they were led by men of their own choosing. Thus contention quickly arose over which group would maintain political power. In June 1839 a meeting of the whole tribe was called to settle the matter. At Takatokah or Double Springs, northwest of present-day Tahlequah, John Ross invited the Old Settlers to join his party in setting up a government. Apparently prompted by Treaty party Cherokees, the Old Settlers insisted that their government should prevail, and the Cherokees reached an impasse. On June 22, the day following the adjournment of the meeting, John Ridge, Major Ridge, and Elias Boudinot—all leaders of the Treaty party—were brutally murdered. Other members of the Treaty and Old Settler parties fled to the military post at Fort Gibson or elsewhere to save their lives, which they feared were in danger.

In the midst of this turmoil, the Ross party called a meeting on July 1 and, with the cooperation of some of the Old Settlers, adopted an act of union that nominally unified all of the Cherokees into the Cherokee Nation. In September a convention was called at Tahlequah, where a constitution was drafted and adopted on September 6. John Ross was elected principal chief by an overwhelming majority. The establishment of the new government did not bring stability to the Nation, however. The next several years were marked by bitter factionalism that was often expressed

in murder, assassination, and house burning. In 1846 the only solution
seemed to be division of Cherokee lands into two separate nations. However, a treaty on August 6 of that year reaffirmed the common title to
Cherokee lands, declared a general amnesty to all who would return to
the Nation by December 1, and abolished the bands of armed police
that had been sanctioned by the Ross government to keep order. After
that, the factionalism declined and became dormant for a number of
years.

The Cherokees' 1839 constitution was the last one they wrote, and,
with amendments, it formed the basis for their government until 1898.
Obviously modeled after the Constitution of the United States, it separated the powers of government into the legislative, executive, and judiciary branches. The Nation was to be divided into eight districts—Skin
Bayou (later renamed Sequoyah), Illinois, Canadian, Flint, Going Snake,
Tahlequah, Delaware, and Saline—from which members would be elected
to the National Committee, or upper house, and to the Council, or lower
house, of the National Council, which met each fall to pass legislation.
The boundary lines were adjusted from time to time, and a ninth district,
Cooweescoowee, was later created. The executive branch of government
consisted of the principal chief and assistant chief, who were elected by
the qualified voters of the Nation, as well as an executive council of five
and a national treasurer selected by the National Council to advise and
assist the chief. The judiciary consisted of a supreme court, four circuit
courts, and a district court in each district.[3]

The Cherokee Nation proper, the lands governed by the constitutional
government, lay in the northeastern part of Oklahoma and embraced all
of present-day Delaware, Adair, Sequoyah, Cherokee, Craig, Nowata, and
Washington counties. It embraced as well the land in Ottawa County west
of the Neosho River, the northern part of Tulsa County, most of Rogers
and Mayes counties, a strip of land on the eastern side of Wagner County,
and the parts of Muskogee and McIntosh counties east of the Missouri,
Kansas, and Texas Railroad. The Cherokees also owned a tract of 800,000
acres, known as the Neutral Lands, in the southeastern corner of Kansas,
and the Cherokee Outlet, a strip of land sixty miles wide south of the
Kansas border between the ninety-sixth and the one hundredth meridian.

When the Ross party Cherokees arrived upon these lands in 1839, they
found the Old Settlers and the recently arrived Treaty party Cherokees
settled in the Cherokee Nation proper between the western border of

Arkansas and the Neosho or Grand River. They had comfortable log cabins, and a few of the more wealthy, who operated grist mills and salt works and traded with the western tribes, had large houses. There was some education through missionaries, but education was not emphasized. In contrast, the emigrants were poverty ridden, except for some mixed bloods who were able to bring their wealth with them from the East. The Cherokees had lost much during removal. A decade before that, the Eastern Cherokees had had 762 looms, 2,486 spinning wheels, 2,843 plows, 10 sawmills, 31 blacksmith shops, and 8 cotton gins.[4] During the twenty years following removal, the emigrants reestablished their domestic industries, took over much of the salt industry from the Old Settlers, and developed merchandising enterprises. Two owned steamboats that plied the waters of the Arkansas, Mississippi, and Ohio rivers. However, the Cherokees were predominantly farmers and stockmen. They still held lands communally, and by law a Cherokee could improve as much of the public domain as he could manage as long as he did not place his improvements—that is, houses, barns, fences, or crops—within one quarter of a mile of another's improvement. The Cherokees farmed vegetables, fruits, and grains and by 1859 had over a hundred thousand acres in cultivation. They also had established an agricultural society that held fairs, had introduced the latest farming machinery, and had developed a great industry in cattle raising, owning nearly a half-million head of cattle in 1859. They had as well sixteen thousand hogs and five thousand sheep.[5]

During this time, the Cherokees underwent changes in their life-styles. They changed from using the clay pots and wooden utensils they were forced to make and use after removal to china and metal utensils, and from cloth of their own manufacture, dyed by home-grown indigo and hickory bark, alum, and sumac, to imported cloth trade goods. While some retained the traditional turbans, hunting shirts, moccasins, and leggings, most adopted the dress of the whites: pantaloons, frock coats, top hats, shoes, overcoats. Most of the Cherokees lived in double log cabins, but some of the mixed bloods had clapboard houses, and some of the more wealthy built fine homes that were painted, carpeted, and furnished with imported furniture. Many had good libraries. John Ross's Rose Cottage and George Murrell's home, which stands today, were prominent examples. Some public buildings such as the supreme court building, which still stands, and the seminaries were made of bricks manufactured by the Cherokees. There were incorporated towns, the most prominent example being Tahlequah, the capital of the Nation, which by 1850 had eight stores, two dentists, a saddler, a tailor, three blacksmiths, a shoemaker, five hotels, and three taverns.[6] The Cherokees enjoyed their traditional racket-ball game called the ball play, dances after the fashion of the Virginia reel, and horse races, several Cherokees owning blooded racing stock. In 1859 the first Masonic lodge was established in the Cherokee Nation. Most of the Cherokees gave up their native ceremonials and medicine, and the distinctions of clan fell into disuse. Most of these changes can be attributed to two causes: education and Christianity.

Education in the Anglo mode had begun among the Cherokees through missionary efforts in 1801, and public schools had been established in 1803. In the West mission schools had been conducted among the Old Settlers since 1820. These were continued, and others were established, after removal. In 1841 the Cherokees established a common school system, which by 1859 included thirty schools with fifteen hundred students, who learned the three Rs, English grammar, geography, and history. In 1851 the Cherokees opened their high schools, the Male and Female seminaries, where basic education was continued, and higher mathematics and the classics were studied. The Cherokees were a literate nation. In 1852 William P. Ross boasted that the number of adults who could not read or write could be counted on one's fingers. Ross no doubt exaggerated, but most could read and write, if not English, at least their own language.[7] Sequoyah had given them his famous syllabary in the early 1820s. Literacy was bolstered by the *Cherokee Advocate,* the national newspaper published in English and Cherokee at Tahlequah. At Park Hill Mission, the Reverend Samuel Austin Worcester set up a press and published books, scriptures, tracts, almanacs, hymnals, and other works in both languages. In 1845 and 1846 he printed 276,000 pages in Cherokee, and in 1855 he printed over a million.[8]

Upon removal, there were an estimated two thousand Christian Cherokees, mainly Methodists, Baptists, and Presbyterians. In the next twenty years, church membership greatly increased, and there was a corresponding growth in temperance work. The Cherokees established the Cherokee Temperance Society, with chapters throughout the Nation, and the Cherokee Bible Society. The Christianization of the Cherokees and the increase in the number of native preachers made inroads on the vestiges of native practices.

Among the Cherokees were a number of distinct racial groups. By far

the largest group was the mixed bloods, often referred to by the pejora-
tive term half-breeds, although many were less than half Cherokee. Intermarriage with European immigrants became commonplace in the late
eighteenth century. During his travels among the Cherokees in the 1770s,
William Bartram met a number of traders who had married Cherokees
and had mixed-blood families. In 1796 Indian agent Benjamin Hawkins
encountered many Cherokee mixed bloods with names such as Adair,
Ross, Vann, Wofford, and Petit. By 1809 the Cherokees numbered 12,395,
of whom an estimated half were of mixed blood, and there were 341 intermarried whites. In 1860, because of the decline in population during and
after removal, the Cherokees by blood numbered only 13,821, but the
number of whites had increased to 716.[9]

Another racial group consisted of full bloods, a term that meant more
than just the amount of Cherokee blood a citizen had in his veins. It indicated a distinct social, political, and economic outlook. The full bloods
were traditionalists who held on to the native ways and language long
after the majority of the tribe had given them up. Although Christianity
made inroads upon those ways, it did not make the full bloods dissatisfied
with their simple lives on their small farms in the remote and more rugged sections of the Nation.[10] Nor did it make them more inclined toward
education. The full bloods represented a decided minority as time passed.
In 1863 Wiley Britton, who was with the Union Army in the Indian Territory, anticipated the problem that the full bloods were later to face:
maintaining their identity and resisting amalgamation into Anglo-Amer-
ican society. Britton wrote, "It will probably not be many generations
before we shall be contriving means, not how to kill off the Indians,
but how to preserve the few which are left." He noted the extensive
amalgamation that had already taken place among the Cherokees and
commented that "a considerable part of the population of the Nation"
were of one-half Cherokee blood or less.[11]

The full bloods differed from the mixed bloods in another significant way: they generally did not hold African slaves. The Cherokees
had begun holding African slaves in colonial days, and by the time of
removal, they owned large numbers of blacks, as did the Choctaws,
Chickasaws, Creeks, and Seminoles. In the West, blacks represented a
significant part of the population of the Cherokee Nation.

The Cherokees held a greater number of slaves than any of the
other tribes in the Indian Territory. In 1835, on the eve of removal,

the Eastern Cherokees owned 1,592, and by 1860 the Cherokees had 2,511. Historians agree that slavery among the Cherokees was little different from that in the white South and that the status of their slaves and free blacks declined with the increasing severity of their laws following removal. Their constitution of 1839 admitted to citizenship the descendants of Cherokee women and black men but not those of Cherokee men and black women, and it excluded from public office all persons of "negro or mulatto parentage." An 1839 law prescribed up to fifty lashes for free citizens who married "any slave or person of color" who was not a citizen and one hundred lashes for a black male convicted of marrying a citizen. A law of 1840 prohibited slaves and free blacks not of Cherokee blood from holding improvements (houses, barns, crops, and fences) and other property. Property then held by blacks was ordered sold to the highest bidder. The same law forbade free blacks to sell spirituous liquors in the Nation. An 1841 law created patrol companies to capture and punish any slaves caught off their master's premises without a pass and to give up to thirty-nine lashes to any black not entitled to Cherokee privileges found carrying a weapon of any kind. Another law prohibited teaching slaves and free blacks not of Cherokee blood to read or write. In the aftermath of a slave revolt in 1842, the Cherokees ordered all blacks not freed by Cherokee citizens to leave the Nation by January 1, 1843. Any who refused to do so were to be reported for expulsion. If a Cherokee citizen freed his slaves, he was responsible for their conduct as free blacks. If he died or left the Nation, the free blacks were to give unspecified "satisfactory security" to one of the circuit judges for their conduct. Any free black found guilty of "aiding, abetting, or decoying" slaves to leave their owners was to receive one hundred lashes. An 1848 law prohibited teaching any black to read or write, an 1855 law prohibited hiring teachers with abolitionist sentiments, and, finally, in 1859, the council passed an act requiring all free blacks to leave the Nation; it was, however, vetoed by Chief John Ross.[12]

It is not surprising that large factions in each of the so-called Five Civilized Tribes joined the war effort of the Confederacy during the Civil War. They were slaveholding peoples who had slave states to the east and south of their lands. As significant as that, however, was that during the Buchanan administration, people of southern sympathy held or had access to every governmental office within the Southern Superintendency of Indian Affairs. They influenced all sources of information. In the early months of conflict, to sway Indian sympathy toward the Confederacy, postmasters told the Indians that the U. S. government had fallen and otherwise undermined the Indians' confidence in the United States. Because of the manpower needs of the war, military posts, government stores, and ordnance depots in the West were abandoned, and the Union was late in recognizing the need to assist the Indians in resisting the overtures of the Confederates. The Indians felt abandoned. [13]

The Confederacy attempted to recruit Indians for its cause. By late January 1861 politicians in Arkansas were looking toward secession from the Union and wanted to make sure that they had Indian allies on their western flank. Governor Henry M. Rector asked Cherokee Chief John Ross to support Arkansas in its action: "Your people, in their institutions, productions, latitude, and natural sympathies are allied to the common brotherhood of the slaveholding States. Our people and yours are natural allies in war, and friends in peace. Your country is salubrious and fertile, and possesses the highest capacity for future progress and development by the application of 'slave labor.'" He continued: "It is well established that the Indian country west of Arkansas is looked to by the incoming administration of Mr. Lincoln as fruitful fields ripe for the harvest of abolitionism, free-soilers, and northern mountebanks. We hope to find in you friends willing to co-operate with the south in defense of her institutions, her honor, and her firesides, and with whom the slaveholding States are willing to share a common future, and to afford protection commensurate with your exposed condition and your subsisting monetary interests with the general government."[14] Elias Rector, the southern superintendent of Indian affairs, supported his cousin's view, but Ross, determined to keep his nation neutral, assured Governor Rector that he would not give in to the abolitionists or freesoilers.[15]

During 1861 Cherokee relations deteriorated into factionalism again as the pro-Union organization of full bloods, the Keetoowah Society, became active. This group was opposed by a pro-Southern organization, the Knights of the Golden Circle. With the internal rift, Cherokee neutrality became less secure as more pressure was applied from southern politicians.[16]

Albert Pike of Arkansas was sent to the Indian Territory as a commissioner for the Confederate government, and before the end of 1861, he had concluded a treaty with each of the Five Civilized Tribes. The Cherokees were the last to yield. Chief Ross successfully rejected his appeals until August, when under military threat from the Confederates, he called an executive council meeting at Tahlequah, the capital. An estimated four thousand Cherokees attended the meeting, at which resolutions were adopted allying the Cherokees with the Confederacy. A Cherokee regiment was raised, and on October 7, the Cherokees signed a treaty with the Confederate States of America. As early as December, however, when Union forces displayed strength in the territory, Cherokees began to defect in great numbers to the Union side, and Ross shortly thereafter left the Nation and settled in Philadelphia. The Cherokee National Council abrogated the Confederate treaty in February 1863, and by the time the war ended, a large majority of the Cherokees were in the Union camp.[17]

At the outbreak of the war, some slaves of the Cherokees and other tribes were taken by their masters to the southern part of the Indian Territory or to Texas. Many, however, escaped to Kansas and other places of refuge. Not all of the slaves or free blacks affiliated with the Five Civilized Tribes survived the war, and not all of those who survived returned to the Indian Territory. Those who did looked to the United States to secure for them a place in the political and economic structures of the various nations. Of the slaveholding Indians in the Indian Territory, only the Cherokees had emancipated their slaves during the war, but they did not entertain the idea of adopting their former slaves or free blacks into the tribe. Yet that was what the United States required of them in the Treaty of 1866.

Although the Cherokees immediately adopted their blacks according to treaty stipulations, many of the Cherokee freedmen were excluded from rights because they had failed to return to the Nation within the six-months' limitation set by the treaty. For others the struggle for rights guaranteed by the treaty lasted throughout the forty-year period from emancipation to the freedmen's admission as citizens of the United States, and the struggle profoundly influenced the direction of the Cherokee history.

Definition of the social, political, and legal status of the freed blacks who lived among the Cherokees was perhaps the most complex problem the tribe had to deal with from the end of the Civil War until the dissolution of the Nation in 1907. The freedman question was constantly before the Cherokee public. Citizenship cases so encumbered the Cherokee judicial and legislative systems that the National Council had to create special commissions to hear them. Officials of the Interior Department refused to recognize the authority of the commissions regarding the freedmen, however, and in so doing denied the Cherokees control over that part of their internal affairs and therefore made serious inroads upon Cherokee autonomy. The freedmen's struggle for rights to citizenship and a share in the tribal lands and funds resulted in long, wearisome, and often legal battles that sometimes achieved nothing more than a sapping of the strength of both groups. That struggle, which began in 1866, had social implications that lasted well into the twentieth century.

NOTES

1. Sources useful in the sketch of the social history of the Cherokees during postremoval days are Grant Foreman, *The Five Civilized Tribes* (Norman: University of Oklahoma Press, 1937), 281-420; Grace Steele Woodward, *The Cherokees* (Norman: University of Oklahoma Press, 1963), 219-252; and Morris L. Wardell, *A Political History of the Cherokee Nation, 1838-1907* (Norman: University of Oklahoma Press, 1938), 3-75. Contemporary sketches appear in Reuben Gold Thwaites, ed., *Early Western Travels, 1748-1846* (Reprint ed., New York: AMS Press, 1966), vols. 13, 17, 20, and Grant Foreman, ed., *A Traveler in Indian Territory: The Journal of Ethan Allen Hitchcock, late Major-General in the United States Army* (Cedar Rapids, Iowa: The Torch Press, 1930).

2. *Laws of the Cherokee Nation: Adopted by the Council at Various Periods* (Tahlequah, Ind. Ter.: Cherokee Advocate Office, 1852), pt. 1: 151-179.

3. Ibid., pt. 2: 5-27.

4. Foreman, *Five Civilized Tribes,* 356.

5. Ibid., 419.

6. Ibid., 400, 406.

7. Wardell, *Political History,* 117.

8. Foreman, *Five Civilized Tribes,* 367, 413.

9. Benjamin Hawkins, *Letters of Benjamin Hawkins, 1796-1806,* Collections of the Georgia Historical Society, vol. 9 (Savannah: The Morning News, 1916), 19; Foreman, ed., *A Traveler in Indian Territory,* 224n; Michael F. Doran, "Population Statistics of Nineteenth Century Indian Territory," *The Chronicles of Oklahoma* 53 (Winter 1975-76): 501.

10. Woodward, *Cherokees,* 120.

11. Wiley Britton, *Memoirs of the Rebellion on the Border, 1863* (Chicago: Cushing, Thomas & Co., Publishers, 1882), 143.

12. Kenneth Wiggins Porter, *The Negro on the American Frontier* (New York: Arno Press and the New York Times, 1971), 109; Foreman, *Five Civilized Tribes,* 54, 83, 420; William G. McLoughlin, "Red Indians, Black Slavery and White Racism: America's Slaveholding Indians," *American Quarterly* 26 (October 1974): 380-381; R. Halliburton, Jr., "Origins of Black Slavery Among the Cherokees," *The Chronicles of Oklahoma* 52 (Winter 1974-75): 496; *Laws,* pt. 2: 7, 19, 44, 53, 55-56, 71, 173-174, 381; James W. Duncan, "Interesting Ante-Bellum Laws of the Cherokees, Now Oklahoma History," *The Chronicles of Oklahoma* 6 (June 1928): 179; J. B. Davis, "Slavery in the Cherokee Nation," *The Chronicles of Oklahoma* 11 (December 1933): 1066-1067. A book-length study of slavery among the Cherokees is Halliburton, *Red over Black: Black Slavery among the Cherokee Indians* (Westport, Conn.: Greenwood Press, 1977). A list of Cherokees owning ten or more slaves in 1860 is as follows: David Vann (21), William W. Buffington (13), Mariah Cunningham (14), Lucian B. Bell (12), Elizabeth Pack (15), William A. Davis (14), John Glass (28), George Whitmire (25), Cornelius Wright (18), J. M. Starr (16), N. B. Dannenburg (13), John T. Adair (22), Mary Rider (10), Eliza Ratlingord (10), James McKey (19), William L. Holt (12), Felix McNair (14), Kasy McNair (16), R. D. Ross (11), Allen Ross (11), David Vann (34), Charles Landrum (12), Betsy Sanders (13), J. L. Martin (29), J. M. Lynch (25), J. D. Alberty (19), William Alberty (18), Susanna McNair (31), Eliza McNair (13), George W. Gunter (19), Benjamin Johnson (30), David Carter (23), Walker Mayfield (20), Joseph Shepherd (13), John Ross (50), Johnson Foreman (11), George M. Murrell (42), James A. Thompson (16), Rachel Ore (13), Cabbin Smith (11), John Drew (11), Stand Watie (17), Charlotte Drew (10), John Vann (13), I. G. Vore (16), Jane Mitchell (14), Lewis Ross (57), Catey Williams (32), William Musgrove (10), Johnny Whitmire (21), James Lowry (15), Mary Starr (16), Robert Webber (20), Alexander Nave (21), R. M. French (14), Ned Smith (18), William P. Ross (12), John Campbell (13), James Brown (12), Nancy Alberty (14), Thomas B. Wolf (10), Thomas Rider (11), Richard F. Martin (11), James Marcum (11), Sarah Martin (14), Eliza May (15), George W. Adair (15), Lucy Martin (18). National Archives Microfilm Publications, *Microcopy M653* (Schedules of Federal Population Censuses)-54.

13. S. S. Scott to Choctaws et al., December 26, 1862, 38th Cong., 1st Sess., *House Executive Document 1,* pt. 3, 342; John T. Cox to W. G. Coffin, March 18, 1864, 38th Cong., 2d sess., *House Executive Document 1,* 477.

14. Henry M. Rector to John Ross, January 29, 1861, 38th Cong.,
1st sess., *House Executive Document 1,* pt. 3, 345.

15. Woodward, *Cherokees,* 255-256.

16. An authoritative treatment of the dissension among the Cherokees
concerning slavery and the Civil War appears in Wardell, *Political History,*
119-141.

17. Report of the Secretary of the Interior (1863) and Ross to William
P. Dole, April 2, 1863, 38th Cong., 1st sess., *House Executive Document
1,* 292-293, 343-344; Charles C. Royce, "The Cherokee Nation of Indians,"
in *Fifth Annual Report of the Bureau of Ethnology* (Washington, D. C.:
Government Printing Office, 1887), 324-332.

EMANCIPATION
AND ADOPTION

chapter **2**

Although the Cherokee Nation as a whole had formed an alliance with the Confederate States of America, upon the outbreak of hostilities in the West, the Indians soon became divided in sentiment. Ultimately about nine thousand deserted to the Union side while about sixty-five hundred remained allied to the Confederacy. In the course of the war, all suffered, and when the war ended, the Cherokee Nation was in ruin. Crossed and re-crossed by both Union and Confederate military units and raided by foraging parties, guerrillas, bushwhackers, cattle thieves, and border bandits, the Cherokee country suffered more destruction than did any of the other Indian nations that comprised the Indian Territory. Their homes were burned, their treasury robbed, their fences and tools destroyed, their capitol burned, and their schools and seminaries ruined. Their herds, estimated in value at $2 million to $4 million, had been stolen, their fields were overgrown, and their slaves had been freed. The people were scattered, those loyal to the Union having sought refuge in Kansas and the disloyal faction having fled to the southern part of the Indian Territory and to Texas.[1]

Slaves as well as Cherokees had been scattered during the war. Most southern sympathizers took their blacks into the Choctaw and Chickasaw nations and to Texas to prevent their running away, and when the war ended, many were in the Red River Valley. Some had been moved by federal troops to Kansas in the summer of 1862, when troops under the command of Brigadier General James G. Blunt invaded the Indian Territory, then in Confederate hands. The army could not hold the territory and retreated, taking thousands of loyal Cherokees, Creeks, and Seminoles and their households as far as Baxter Springs, Kansas. Most of the Cherokee blacks who went to Kansas remained in refugee camps until the war ended,

while many of the men joined black units of the army. There were a few
blacks at the Sac and Fox Agency, and large groups were camped at Neosho Falls, Mapleton, Garnett, and Osawatomie.[2]

Many of these blacks did not know that early in 1863 they had been
freed. Thomas Pegg, acting principal chief of the pro-Union Cherokees,
called an extraordinary session of the Cherokee National Council, which
convened under federal military protection at Cowskin Prairie in Delaware
District. On February 19 the body passed an act, to become effective on
June 25, 1863, emancipating all slaves within the limits of the Nation.[3]

By late spring of that year, large numbers of freed blacks had come
back to the Cherokee Nation. Their return was made possible by troops
under the command of Colonel W. A. Phillips, who occupied and fortified
an enclosed area of one and one-half square miles at Fort Gibson, where he
remained in command of federal Indian troops north of the Arkansas
River until the end of the war. Anxious to return home, many Indians and
blacks followed the army from Kansas to Fort Gibson. Most were related
to the Indian troops stationed there; others came in from the surrounding
countryside. By midsummer the refugees numbered about six thousand.
Some of the blacks were starving, some lived with their former owners,
and others indiscriminately appropriated for their own use the abandoned
property of Union and Confederate Cherokees alike. This latter the Cherokees considered national property, to which the freedmen had no rights.[4]

The pro-Union Cherokees managed their national affairs through councils. Acting Chief Pegg called for the confiscation of property abandoned
by Cherokees who had joined the Confederacy and for regulations concerning the freed slaves, whose status was unclear. In response, on October
24, 1863, the council provided for the confiscation and sale of the property abandoned by Confederate Cherokees, and in November it declared
that the freedmen had no rights or privileges as Cherokee citizens and
were to be treated as members of other nations or communities. They
could, however, become laborers in the Cherokee Nation on the same
terms as other noncitizens by permit obtained by their employers from
the district courts. The aged were allowed to remain where they could
best be cared for. Those who were formerly held as slaves by Cherokees
and who violated the laws were subject to the laws of the Cherokee Nation. Blacks formerly held by others were subject to immediate expulsion
from the Nation. The council also repealed former laws that prohibited
teaching blacks to read and write or trading with them and that oppressed

blacks, such as forbidding them to own and use firearms. They did not, however, repeal the law forbidding amalgamation of the races.[5] Such were the laws regarding freedmen until a formal end to hostilities between the United States and the Cherokee Nation was obtained.

In May 1865 the tribes and tribal factions who had been allied with the Confederacy met in council and appointed delegates from each tribe to visit Washington and confer with the government. Instead the government sent a board of commissioners to meet the delegates at Fort Smith. It consisted of Dennis N. Cooley, commissioner of Indian affairs, Elijah Sells, superintendent for the Southern superintendency, Thomas Wistar, a leader among the Society of Friends, Brigadier General W. S. Harney of the U. S. Army, and Colonel Ely S. Parker of General Grant's staff.[6]

When the meeting convened at Fort Smith on September 8, 1865, the Confederate Indians had not arrived. Nevertheless, Cooley presented to those already in attendance the President's wishes to renew alliances with the Indians. The Indians were told that by aligning themselves with the Confederacy, they had forfeited all rights due them under former treaties with the United States and must consider themselves at the mercy of the government. The commissioners, however, assured them that the government would recognize the loyalty of those who had fought for the Union and had suffered in its behalf.[7]

Cooley made plain the penalties that the government would assess for the Indians' disloyalty. By way of new treaties, the President would insist on certain stipulations, among them that slavery be abolished and that all persons held in bondage be unconditionally emancipated and incorporated into the tribes on an equal footing with the original members or that they be otherwise provided for. Another condition was that slavery or involuntary servitude could never exist in the tribes except in punishment of a crime. However, Cooley insisted that those who had remained loyal, even though their nation may have gone over to the enemy, would be liberally provided for. After a few days of the council, the commissioners became convinced that no final treaties could be concluded until the differences between the pro-Union and pro-Confederate factions were resolved. Therefore they drafted a preliminary treaty to be signed by those delegates present, rejecting treaties with all other parties, reaffirming allegiance to the United States, and agreeing to reestablish peace with them. Both factions of Cherokees signed the document.[8]

The southern Cherokees had reservations regarding certain stipulations the government wanted written into the final treaty, however. Although they accepted the abolition of slavery as an accomplished fact and were willing to recognize it by proper acts of council, they objected to incorporating the freedmen into the tribe on an equal footing with the Indians. Doing so would benefit neither the blacks nor the Indians, they insisted. "That the emancipated negro must be 'suitably provided for' is a natural sequence of his emancipation," the Cherokees said, but it was such a "serious and delicate" question that they wanted more time to consider and act upon it.[9]

Throughout the remaining days of the meeting, the commissioners accomplished little more than making arrangements for delegations from both factions to go to Washington at a later date and work out a treaty. Cooley warned the Cherokee factions that should they not settle their differences, the government would do so for them.[10]

During the next several months, Cherokees and freedmen returned to the Nation, many straggling in. One large group, including over two hundred freedmen, asked the government to remove them from Mapleton, Garnett, and Osawatomie, Kansas, during the winter of 1865-66 under the direction of Dr. W. L. G. Miller of the Cherokee Nation. Several of the freedman families had wagons, teams, ponies, and oxen, but most needed assistance in removing to the Nation. Elijah Sells, the superintendent of Indian affairs in charge, sympathized with the blacks but was unsure of their legal status. They belonged to the Indians, and he had ordered rations issued to them as destitute refugees. But were they to be officially recognized as Indians? Uncertain, he sent the issue to Commissioner Cooley, whose answer was clear: the blacks were to be removed to the Cherokee Nation, and no distinction was to be made between members of the tribe who had been held in bondage and those who had been free. In all cases the blacks were to receive the same annuities, lands, and educational advantages as the Cherokees.[11] Although these policies had not yet become the law of the land, Cooley's answer showed the government's determination to impose its views upon the Indians.

Government officials anticipated problems in instituting their policy of equal status for the freedmen. In late October 1865 Brevet Major General John B. Sanborn was assigned to regulate "the relations between the Freedmen in the Indian Territory and their former masters as the Secretary of the Interior may indicate." Where Sanborn found relations between the freedmen and the former masters amicable and satisfactory to both, he was not to interfere or to disturb them. But where he found rights denied or abuses existing, he was to give immediate relief. He was to encourage the freedmen to support themselves by making written contracts with persons who were willing to hire them for up to one year as laborers either for wages or as sharecroppers. Sanborn and the Indian agents were to cooperate in seeing that the freedmen were allowed to occupy lands of their own so that they could realize the profits of their own labor. He was to impress upon the Indians the justice of admitting the freedmen to rights of person and property and to the equal enjoyment of what bounty the Cherokee national government might thereafter bestow. Sanborn was also to broach the idea of an equal enjoyment of civil rights, using the arguments that in granting it, the Indians would be following the example of the whites, as well as increasing the strength of the Indian nation.[12] Ironically the government was asking the Indians to do something that the whites were ultimately not willing to do.

At the time of Sanborn's appointment, rumors were rife in the Indian Territory that murder and other violence were being perpetrated upon the freedmen. Freedmen complained to General H. J. Hunt, commanding the Frontier District of the Department of Arkansas at Fort Smith, yet they were not able to testify first hand to the murders. Hunt ascribed the rumors to the general uneasiness that gripped the freedmen. Some Indians said that they were free, while others insisted that they were still slaves. Hunt took the safe route, telling them that they must support themselves and work quietly with their present owners, making contracts for wages when suitable wages were offered. For the meantime, he asked them to "keep quiet and bear the evils that attend their change in condition as well as possible." Hunt thought the freedmen "very reasonable" concerning his advice, and they seemed content with their prospects. Upon his inquiry concerning official views of the freedmen's status, Hunt was informed by Commissioner Cooley that "the constitutional number of states having ratified the anti-slavery amendment, there is not, in fact, a slave within the limits of the United States."[13] The question, of course, was whether the laws of the United States extended to the Indian Territory.

When Sanborn arrived in Fort Smith near the end of 1865, he held preconceived ideas concerning the status of the freedmen of the Indian Territory. He believed, mistakenly, that before the war the blacks of the ter-

ritory were not legal, but voluntary, slaves who had the right to leave
their masters and go anywhere. If they had escaped to a free state, he
reasoned, they could not have been returned by process of court. Sanborn
disagreed with Hunt, who thought that it would be disastrous to inform
the blacks that they were now free. Hunt argued that they would abandon
their homes, rush to the military posts, and become completely dependent
on the government. Sanborn felt that if they were informed of their pro-
jected rights among the Indians, they would remain where they were. They
would have to be told sometime, he argued, and the sooner, the better. To
Sanborn, the best course for the government was to consider the blacks as
parts of the tribes to which they belonged and to give the freedmen a
choice of staying or leaving. Those who remained, he believed, should
have all the rights, interests, and annuities of Indians. Sanborn thought
it important to confer upon the freedmen at once the right to hold and
acquire real estate to make them feel responsible for the contracts they
made by making their property liable if the contracts were broken.[14]

Sanborn established headquarters at Fort Smith and made his policies
known through circulars. The first, released on January 1, 1866, directed
the agents to impress upon the Indians a "correct idea" of the new relation between them and their former slaves, stressing that the freedmen
were now invested with all the rights of free men. It confirmed the government's commitment to protecting the freedmen in their persons. An outrage committed upon a freedman would be considered an outrage upon
the United States. The circular instructed the agents to see that fair contracts for wages were made between Indians and freedmen and required
contracts for periods longer than a month to be put in writing. It also announced that the government would no longer tolerate the system of
polygamy, which had always existed to some extent among the Indians
and therefore had been practiced by some of the freedmen. Freedmen
would be allowed to take only one wife; those cohabiting at that time
would be considered legally married. Marriages that had been solemnized
by Indian custom were binding and valid, and until further provisions
were made, the agent could take the mutual pledges of couples and issue marriage certificates. Finally, the circular committed the government
to removal of all prejudice against the freedmen on the part of the Indians.[15] This last point reflected the obvious naiveté of government officials in assuming that absorption of the freedmen into the Indian tribes
could be effected without discrimination or social and racial prejudice.

The second circular, issued on January 2, authorized Indian agents to sign ration returns for destitute freedmen and commissaries of subsistence to issue rations "in case of great destitution."[16] On his first visit to the Cherokee country a few days later, Sanborn found the freedmen "the most industrious, economical, and, in many respects, the more intelligent" segment of the population. They wanted to remain in the Cherokee Nation on land set apart for their exclusive use. The matter of segregated lands had been much discussed in the Indian Territory, he found, and the freedmen therefore were inclined to do no more work than was necessary in improving the lands they occupied because they expected to be relocated. Sanborn urged that some decision about separate lands be made before spring, for plowing and planting would begin as early as the first of March. If the blacks were not to be resettled, they should know at once. Sanborn believed that they could survive by themselves because most of them had ox teams, and among their numbers were blacksmiths, carpenters, and wheelwrights.

The Cherokees were divided concerning the freedmen. A large number argued that the government should remove the freedmen from the Cherokee Nation since the government was responsible for their freedom. Another group, including Lewis Downing, who was then acting as principal chief, favored their remaining in the Nation on land set apart for their use, and he expected civil rights to be granted to the freedmen before long. Sanborn doubted the propriety of leaving the freedmen to the laws and customs of the Indians; such action would make their position anomalous. Therefore he suggested that if the lands were set apart for the freedmen, the civil government of the United States should be extended to them or a military government be established.[17]

In late January Sanborn reported a "great improvement" in the public sentiment concerning the freedmen. Ill will and prejudice were rapidly disappearing, he thought, and most of the freedmen were finding employment at fair wages. Most Indians seemed disposed to admit their rights and to treat them reasonably well. Of prime concern to Sanborn were the destitute refugee freedmen who were just arriving from outside the Nation. A large number were still on the Red River, where they had been taken by their masters during the war. Because most of them had no means of transportation, Sanborn requested that the agent be authorized to arrange their removal to and their proper location in the Nation.[18]

In early February Sanborn made another tour of the Indian country and changed his mind. From what he saw, he became less optimistic about the future of the freedmen and more convinced that land should be set aside for their exclusive use. He recommended, first, that each male over twenty-one be allowed to enter a homestead of 160 acres, which he could not sell. Second, there were a large number of freedwomen who had had from one to several children during slavery but had never had husbands. It would be difficult for them to find husbands, so Sanborn recommended that they be allowed to enter 160 acres as heads of households. Finally four sections in every township of freedman land should be set aside as school lands for the children. Commissioner Cooley liked Sanborn's idea and asked him for suggestions for the proper location of freedman colonies.[19] The idea of separate lands, however, was soon dropped.

As spring progressed, the Cherokee freedmen tried to make a crop, despite obstacles the Cherokees placed in their way. According to Cherokee law, a citizen could improve as much land on the public domain as he could successfully tend, so long as his improvements did not come within one quarter of a mile of another citizen's. The Indians argued that since the freedmen had not been admitted to citizenship, they could not improve property. They wanted the blacks removed and were unwilling for them to cultivate even leased land. For the most part, the freedmen had returned to the land they had worked for their masters before the war. They had built cabins and farmed the plantations formerly owned by rebel Cherokees who had fled the Nation. Cherokees who had bought improvements under the confiscation laws began notifying the freedmen to vacate. Major Pinkney Lugenbeel, the commander at Fort Gibson, sympathized with the blacks and believed that the Cherokees should pass laws permitting the freedmen to buy, lease, and rent lands in the Nation. He appealed to his superiors for a clarification of his duties regarding their protection.[20]

The matter was the domain of Sanborn, who issued another circular, this one authorizing the freedmen to remain in the Indian nations and cultivate the land they occupied. He instructed Lugenbeel to report every Indian who denied those rights or who appeared unwilling for the freedmen to occupy and cultivate land during the current season. Sanborn declared the confiscation laws void concerning the freedmen until further directions arrived from the Department of the Interior and promised that no freedman would be dispossessed of any land, tenements, or improvements by virtue of any titles acquired under confiscation proceedings. The freedmen's rights to remain on the farms where their cabins were built and where they had been held as slaves would be maintained in all cases where their masters had abandoned the farms during the war and had gone south.[21]

Circular 6 stressed the importance of making as large a crop of corn and other cereals as possible during the current season. Sanborn encouraged the freedmen to take any land not likely to be occupied by Indians during the season and to make a crop. He requested the military officers to protect freedmen who thus settled and to enforce contracts in which they owed part of the crop to Indians. Sanborn adopted these measures because he believed that the only people who would reestablish the old fields and make a crop were the freedmen, who had made improvements and had always lived on the plantations. He wanted possession to remain where it was until the proper authority determined whether the confiscation titles were good. If they were, then those in possession could pay rent and be allowed to remain. Sanborn did not want to interrupt the freedmen's progress. They were working constantly and hard, and the prejudice against them seemed to him to be dying. All were reasonably well supplied with farming implements and seeds, and Sanborn expected a good crop if the season permitted it. By that time, few of the freedmen were calling on Sanborn for assistance.[22]

Sanborn considered relations between the freedmen and their former masters "generally satisfactory." Fair wages were paid for their labor; the Cherokees allowed the freedman sharecroppers a fair part of crops they raised on the old plantations; there was plenty of labor for the freedmen; and nearly all of them were self-supporting. Only 150 in the entire Indian Territory applied to Sanborn for assistance during April 1866, and much of that was rendered to those who had been taken south and were just returning to their old homes. Sanborn saw little reason to continue his commission beyond early May. Some abuses would undoubtedly require correction, and general supervision of freedman matters would be more necessary at the time the crops matured and contracts were due. But Sanborn believed that the agents, under proper instructions, could attend to and perform all of the duties that pertained to his office.[23]

Sanborn was mustered out of service on April 30, 1866, and freedman relations were put under the supervision of Elijah Sells, the superintendent of Indian affairs for the southern superintendency. Sells found that Chero-

kee agent Justin Harlan wholly agreed with Sanborn's policies and methods. He asked that the protection afforded the freedmen continue and
be enforced; freedmen who had built cabins on confiscated lands should
be protected until the new treaties were confirmed. Harlan thought that
the confiscation laws were well within the constitutional powers of the
Cherokees and that the disloyal Cherokees had no right to contend for
the lands, for under Cherokee law, any improvements abandoned for
more than two years were open to claim by anyone. Most of the rebel
Cherokees had been gone for more than two years; thus the only Cherokees who had right to complain were those who had purchased or otherwise taken up the improvements under the confiscation laws. Like Sanborn, however, Harlan advocated that matters be left where they stood
to ensure the well-being of the freedmen.[24]

In general, the freedmen fared better than their Cherokee neighbors,
who still depended on the government to keep them from want. They
had been unable to make a crop in 1865.[25] Many were apparently not
as adept at farming as the freedmen were. Other reasons no doubt contributed to the more rapid progress of the freedmen. Their incentive for
maintaining their freed status was strong, while the Cherokees were de-
moralized. Once the most prosperous of the Five Civilized Tribes, they
had seen their nation totally wasted by war, and they were split by factional interests.

The Cherokees had carried their factionalism with them when they
went to Washington in January 1866 to continue treaty negotiations.
Commissioner Ely S. Parker and Elijah Sells received the delegations of
both the Union and Confederate Cherokees. They were particularly
concerned with the settlement of affairs between the factions, especially
regarding the confiscation laws, compensation for the losses of those who
had remained loyal, cession of Cherokee lands to be used for the settlement of western Indians, land grants to railroads, the establishment of a
territorial government, and the future relation between the freedmen and
the Cherokees.[26]

The Cherokees were the last of the five tribes to conclude a treaty.
The difficulties that had caused the negotiations to break down at Fort
Smith were still evident. Conference after conference was held between
the factions. Several drafts of treaties were made and, at times, apparently
agreed upon, but some new point would cause one faction or the other
to withdraw. A particularly difficult point was the division of the Cherokee Nation. The Confederate party wanted a portion of the Nation set

aside for their exclusive use. The Union Cherokees could agree to that proposition if the separation were effective until the President revoked the exclusive right, but they rejected a permanent separation. They also objected to the proposals of the Confederate Cherokees to sell the Neutral Lands in Kansas and the lands west of the ninety-sixth meridian and to grant railroad rights of way through the Nation. The Union Cherokees believed that it was not right for the government to destroy the Nation when they had remained loyal to the United States. On one point the two factions generally agreed: slavery should be abolished.[27]

The Confederate Cherokees were willing to negotiate a treaty with the government on practically any terms, but the Union Cherokees maintained that the power of the Cherokee government rested in them and that they were the only legitimate faction with which the government could negotiate. The U. S. commissioners despaired of coming to an agreement with them, and about mid-June, they made a treaty with the Confederate faction, in which they agreed that the Confederate party would have a certain part of the territory set aside for their use, although they would not be formally separated from the Nation. In return they would sell their right to certain portions of the national lands. The treaty never reached the Senate, and it was apparently just a maneuver to bring the Union faction to terms. Subsequent negotiations finally resulted in a treaty, concluded on July 19, 1866, in which both factions made concessions.[28]

Article 4 of the treaty was important for the freedmen:

All Cherokees and freed persons who were formerly slaves to any Cherokee, and all free negroes, not having been such slaves, who resided in the Cherokee Nation prior to June 1, 1861, who may within two years elect not to reside northeast of the Arkansas River and southeast of Grand River, shall have the right to settle in and occupy the Canadian district southwest of the Arkansas River and also the country northwest of Grand River, and bounded southeast by Grand River and west by the Creek country, to the northeast corner thereof; from thence west on the north line of the Creek country to 96° so far that a line due east to Grand River will include a quantity of land equal to 160 acres for each person who may so elect to reside therein, provided that the part of said district north of Arkansas River shall be found insufficient to allow 160 acres to each person desiring to settle under the terms of this article.

The article meant that the disloyal faction and any blacks who wanted to settle with them had a land of their own. Of course, it would apply mainly to Cherokees, for few freedmen would likely want to settle among the former slaveholding element of the tribe. Those who chose to settle in the designated areas could select their own judges, make their own police regulations, and elect delegates to the National Council. The President had the power to review police regulations passed in the district, and all suits arising between members of the factions were to be adjudicated in the U. S. district court at Van Buren, Arkansas. The stipulations regarding Canadian District were to remain in force until a majority of the voters in the district asked the President, by special election, to abrogate them.[29]

Article 9 of the treaty was of most significance to the freedmen. "The Cherokee Nation covenant and agree that slavery shall never hereafter exist in the nation. All freedmen, as well as all free colored persons resident in the nation at the outbreak of the rebellion and now resident therein or who shall return within six months and their descendants, shall have all the rights of native Cherokees. Owners of emancipated slaves shall never receive any compensation therefor."[30]

The treaty declared amnesty in the Cherokee Nation, provided for repeal of the confiscation laws and restoration of the property of the southern Cherokees, the establishment of a U. S. court in the Cherokee Nation, the granting of rights of way to a railroad to run north and south and one to run east and west across the Nation, the settlement of western tribes on Cherokee lands, the cession of Cherokee lands in Kansas, and the establishment of a general council for the Indian Territory to provide legislation on matters concerning the entire territory. The treaty was proclaimed on August 11, 1866.[31]

In October the Cherokee National Council repealed the confiscation laws of 1863 and nullified all purchases of confiscated property. Purchasers of the property, who were given until December 1 to turn it over to the former owners, could apply to the National Council for reimbursement for their losses.[32] This action placed in jeopardy some of the improvements occupied by the freedmen.

In November 1866 the treaty articles concerning the freedmen were incorporated as amendments into the Cherokee constitution. Article 5 was amended to say that only citizens of the Nation who were at least twenty-five years old and had lived in the district for six months could

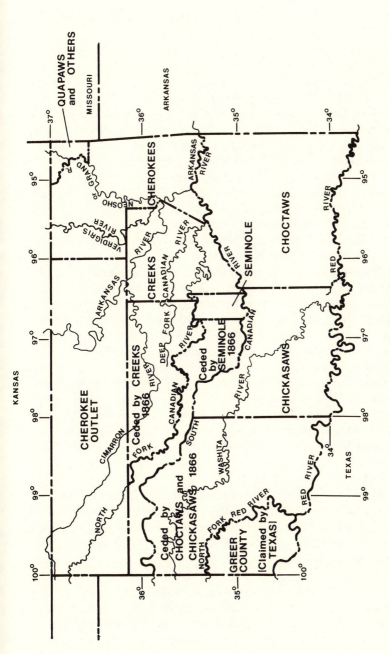

Indian Territory in 1867

hold a seat in the National Council. It defined citizens as all native-born
Cherokees, all Indians and whites legally members of the Nation by adoption, all freedmen liberated by voluntary acts of their former owners or
by law, all free blacks who were in the country at the beginning of the
rebellion and were then residents or who might return within six months,
and their descendants. All male citizens of eighteen or older were designated qualified voters of the Nation. Article 7 of the constitution abolished slavery forever except in the punishment of crime for which a person was duly convicted. At a general convention of the people of the
Cherokee Nation at Tahlequah on November 28, the amendments were
read, considered severally, and approved. On the following day they
were formally adopted by the National Council.[33]

At the time of the Treaty of 1866, there were an estimated 17,000
residents in the Cherokee Nation, about 10,500 of them considered
loyal Cherokees. Since so many citizens had died during the war, since
the Nation had acquired new citizens by virtue of the treaty, and since
it was necessary to determine the number of representatives for each
district, the constitutional amendments adopted by the people provided
for a census, to include the freedmen, to be taken as soon as practicable
and another to be taken in 1870 and each ten years after that.[34]

Returns from the census of 1867 are incomplete, but a contemporary
estimate set the number of freedmen at 2,000 to 2,500. The returns that
are available give some indication of their number in the various districts
and of their distribution throughout the Nation. There were 117 freedmen in Sequoyah District (38 were listed as voters), 148 in Saline, 25 in
Canadian (16 were listed as voters), 499 in Illinois, and 13 in Flint, of
whom 6 were listed as intruders, that is, noncitizens squatting on Cherokee land.

The great concentration of freedmen in Illinois District was a result
of Fort Gibson's location there. When the freedmen had begun to return
to the Cherokee Nation, the federal troops had offered a source of refuge
to them. Fort Gibson was the hub of activity, and most of the main routes
of travel into the Nation ended there. During the winter of 1866, many
of the freedmen were unemployed. Major Lugenbeel tried to induce them
to enlist in the army but none did so. Although Lugenbeel accused them
of being lazy, several families had moved from the vicinity of the post
into the surrounding countryside and had begun farming. Lugenbeel
thought they would do better during the next year, and he expected to

succeed before the spring of 1867 in scattering others who persisted in living around the garrison, doing and earning nothing.[36]

Many of the Cherokee freedmen did not return within the six-months' limit established by the treaty. In some instances slave families had been separated during the war. Children who had been sold and separated and were not old enough to travel alone could not get back to the Nation. In other instances children became subject to the laws of the states in which they resided at the end of the war. They were bound out until they reached maturity and were therefore prevented from returning to the Nation. Freedmen of mature age sometimes did not know about the treaty; others did not know about the six-months' limit; still others did not have the means to return in time. Some had been taken by their masters to the Choctaw and Chickasaw nations and Texas. In the spring of 1864, many of those slave owners, concerned about the direction the war was taking, had sent their slaves to the Brazos River in Texas to prevent their escape. John N. Craig, who became Cherokee agent in 1869, believed that some of the blacks were held as slaves in Texas for several years after the war had ended. Others were allegedly prevented by violence from returning to the Nation. One group of former slaves claimed to have left Osawatome, Kansas, bound for the Nation in July 1866. On Horse Creek, about fourteen miles north of the line, they were met by an armed force of Cherokees who killed some, wounded others, and drove them back into Kansas. Other freedmen apparently were taken by their Cherokee masters to Mexico at the close of the war, and some of them were several years in returning to the Nation.[37] Thus many of the Cherokee freedmen returned too late to be embraced by the treaty stipulations. Legally they were intruders, whom the agent was obligated to remove.

The Treaty of 1866 formed the legal basis for the rights of the Cherokee freedmen to citizenship in the Cherokee Nation. Yet the same treaty, by its six months' limitation clause, denied rights to many blacks who had been as much a part of the antebellum Nation as had those admitted to citizenship. For the next forty years, freedman rights were a constant source of conflict between the Cherokees and U. S. officials, the former insisting on a strict enforcement of the treaty and the latter insisting on the morality of a more flexible interpretation. That insistence made inroads upon Cherokee autonomy by officials' refusal to recognize the Indians' right to determine who were citizens of the Cherokee Nation.

NOTES

1. Report of the Secretary of the Interior, 39th Cong., 1st sess., *House Executive Document 1*, 205-206, 438, 468, 470-471.

2. Colonel W. A. Phillips to W. P. Dole, March 22, 1864, Phillips to Major General S. R. Curtis, March 17, 1864, and John T. Cox to G. W. Coffin, March 16, 1864, 38th Cong., 2d sess., *House Executive Document 1*, 472, 473, 476; statement of Wiley Martin, in Leo Bennett to Commissioner of Indian Affairs, May 28, 1891, National Archives Record Group 75 (Records of the Bureau of Indian Affairs), *Letters Received*, 19625-91; Wiley Britton, *Memoirs of the Rebellion on the Border, 1863* (Chicago: Cushing, Thomas & Co., Publishers, 1882), 93; Coffin to Dole, January 25, 26, 1864, National Archives Microfilm Publications, *Microcopy M234* (Records of the Office of Indian Affairs, Letters Received)-835, C664-64, C649-64; William Hayes to Elijah Sells, October 20, 28, 1865, *Microcopy M234*-836, S829-65. Blacks at the Sac and Fox agency were Ned, his wife and child, Adam, his wife and child, Jackson, and his wife and child.

3. Indian Archives Division, Oklahoma Historical Society, *Cherokee Volume 248*, 508; Gaston L. Litton, "The Principal Chiefs of the Cherokee Nation," *The Chronicles of Oklahoma* 15 (September 1937): 263.

4. Britton, *Memoirs*, 154; Edwin C. McReynolds, *The Seminoles* (Norman: University of Oklahoma Press, 1957), 305-306; Coffin to Dole, July 18, 1863, *Microcopy M234*-835, C366-63; *Cherokee Volume 248*, 14, 34.

5. *Cherokee Volume 248*, 13-14, 34-35; *Laws of the Cherokee Nation Passed During the Years 1839-1867* (St. Louis: Missouri Democrat Print, 1868), 128.

6. Report of the Secretary of the Interior, and Major General J. J. Reynolds to James Harlan, June 28, 1865, 39th Cong., 1st sess., *House Executive Document 1*, 202, 479.

7. Report of D. N. Cooley, October 30, 1865, and report of the Secretary of the Interior, 39th Cong., 1st sess., *House Executive Document 1*, 481-482, 202; Annie Heloise Abel, *The American Indian Under Reconstruction* (Cleveland: Arthur H. Clark Company, 1925), 189.

8. Report of the Secretary of the Interior, and Report of Cooley, 202, 203, 482-483; Abel, *American Indian*, 189.

9. Report of Cooley, 490.

10. Report of the Secretary of the Interior, 491.

11. Hayes to Sells, October 20, 28, 1865, and Harlan to Cooley, November 14, 1865, *Microcopy M234*-836, S829-65, P1376-65. Freedmen

from Mapleton included Orange Vann, one child; Sam Vann, wife, ten children; Jesse Rowe, wife, two children; Charles Martin, two children; Sam Webber, six children; Billy Foreman, wife, two children; George Brown, wife, four children; Mrs. M. Taylor (war widow), three children; Harry Martin, wife, four children; Charles Vann, wife, six children; Tobe Vann, wife, four children; Will Adair, wife, four children; Austin Martin, wife; Mrs. Gilbert Vann; Mrs. Suky Vann, three children, mother; Charles Nave, wife, seven children; Riley McNair, wife, eight children; Nelson Martin, wife, eight children; Warren Martin, wife, two children; Sandy Bean, wife, four children; Adam Martin, wife, three children; Henry Griffin, wife, three children; Reuben Downing, three children; Helen Vann (war widow), child; James Martin, wife, four children. From Osawatomie were Sam Vann, wife, two children; Joe Rogers, wife, two children; Jesse Vann, wife, five children; Gilbert Vann, seven children; Mrs. R. Vann (war widow), nine children; Jem Vann, wife, six children; Toby Chouteau, wife, two children; Johnson Vann, wife, ten children; Ben Sancho, wife, child; Emily Clark, half Cherokee; Nancy Butterfly, half Cherokee; Toby Drew, wife, six children; Jesse Vann, wife, two children. Apparently not all of these freedmen were removed by Miller.

12. Harlan to Cooley, November 18, 1865, and circular 1, January 1, 1866, *Microcopy M234*-836, I1382-65 and 156-66.

13. General H. J. Hunt to Cooley, November 28, 1865, *Microcopy M234*-836, H1323-65; Cooley to Hunt, December 15, 1865, National Archives Record Group 393 (Records of the United States Army Continental Commands, 1821-1920), *Frontier District,* Seventh Army Corps and Department of Arkansas, Letters Received, 1865-66 (hereafter cited as Seventh Army Letters Received).

14. Sanborn to Cooley, December 26, 1856, *Microcopy M234*-837, S101-66.

15. Circular 1, January 1, 1866, *Microcopy M234*-837, I56-66.

16. Sanborn to Harlan, January 10, 1866, *Microcopy M234*-837, S91-66.

17. *Report of the Secretary of the Interior* (Washington, D.C.: Government Printing Office, 1866), 283-285 (hereafter cited as *Report, 1866);* Litton, "Principal Chiefs," 264.

18. Sanborn to Cooley, January 29, 1866, *Microcopy M234*-837, S89-66.

19. *Report, 1866,* 286.

20. Major Pinkney Lugenbeel to John N. Craig, March 7, 1866, *Microcopy M234*-837, S216-66, and National Archives Record Group 393, Fort Gibson, Letters Sent, vol. 20.

21. Sanborn to Lugenbeel, April 7, 1866, *Microcopy M234*-837, S216-66.

22. Circular 6, March 27, 1866, and Sanborn to Cooley, April 10, 1866, *Microcopy M234*-837, S203-66, S216-66.

23. Sanborn to Cooley, April 13, 1866, in *Report, 1866,* 287.

24. E. D. Townsend to Sanborn, April 11, 1866, and Harlan to Sells, April 30, 1866, *Microcopy M234*-837, S237-66; Cooley to Harlan, April 30, 1866, National Archives Microfilm Publications, *Microcopy M348* (Records of the Office of Indian Affairs, Report Books)-15, 240.

25. *Report, 1866,* 55.

26. Ibid., 8-9; Hanna R. Warren, "Reconstruction in the Cherokee Nation," *The Chronicles of Oklahoma* 45 (Winter 1967-68): 182.

27. *Report, 1866,* 12; interview between the chiefs and headmen of the Cherokee Nation, March 30, May 3, 1866, National Archives Microfilm Publications, *Microcopy T496* (Documents Relating to the Negotiation of Ratified and Unratified Treaties with Various Indian Tribes, 1801-1869)-7, frames 378, 302.

28. *Report, 1866,* 12.

29. Charles C. Royce, "The Cherokee Nation of Indians," *Fifth Annual Report of the Bureau of Ethnology* (Washington, D.C.: Government Printing Office, 1887), 334-335; *Report, 1866,* 12.

30. Royce, "Cherokee Nation," 336.

31. Ibid., 334-336; Warren, "Reconstruction," 183.

32. *Laws, 1839-1867,* 128-129; *Cherokee Volume 248,* 107.

33. "Copy of Proposed Amendments to the Constitution of the Cherokee Nation with the Action Thereon of the National Council," *Microcopy M234*-101, B51-67; *Constitution and Laws of the Cherokee Nation, Published by an Act of the National Council, 1892* (Parsons, Kan.: Foley R'y Printing Co., 1893), 33, 35; *Laws, 1839-1867,* 132.

34. *Report, 1866,* 283; "Copy of Proposed Amendments to the constitution of the Cherokee Nation"; *Laws, 1839-1867,* 135-136.

35. John J. Humphreys to William Byers, January 18, 1867, *Microcopy M234*-101, B51-67; census, 1867, *Microcopy M234*-101, R183-67.

36. Lugenbeel to Major O. D. Greene, December 27, 1866, *Fort Gibson,* Letters Sent, vol. 20. The recruiter who replaced Lugenbeel had no luck in recruiting for the Tenth U. S. Colored Cavalry. Various letters, January-February 1867, of Lieutenant John S. Appleton to Lieutenant John G. Leefe, National Archives Record Group 393, *Fort Gibson,* Letters Received, 1865-1868.

37. *Report of the Secretary of the Interior* (Washington, D. C.: Government Printing Office, 1868), 741; Phillips to Dole, March 22, 1864, Phil-

lips to Curtis, March 17, 1864, and Cox to Coffin, March 16, 1864, 38th
Cong., 2d sess., *House Executive Document 1,* 472, 473, 476; statement
of Wiley Martin in Bennett to Commissioner of Indian Affairs, May 28,
1891, Frank Pack to Commissioner, January 19, 1894, and affidavit of
Anderson Starr, April 18, 1892, *Letters Received,* 19625-91, 3572-94,
15119-92; testimony of John Price, January 14, 1892, affidavit of George
Downing, January 14, 1892, and affidavit of Carter D. Markham, January 25, 1892, National Archives Record Group 75, *Affidavits, 1891-92,*
box 2; D. M. Browning to Secretary, January 16, 1897, C. F. Larrabee to
Secretary, January 5, 1906, and protest of Burrell Daniels, n.d., National
Archives Record Group 75, *Central File,* 8545-1927 Cherokee Nation
175.2 (part 4), 39865-08 Cherokee Nation 953 Spl., 21122-07 and
104528-05, respectively. Decades later the Cherokees claimed that the
Horse Creek fight occurred in 1867 rather than 1866. Troops were allegedly sent from Van Buren, Arkansas, but the War Department, in a
search of the records in 1902, found no reference to it. W. A. Jones to
Secretary, October 30, 1902, Elihu Root to Secretary of War, November
21, 1902, and Root to Secretary, January 28, 1903, National Archives
Record Group 48 (Records of the Department of the Interior, Office of
the Secretary), Indian Territory Division, *Chickasaw Freedmen,* box 60a,
6711-02, 7497-02, 1060-03.

chapter 3   RECONSTRUCTION

Following the Civil War, the Cherokees and other tribes in the Indian Territory suffered a social demoralization somewhat like that in the Southern states.[1] For many reasons, a kind of apathy set in, and the Cherokees began to distrust their future. First, the war had revived the old factionalism, the Union finding its support among the old Ross party and some of the Old Settlers, while the Confederacy found its support, for the most part, among the old Treaty or Ridge party Cherokees. Second, the Treaty of 1866 had seriously weakened their ability to maintain autonomy over their affairs. It had given the railroads a foothold in the Indian Territory, which they were making plans to cross, and the Cherokees were convinced that the railroads would be accompanied by a great influx of whites. The treaty had also opened the way for the establishment of a territorial government by providing for the creation of a grand council of all of the tribes. To the whites, the council was the first step toward creating a territorial government, extinguishing the Indian title, and establishing a new state. Third, whites began to agitate, through Congress, for the establishment of a territorial government and the ultimate opening of surplus lands to non-Indian settlement. Finally, in the postwar years, the Cherokees watched as whites crowded their borders, intruded upon their lands, especially along the Kansas border, and cut their timber. These problems that emerged during Reconstruction require a detailed analysis, for they are the bases of the final destruction of the Cherokee Nation. The antagonism they generated set the tone for Cherokee relations with the United States and greatly affected the Nation's policies regarding the most serious domestic issue to face it during the next forty years: the status of the freedmen and other citizens of the Nation. The postwar problems with which the Cherokees had to deal formed the backdrop against which the freedmen's struggle for civil, political, and economic rights occurred.

The factionalism that had marked Cherokee affairs in postremoval days resurfaced at the Fort Smith negotiations in the fall of 1865. Commissioner D. N. Cooley, acting on orders from Secretary of the Interior James Harlan, accused Chief John Ross of being an enemy of the United States and refused to recognize him as chief of the Cherokee Nation. Harlan, a former senator, was apparently angered because during the previous winter and spring, Ross had opposed his Senate bill to create a territorial government in the Indian Territory. Cooley was supported and encouraged in his attempt to depose Ross by Elias C. Boudinot, a Confederate Cherokee whose father had been among the Treaty party leaders murdered in 1839. Whether in factional spirit, from conviction, or from poor judgment, Boudinot supported the idea of territorial government as a grand scheme for the Indians. If his support was an attempt to ingratiate himself with the commissioners and to help depose Ross, he failed. When the Union delegation went to Washington to negotiate a final treaty in 1866, they rallied to Ross's cause and defended him before the President of the United States.[2] Ross, old and ill, lived to see the treaty negotiated and signed. He died less than two weeks later, on August 1, 1866.

Lewis Downing, the second chief, served in Ross's stead until the fall of 1866 when the Cherokee National Council selected Ross's nephew, William P. Ross, to fill the unexpired term. In his address to the people, Ross expressed concern for the future of the Nation, citing the factionalism, poverty, railroads, territorial government, the proposed establishment of a U. S. court in the territory, and intruders as threats to Cherokee national integrity. Although he called for unity, many of the Confederate Cherokees who had not returned to the Indian Territory after the war refused to do so with Ross in office, for to them there was no difference between him and his uncle. Thus, many did not return until he left office.[3]

The Southern Cherokees returned with less trepidation because of political developments in 1867. William P. Ross stood for reelection, but dissatisfaction with his candidacy developed in the ranks of the Ross party. The breakaway group, comprised mainly of full bloods who had formerly followed Ross, put forth Lewis Downing, a Baptist preacher, as their candidate. The Confederate Cherokees, hating the Rosses as they did, supported Downing, who won the election that summer. Public officials hailed the coalition of factions as an end to the factional strife and called 1867 a year of peace and quiet among the Cherokees. That year, the two major factions combined their delegations in Washington, thus taking another major step toward reunification.[4]

Despite officials' hopes, however, factionalism was still alive. Fights had occurred at the polling places during the summer elections, and when Downing was announced the winner, more fighting broke out between Ross and Downing men. Treaty stipulations maintained distinctions between the factions. As concessions to the Confederate Cherokees, framers of the treaty had tried to avoid the factionalism they feared would be revived because most of the Cherokees who had remained loyal to the Confederacy when the rest returned to the Union fold had been, for the most part, old Treaty party Cherokees. To prevent oppression by the Ross party, the treaty stipulated that those who desired could move to Canadian District, which was separated from the rest of the Nation by the Arkansas River, and there elect their own local officers and judges and conduct their own affairs in a manner not inconsistent with the Cherokee constitution. The treaty also provided for the establishment, at some undesignated time, of a U. S. district court in the Indian Territory. Until that time, the district court for the Western District of Arkansas at Van Buren had exclusive original jurisdiction in "all causes, civil and criminal," between inhabitants of Canadian District and other citizens of the Cherokee Nation. The stipulations regarding Canadian District were to remain in effect until a majority of the voters in the district, by special election, asked the President to abrogate them.[5] Most of the Confederate Cherokees settled in Canadian District.

As time passed, the prewar factionalism became dormant or disappeared altogether, and the divisiveness expected by government officials did not develop. The Cherokees had emerged from the war much wiser in the ways of the white man than they had been before. They apparently realized that only in unity could they resist white encroachment upon their national integrity. Said one observer in 1869, "All of them see they must be united, or the Cherokee nation goes to the wall."[6] In the place of the old factionalism was a political realignment, more or less along racial lines. The Downing party, which had emerged as a coalition party during the 1867 election, became the party of the mixed bloods during the 1880s and remained so throughout the last years of the Nation's existence. The Ross party of the 1860s was replaced by the National party; its adherents were the full bloods, the lower-class, native-speaking, traditional Cherokees, who insisted on the strictest interpretation of the Treaty of 1866 and generally held the position that the Cherokee Nation was the property of the Cherokees by blood. Needless to say, the freedmen found little support among the National party members. The mixed bloods of the Downing party were well-educated, English-speaking, shrewd politicians, among whom were the more wealthy Cherokee citizens. An odd coalition of former Old Settler, Treaty party, and Ross party Cherokees, they liked the freedmen little more than did the full bloods, but being more politically astute, they often convinced the freedmen that their interests lay with the Downing party.

There was one point on which the political parties agreed: their opposition to the railroads. Railroad lobbyists had attended the council at Fort Smith in 1865 and were successful in inserting into the treaties with the Indians provisions for railroads to be built across the territory. The treaties had no sooner been negotiated than Congress gave franchises to two railroad companies to build roads across the territory from the east and from the north. Congress held out to the companies the promise of generous grants of land along the right of way as soon as the Indian title was extinguished and the lands became part of the public lands of the United States.[7] The Cherokees were afraid that if railroad corporations built the roads, they would look upon Cherokee "nationality as an incumbrance" and that the Cherokees would lose their lands; should they be able to prevent that catastrophe, they would be faced with hordes of intruders who would follow the railroads into the territory. By 1869 it was reported, "It is well known that there is, at present, more speculation in the West in building roads than in running them."[8]

The north and south right of way was granted to the Missouri, Kansas, and Texas Railroad Company, and in 1870, without the Cherokees' consent, the company built a road from the Kansas line near Chetopa across the Nation and into the Creek Nation. The following year, the Atlantic and Pacific built a road from Seneca, Missouri, to Vinita, which had sprung up on the MK&T line in 1871. Through diplomatic maneuvering in Washington, the Cherokees thwarted attempts to build other roads for several years, but in 1886, Congress put the Indian lands under federal jurisdiction and granted rights of way to other railroad companies. After that date, Cherokee opposition was useless.[9]

The Cherokees opposed the railroads, viewing them as "the introducers of calamities rather than of blessings." And when they were built,

Cherokee fears were realized. The builders stripped the timber from the
countryside along the right of way. Tent towns sprang up and attracted
criminals and other lawless elements, who with the disorderly construction crews disturbed the peace of the citizens. When the building boom
subsided, there remained adventurers and land speculators, who with
singularity of purpose, set about finding ways to extinguish the Indian
title to the land, upon which depended the acquisition of land grants to
the railroad companies.[10]

As people began to travel across the Indian Territory, often exaggerated
reports of good land went out, and a clamor grew in the United States
to extinguish the Indian title, allot lands in severality to the Indians, and
open the surplus lands to non-Indian settlement. Most Cherokees opposed
allotment and feared that the power of the railroad companies would prevail, resulting in a loss of more land for right of way, loss of more timber
and coal, and an influx of whites.[11]

One way the government had sought to force the extinguishment of
the Indian title was the treaty provision for the establishment of a grand
council for the tribes in the territory, which the government hoped would
lead, finally, to a territorial government. When the council first met in
1870, the delegates adopted resolutions protesting the territorial bills
then pending before Congress. That December, the council met at Okmulgee in the Creek Nation and adopted a constitution that organized the
Indian Territory like a state with a governor, a legislature, and supreme
court. The Cherokees did not approve the constitution and tried to use
their refusal as a means to force Congress to repeal the acts giving conditional land grants to the railroad companies. The President and Congress
wanted veto and appointive power, concessions that the Indians would not
accept. Thus the constitution was rejected by the tribes. The council convened several more times as the delegates attempted to write another constitution. In 1875 Congress stopped appropriating funds for its expenses,
for it had proved to be a force for uniting the tribes in their resistance to
the policies of the government and had been the source of numerous protests against the territorial bills introduced in Congress. Nevertheless the
council convened regularly until 1878.[12]

Bills providing for the establishment of a territorial government in the
Indian Territory were introduced in every session of Congress from 1870
until the Curtis Act of 1898 extinguished the Indian title without the
Indians' consent. Politicians, speculators, and would-be land grabbers were

assisted in their efforts by Elias C. Boudinot, who spoke before Congress
in behalf of the territorial bills, but for the most part, Cherokees presented
a united front against the bills, even after the Dawes Commission was established in 1893 to treat with the Five Civilized Tribes. Most of the Cherokees believed that their welfare depended on being separated from the
whites and on their living under their own laws.[13] In 1869 the leading
Cherokees wrote, "To mingle the Cherokees and white men together in
the same community would result in the white men soon owning everything, the Indian nothing; and he becomes a worthless outcast in the
country which was once all his own—his home."[14] Much of the agitation
for establishing a territorial government came from the railroad companies, who even went so far as to sell stock abroad on the basis of their
conditional land grants.[15] After 1879 the strong agitation for territorial
bills was eclipsed by agitation for opening to settlement several million
acres of land in the central part of present-day Oklahoma. Ceded by the
Indians by the Treaty of 1866, these lands had not been assigned to any
tribe. Whites attempted to establish a colony there in 1879, and in 1880
the famous "boomer" David L. Payne tried to so do. Attempts to settle
the unassigned lands, popularly called Oklahoma, and the Cherokee Outlet during the next few years became common. In 1885 an Indian appropriations act provided for negotiation with the Cherokees, Creeks, and
Seminoles to open Oklahoma to settlement under the homestead laws of
the United States. The Creeks and Seminoles finally gave in, and the lands
were opened in 1889.[16]

The Cherokees were also faced with squatters in the Cherokee Nation
proper. By 1869 noncitizens by the thousands were pushing into Cherokee territory. The intruders believed that the Indian title was worthless
except for the land actually improved by the Indians, and they were convinced that it was just a matter of time until the land would be opened
to settlement.[17] Wrote one observer in 1869, "To this class of frontiers-
man, an Indian reservation is a God-send."[18]

When John N. Craig became Cherokee agent in July 1869, the Cherokees complained immediately about intruders or squatters, a problem
that had grown to great proportions during the preceding months. It was
in many respects a problem that the Cherokees had brought upon themselves as they sought economic recovery, for when Craig investigated, he
found that many of the new settlers were mechanics and farm laborers
who were working in the Nation under permits issued by the Cherokees.

Others, and among them some of the most lawless characters in the Nation, were married to Cherokees and therefore held rights of Cherokee
citizenship under the law. Craig felt that some of these should be removed regardless of their claims to citizenship. Still others were Indian
and freedman citizens of the Creek Nation, and upon complaint of the
principal chief, Craig requested the Creek agent to remove them according
to his instructions.[19]

The increasing problem with the white intruders brought the attention
of the Cherokees to focus more sharply on the freedmen as well, especially
those who had returned to the Nation too late to be adopted as citizens.
To this point, the Cherokees had taken no steps to enroll or register those
freedmen entitled to citizenship. Those not entitled were allowed by common consent to exercise the rights of citizens and were practically recognized as citizens. Now, however, the Cherokees began steps to effect their
removal. The district solititors were directed to make lists of all persons
considered intruders in their respective districts. As soon as the lists were
received, the district sheriffs served notice on the intruders and listed the
time and place of service to be used in deciding if force were necessary
to ensure compliance with the notice. In most instances, notice to remove
sufficed. Those who ignored removal notices were usually involved in illegal activities. Among these was timber theft on Cherokee lands adjoining Kansas. There, Cherokees and freedmen who claimed citizenship cut
timber for sale in Kansas. These, among others Craig investigated, determined to remove those who had no rights in the Nation.[20] His efforts,
however, did little good.

As years passed, the intruder problem became worse. As the number
of intruders grew dramatically, the Cherokees received increasingly less
cooperation from the government in removing them from Cherokee lands.
When the United States took its first census of the Indian Territory in
1890, people were recorded according to their physical appearance. The
census takers listed 29,166 whites and 22,015 Indians in the Cherokee
Nation.[21] Of course, some of the whites were citizens of the Nation, and
many of the Cherokees were of such mixed blood that they appeared
white. Nevertheless thousands of the whites were not citizens, and the
Cherokees thus had no legal jurisdiction over them. Their presence in the
Cherokee Nation made a strong argument for those who wished the Indian title extinguished.

The increasing numbers of settlers in the Cherokee country resulted in an increase in violence and crime, and there was constant conflict between the Cherokee Nation and the United States over judicial jurisdiction. The Treaty of 1866 had guaranteed that the Cherokee courts would retain exclusive jurisdiction in all civil and criminal cases arising within the Nation in which members of the Nation, by nativity or adoption, were the only parties, or where the cause of action arose in the Cherokee Nation, except as otherwise provided in the treaty. This provision meant that the federal government had jurisdiction over cases involving only noncitizens in the Cherokee Nation and over those involving both citizens and noncitizens.

The Cherokees' criminal code was not adequate for the situation. Except for capital crimes, they punished by fines or by whipping. They had no jails. Judges were chosen for their character, not their knowledge of the law, and they followed no prescribed rules of procedure. In 1869 Agent Craig recommended that the penal laws of the United States be extended to the Indian Territory "in all cases of crimes accompanied by violence, committed within the territory by Indians, whether against the persons of Indians or white men." He complained that the U. S. district court at Van Buren (and later, Fort Smith), Arkansas, because it was outside the Nation, exercised a "wholly inefficient criminal jurisdiction" over cases under the treaty stipulations and offered "many opportunities for partiality and discrimination against the Indian." Few crimes were punished, and violators held the law in contempt. Craig concluded , "The increase of population and travel through the country renders the means that were once partially adequate wholly inefficient."[22]

As the Cherokee judiciary proved more ineffectual, the U. S. court and its agents, the U. S. marshals, encroached increasingly on the jurisdiction of the Cherokee courts. The court exercised its authority rather loosely regarding the treaty. Adopted citizens of the Nation were treated as though they were citizens of the United States. The Cherokees came to look upon the marshals as foreigners, "exercising over them a usurped and oppressive authority."[23]

Many of the abuses of authority resulted from the fee system under which the marshals worked for twenty years following the war. Indian citizens were arrested under any pretense so the marshals could collect their fees. The marshals were particularly abusive in suppressing the liquor traffic, which flourished during the years just after the close of the war. When violators were apprehended, their goods were confiscated, and half of them went to the informers. In 1869 Agent Craig accused marshals of hiding whiskey on steamboats and in traders' stores bound for the Cherokee Nation, thus guaranteeing an arrest. Some marshals hired informers who would share confiscated goods. They also developed the attitude that the possession of whiskey by a resident in the Nation was prima facie evidence of its introduction into the Nation by the person possessing it and put the burden on the citizen to prove that he did not introduce it. The Cherokee agent wrote in his report for 1872: "It has become a very common occurrence for innocent men to be arrested by these marshals, and dragged to Fort Smith, Arkansas, a distance of perhaps fifty, one hundred, or even one hundred and fifty miles, and compelled to give bail in a city of strangers, of whose language they are ignorant; or in default of such bail to be incarcerated in the common jail, until the meeting of the court. To all appearance the whole court, together with the deputy marshals and attorneys, cooperate to increase the business of the court—thus increasing their business and profits, and to oppress the Indians and take from them the little they possess."[24]

Tensions between the court at Fort Smith and the Cherokee Nation rose steadily until 1872, when, acting on a writ issued by the U. S. court at the request of a white adopted Cherokee citizen, a posse of marshals attempted to take a full-blood Cherokee prisoner from a court in session at the Going Snake District courthouse.[25] A fight ensued; eight were killed and many were wounded, including the presiding judge and the prisoner, Ezekiel Proctor. This event, known as "the Going Snake tragedy," was followed by a gathering of forces on both sides, the arrest of several Cherokees, some of whom were national officials, threats of federal troops being called out, and a good deal of bitterness.

The incident focused attention on the Cherokee Nation and its courts and brought charges that lawlessness prevailed in the Indian Territory. Those accusations became an argument for the cause of those who sought to establish a territorial government there. A typical rendering by reporters of conditions in the Indian Territory was that the male inhabitants habitually carried weapons and the people held life in low esteem. The Indians and blacks who lived there were thought lazy and shiftless, and the whites were considered "adventurers, professional thieves, escaped convicts and other grades of refugees from justice." Terror reigned; the people were afraid to assist the marshals or to appear as witnesses because they feared reprisals. Writers who presented such accounts argued against the establishment of a U. S. court inside the territory, which they said would be useless without a territorial government to back it up. The Cherokees countered that the marshals were unconcerned with the rights of the Cherokees, that they often committed lawless acts themselves, and that most of the crimes were committed by whites over whom the Indians had no control. Some Cherokees came to believe that the solution lay in the establishment of a U. S. court within the territory, a solution made necessary by unavoidable intercourse with whites.[26]

The Going Snake tragedy and the furor it sparked over lawlessness in the Cherokee Nation caused the Cherokees to begin to look critically at their judiciary. The National Council of 1873 provided for the revision of the Cherokee laws into what became known as the New Code, written by William P. Boudinot, D. H. Ross, and J. A. Scales. The National Council adopted the code on December 5, 1874, and provided for the erection of a national prison in Tahlequah.[27]

The New Code made significant changes in the role of the Cherokee courts. The supreme court was given the power to decide upon the constitutionality of any act of council brought into question by an appeal from a lower court. It also was empowered to prescribe rules of practice for regulating the procedure in the trial of cases in the lower courts. The judges were required to present written opinions on points of law to be used as precedent in subsequent cases, and their decisions were given the force of law. The court was given jurisdiction in all cases of manslaughter and in those involving the death sentence. The Nation was divided into three supreme judicial circuits, with one of the judges presiding over each in the trial of the cases indicated above.[28] The code clearly defined as well the roles of the circuit and district courts.

The New Code spelled out in great detail the rules of procedure·in impaneling juries, calling grand juries, conducting criminal trials, taking testimony, and calling witnesses and issuing subpoenas. It also prescribed some general rules of procedure and required the inferior courts not only to abide by the rules prescribed by law and by the supreme court, but to report to the latter any rules of their own that they adopted in court.[29]

The new laws corrected a long-standing weakness in the judiciary by defining murder and manslaughter in degrees, excusable and justifiable homicide, and other crimes and misdemeanors. It prescribed the death sentence for treason, murder, rape of a child under twelve, and arson and prison terms and fines for lesser crimes and misdemeanors. Violent

crimes were punishable by the harshest sentences. The editor of the
Cherokee Advocate hailed the New Code and the erection of the jail
as an accommodation of the Cherokees' "new condition."[30]

When a fire delayed publication of the code, which was to have gone
into effect on November 1, 1875, the National Council passed an act
suspending the sections of it relating to punishment of criminal offenses
until August 1, 1876. Nevertheless the supreme court—comprised of
John T. Adair, George W. Scraper, and Richard Fields—began to try
cases under the New Code, claiming that the act, by its phrasing, suspended
only the punishment of criminal offenses, not the trial of them. Their
action resulted in a confrontation between the court and Chief Charles
Thompson, a conservative full blood who took office in the fall of 1875.
The constitutional crisis, which threatened to subvert the New Code before it could take effect, ended in the removal of Chief Justice Adair
and a proclamation from Chief Thompson directing judges to continue
their duties in criminal cases under the old law.[31]

Under the New Code, which took effect in 1876, the Cherokee judiciary was more effective than it had been previously, but the agitation
for a territorial government did not stop. For a decade after the code
was adopted, white and black intruders flocked to the Cherokee Nation.
The Cherokee judiciary still had no authority over them. By the time an
Indian reported a felony or misdemeanor to the principal chief and he
reported it to the agent, who reported it to the proper authority, the
accused had moved on. Congress took the matter in hand in 1885 by
giving the U. S. federal courts jurisdiction over cases of murder, manslaughter, rape, assault with intent to kill, burglary, larceny, and arson
in which an Indian was involved, even if the act had been committed on
Indian land. In 1889 Congress gave those convicted of capital crimes
the right to appeal to the Supreme Court of the United States. Finally,
on March 1, 1889, a U. S. district court was established at Muskogee,
Creek Nation. Other courts were subsequently established at Vinita and
elsewhere in the Indian Territory.[32]

One further complexity of Cherokee affairs during Reconstruction and
the subsequent years resulted from the heterogeneous characteristic of
the population, which was composed of ten identifiable classes: full
bloods, mixed bloods, Delawares, Shawnees, intermarried white men
and women, a few Creeks who had become citizens in the 1840s, a few
Creeks who were not citizens, a few Natchez Indians who were citizens,

the adopted freedmen, and the freedmen who had not been admitted but whom the government refused to remove.[33] The Delawares, numbering 985, were adopted in 1867, and 770 Shawnees were adopted in 1869. Although under the treaties both of these groups initially paid large sums of their tribal funds into the Cherokee national treasury, the Cherokees later tried to deny their rights and those of the freedmen to share in the common title to the land and in the tribal funds.

The matter of freedman rights was eclipsed by the external pressures brought to bear on the Cherokee Nation following the Civil War. Preoccupied with other matters, the Cherokees apparently paid the freedmen little attention until 1870. By that time, the freedmen had settled into the role of productive members of Cherokee society. In 1867 the seasons had been good and the crops abundant. Some of the freedmen were reported industrious and prosperous, while others were inclined toward indolence and were willing to live upon those more industrious than they. By the following year, the freedmen were becoming an element of discord among the Cherokees, who looked at their recent treaty and believed, in retrospect, that the freedmen had been forced upon them. According to Southern Superintendent L. N. Robinson, there was a growing feeling among both Indians and blacks that both would be better off if separated. He therefore urged the department to make arrangements with the Cherokees in a supplemental treaty for lands and pro rata of funds for the freedmen to enable the department to colonize them in the western part of the Indian Territory. Both parties would be satisfied with such an arrangement, he thought.[34]

Cherokee Agent William B. Davis described the freedmen in 1868 as a "generally peaceable and well disposed" people, who "with their advantages of climate and soil will soon present the appearance of a thriving, industrious community." The growing season had been a good one, and there had been produced an abundance of grain and vegetables. Horses, cattle, and hogs fattened without feeding. But the peace and prosperity of many freedmen were subject to a constant threat: strict enforcement of the treaty concerning the six-months' limit. It was Davis's duty under the treaty to remove those who did not return in time, for they were legally intruders. However, to do so he would have to separate families in instances where some members did not return in time, did not know about the six-months' limitation, or did not have the means to return. Davis found that prospect distasteful and asked

the department to adjust that treaty stipulation.[35] The department did
nothing, however, and it would be two years before the Cherokees would
take any action themselves.

The Cherokee failure to act concerning the matter of the freedmen
who had returned too late created a much greater problem for them when
they finally turned their attention to the matter, for as time passed, the
facts of individual freedman cases became vaguer and more confused. The
problem was made more complex as subsequent U. S. officials insisted
that the Cherokees were morally obligated to adopt the freedmen whether
they had returned in time or not. That insistence touched a raw nerve in
the Cherokees, who were always strongly opposed to any act that would
give their land to anyone who was not a member of their nation. In time
the problems engendered by the presence of the freedmen became mag-
nified and merged with national concerns about threats to Cherokee
autonomy over its own affairs and to the security of its borders. That
merger resulted from the determination of U. S. officials to dictate policy
in two important areas of freedman matters: determination of the rights
to citizenship of the freedmen who had failed to return within the six-
months' limit and who, in fact, had returned; the determination of the
right of the citizen freedmen to participate in land and monies of the
Nation.

NOTES

1. Report of the Secretary of the Interior, 41st Cong., 2d sess.,
House Executive Document 1, 847 (hereafter cited as *Report, 1869*);
report of the Secretary of the Interior, 41st Cong., 3d sess., *House
Executive Document 1,* 753 (hereafter cited as *Report, 1870*). A general
and poorly documented treatment of Reconstruction in the Cherokee
Nation appears in Minnie Thomas Bailey, *Reconstruction in Indian Territory* (Port Washington, N.Y.: Kennikat Press, 1972), 159-190.

2. Grace Steele Woodward, *The Cherokees* (Norman: University of
Oklahoma Press, 1963), 295-300.

3. Ibid., 306-308; Morris L. Wardell, *A Political History of the Cherokee Nation, 1838-1907* (Norman: University of Oklahoma Press, 1938),
209.

4. Wardell, *Political History,* 209-210; Woodward, *Cherokees,* 309;
Hannah R. Warren, "Reconstruction in the Cherokee Nation," *The Chron-*

icles of Oklahoma 45 (Winter 1967-68): 184; Gaston L. Litton, "The Principal Chiefs of the Cherokee Nation," *The Chronicles of Oklahoma* 15 (September 1937): 266; John Bartlett Meserve, "Chief Lewis Downing and Chief Charles Thompson (Oochalata)," *The Chronicles of Oklahoma* 16 (September 1938): 319-320; *Report of the Secretary of the Interior* (Washington, D.C.: Government Printing Office, 1868), 736 (hereafter cited as *Report, 1868).*

5. Charles J. Kappler, comp. and ed., *Indian Affairs: Laws and Treaties* (Washington, D.C.: Government Printing Office, 1904), 2: 943-944.

6. *Report, 1869,* 517, 849.

7. Woodward, *Cherokees,* 295; Angie Debo, *The Road to Disappearance* (Norman: University of Oklahoma Press, 1941), 175; Wardell, *Political History,* 258-259.

8. *Report, 1869,* 515, 541.

9. Report of the Secretary of the Interior, 42d Cong., 2d sess., *House Executive Document 1,* pt. 5, 982 (hereafter cited as *Report, 1871*); Joseph B. Thoburn and Muriel H. Wright, *Oklahoma: A History of the State and Its People* (New York: Lewis Historical Publishing Company, 1929), 2: 475, 481, 482; Charles C. Royce, "The Cherokee Nation of Indians," *Fifth Annual Report of the Bureau of Ethnology* (Washington, D.C.: Government Printing Office, 1887), 366-367; Woodward, *Cherokees,* 316; *Report, 1870,* 751; Wardell, *Political History,* 259-260.

10. *Report, 1871,* 982; Debo, *Road to Disappearance,* 197, 199; Woodward, *Cherokees,* 317.

11. *Report, 1871,* 979-980, 982; James D. Morrison, "The Union Pacific, Southern Branch," *The Chronicles of Oklahoma* 14 (June 1936): 174-175; *Cherokee Advocate,* April 22, 1876.

12. Woodward, *Cherokees,* 315-316; "Journal of the General Council of the Indian Territory," *The Chronicles of Oklahoma* 3 (April 1925): 33-44; "Journal of the Adjourned Session of First General Council of the Indian Territory," *The Chronicles of Oklahoma* 3 (June 1925): 120-140; "Okmulgee Constitution," *The Chronicles of Oklahoma* 3 (September 1925): 216-228; Wardell, *Political History,* 292-296.

13. *Report, 1870,* 750.

14. *Report, 1869,* 541.

15. Wardell, *Political History,* 260, 297.

16. Ibid., 301-306.

17. Report of the Secretary of the Interior, 42d Cong., 3d sess., *House Executive Document 1,* pt. 5, 617 (hereafter cited as *Report, 1872*).

18. *Report, 1869,* 515.

19. Ibid., 478-479, 845-846; *Report, 1870,* 748.

20. *Report, 1869,* 478-479, 845-846; Henry Ward and Cyrus Beede to H. M. Teller, June 2, 1883, National Archives Record Group 75 (Records of the Bureau of Indian Affairs), *Letters Received Relating to Cherokee Citizenship,* box 2, 12339-83; *Report, 1870,* 747-748.

21. Angie Debo, *And Still the Waters Run* (Princeton: Princeton University Press, 1972), 13.

22. *Report, 1869,* 847.

23. *Laws of the Cherokee Nation Passed During the Years 1839-1867* (St. Louis: Missouri Democrat Press, 1868), 178-179.

24. *Report, 1868,* 847-848; *Report, 1871,* 984; *Cherokee Advocate,* June 1, 1872; *Report, 1872,* 618.

25. *Report, 1872,* 619.

26. *Cherokee Advocate,* May 4, 1872, October 11, 1873, March 11, 1876, May 14, June 1, 1872, October 11, 1873, February 28, 1874, March 11, 1876.

27. *Constitution and Laws of the Cherokee Nation* (St. Louis: R & T. A. Ennis, 1875), 27.

28. Ibid., 71-77.

29. Ibid., 82-118.

30. Ibid., 118-146; *Cherokee Advocate,* November 14, 1874.

31. *Cherokee Advocate,* March 1, 11, 25, April 8, 15, 22, 1876.

32. Wardell, *Political History,* 309-310.

33. Report of the Secretary of the Interior, 43d Cong., 1st sess., *House Executive Document 1,* pt. 5, 570.

34. *Report of the Secretary of the Interior* (Washington, D.C.: Government Printing Office, 1867), 318; John J. Humphreys to William Byers, January 18, 1867, National Archives Microfilm Publications, *Microcopy M234* (Office of Indian Affairs, Letters Received)-101, B51-67; *Report, 1868,* 736-737.

35. *Report, 1868,* 741-742.

FREEDMAN LIFE AMONG THE CHEROKEES

chapter **4**

For a few years following the Civil War, most of the freedmen lived in Illinois District, near Fort Gibson. As the Cherokee Nation progressed through Reconstruction, the freedmen began to scatter and establish themselves firmly on Cherokee soil. In the succeeding thirty years, they developed a life-style that most blacks in the South would have envied.

When settlement patterns finally stabilized, Cooweescoowee and Illinois districts had the greatest number of freedmen citizens. Tahlequah District was next, followed by Sequoyah, Saline, Delaware, Canadian, Flint, and Going Snake.[1] Cherokee settlement patterns had something to do with the distribution of freedmen. The former Confederate Cherokees settled Canadian District, and Flint and Going Snake were settled mainly by full bloods, who had held few slaves before the war. Illinois and Tahlequah districts absorbed the freedman refugees from Fort Gibson, and Cooweescoowee received many refugees from Kansas. Sequoyah's proximity to Arkansas apparently was one reason for the size of its freedman population, and Saline's perhaps can be explained by the fact that it had had a high density of slave population.

In Cooweescoowee District, the freedmen settled on farms along Cedar Creek, Snow Creek, Big Creek, and Lightning Creek, all right-hand tributaries of the Verdigris River. They also settled on Hickory Creek, a left-hand tributary of the Verdigris, and Cabin Creek, a left-hand tributary of the Grand. Some settled in or near the villages of Alluwe, Elliott, Lenapah, Hudson, Ruby, and Hayden. The last, two miles south of present Nowata, was named for Henry C. Hayden, a freedman who operated a store and blacksmith shop there.[2] In Saline

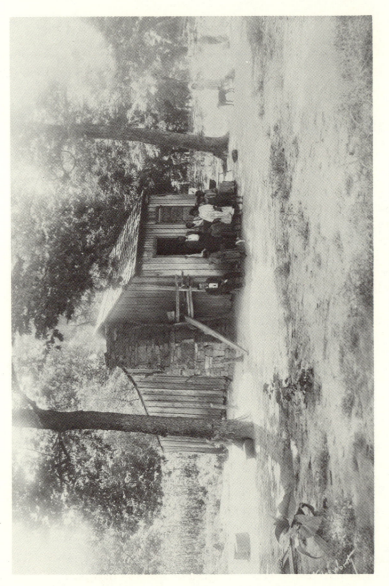

A typical freedman home in Indian Territory. Courtesy of the Oklahoma Historical Society.

District, the freedmen settled along Grand River and near Lynch's
Prairie; in Tahlequah, near the town of Tahlequah and on Four Mile
Branch east of Fort Gibson; in Illinois, near Fort Gibson and along Four
Mile Branch and Greenleaf Creek; in Delaware, at Vinita; and in Sequoyah,
in the Arkansas River bottom and near the villages of Muldrow and
Redland.

Most of the freedmen were farmers, improving from fifteen to seventy-
five acres under the Cherokee laws regarding the public domain.[3] Those
in the northern sections of the Nation were generally more prosperous
than those in the south. Cooweescoowee and northern Delaware District
were predominantly prairie lands, while southern Delaware, Saline, and
northern Tahlequah were rugged hills interspersed with small prairies.
Southern Tahlequah and Going Snake, Flint, Illinois, and Sequoyah, consisting mainly of flint and limestone-covered hills, contained the most
rugged land in the Nation. Canadian District, south of the Arkansas River,
was dominated by gently rolling hills and wide river bottom land. Corn
was the major grain-crop throughout the Nation, and wheat was raised
in the northern districts. Cotton was a major crop in the southern districts. The freedmen also raised vegetables and fruit and engaged in hus-
bandry.

Some freedmen owned businesses such as barber shops, blacksmith
shops, general stores, and restaurants. Others worked for the Cherokees
as ferry operators, printers' devils, and cotton gin operators. Still others
were teachers, and at least two were postmasters, Henry C. Hayden at
Hayden and G. W. Lane at Elliott.[4]

The census of 1867 offers other insights into the condition of the
freedmen. First, their families were large. Second, in many instances,
the census of the freedmen could not be distinguished from a census
of the Cherokees without the labels. Most of the freedmen took the
names of their former masters; thus the rosters contain great numbers
of freedmen by the name of Vann, Ross, Baldridge, Rogers, Benge, and
West, to name a few. However, many had not yet progressed from the
naming system among slaves and had only single names—Betsy, Isaac,
Joe, Sam, Mose. Some names reflected the freedmen's former lives among
the full-blood Cherokees: Sac-le-cah, Cher-ne-we-yher-he-tah, Tac-car-
skillah, Kar-ter-nars-tah, Wha-lac-loo, Wah-lec-zah, and Frog. Later these
single names or native names were dropped in favor of Cherokee sur-
names. Some freedmen were known by more than one name. Such

naming practices often caused confusion in legal matters, as did some marital practices. Some of the blacks had practiced polygamy during slavery days and still did so as late as 1897. Some spoke only the Cherokee language.[5] As a whole, the freedmen were poor, superstitious, and ignorant.

The freedmen quickly realized that their status as Cherokee citizens depended in great measure upon educating their youth. As one said in 1876, "It is our extreme ignorance now, that is the barrier to social and political consequence to-day, and if we sit still and do nothing, our children will, when they grow up, labor under the same disadvantage."[6]

The freedmen had the same access to the public schools as did the Cherokees, who had established their public school system in the West in 1841 by building eleven common schools in the areas of densest population in the Nation. The system was under the direction of a superintendent who appointed a board of directors for each school to oversee the erection of buildings and, with the concurrence of the superintendent, to examine and hire teachers and to prescribe curricula and texts. Except in extraordinary cases, no school could go into operation with fewer than twenty-five students. This system was revived following the Civil War but underwent changes under the New Code of 1876. At that time the principal and second chiefs, the executive council, the treasurer, and three commissioners appointed by the chief sat as a board of education, which supervised educational matters in the Nation. The Nation was divided into three school districts: the first embracing Cooweescoowee, Delaware, and Saline districts; the second, Tahlequah, Going Snake, and Flint; and the third, Sequoyah, Illinois, and Canadian. The board appointed in each district a commissioner who met in Tahlequah semiannually to examine candidates for teaching positions. The best-qualified teachers received first-class certificates, and the lesser-qualified received certificates of second- and third-class teachers. They were assigned to schools by the board. The school year consisted of two terms of twenty weeks each, and the board adopted uniform textbooks and other educational materials.[7]

Public education for the freedmen began with the establishment of two segregated primary schools in 1869. The number was expanded to three by 1871 and seven in 1874. Because the schools had to maintain enrollments of twenty-five to remain in operation, the number of schools fluctuated. In 1876 and 1877, only six of the seventy-one day schools were freedman schools. By 1879 there were 102 public schools, but the freedmen had only ten of them. The number then remained constant throughout the 1880s. Between 1892 and 1896 there were fourteen freedman primary schools, and in 1900, when the United States had begun to share the responsibility for education in the Indian Territory, there were fifteen.[8]

Incomplete records prohibit a complete list of the freedman schools during this period. However, during the 1870s there were Tahlequah, Grant, and Four Mile Branch in Tahlequah District, Lightning Creek in Cooweescoowee, Fort Gibson and Greenleaf in Illinois District, and Vann's Valley in Saline District. In 1879 were added Goose Neck in Cooweescoowee District, and the first schools in Delaware and Sequoyah districts were established at Island Ford and Timbuctoo, respectively. In the early 1880s schools were established at Flat Rock and Big Creek in Cooweescoowee District. Among the schools later opened were Vinita Colored School, Lynch's Prairie, and Claremore.[9] The establishment of these schools clearly reflects the settlement patterns of the blacks within the Cherokee Nation.

The location of these schools meant that many freedman children were deprived of school privileges. A school census of 1876 for the third educational district (Illinois, Sequoyah, and Canadian districts) indicates the problems of education in the Cherokee Nation. There were 366 Cherokee, 14 Creek, and 134 freedman children between seven and twenty-one years of age in Illinois District. Of those, 178 were not in reach of a school. The freedmen in the last two districts, who had no access to schools because there were not enough to maintain the enrollment required by Cherokee law, complained. In 1878, for instance, a group from Cooweescoowee and Saline districts petitioned President Rutherford B. Hayes to intervene in behalf of their children.[10] Some of these blacks, however, were not recognized as citizens by the Cherokees and were denied educational privileges altogether.

In 1876 Cherokee educator S. S. Stephens encouraged the freedmen to congregate in colonies large enough to get together enough children to qualify for a Cherokee public school. That same year Arthur Bean admonished his freedmen neighbors: "Complaints are made that we do not get a free school, suppose we do not? Must our children go neglected if we cannot get a free school? Let us have a subscription school, by all means let us have some sort of a school. I say that he is no man at all who cannot pay one dollar a month to have his children educated."[11]

If a community had enough children to qualify for a school, the residents bore the expense of building the schoolhouse and paid for its upkeep. When the blacks at Tahlequah built a new house for their school in 1878, the editor of the *Cherokee Advocate* wrote, "The interest that the majority of these people manifest in educational matters is commendable." Once the building was erected, the Cherokee board of education assigned a teacher, who was paid out of national funds. The freedmen who did not qualify for a Cherokee-supported school because of numbers or lack of recognition as citizens built their own schoolhouses and paid their own teachers. One such school, for example, established at Lightning Creek, was taught by a young missionary, Edward Derrick, who left that post in the spring of 1877. These "subscription" schools, as they were called, were decidedly inferior to the public schools. The expense of a school building was more than some communities could bear, so quite often the church building served also as the school. In 1901, for instance, the Four Mile Branch school in Tahlequah District was a new frame church, thirty by fifty feet, with high walls, wainscoting, linings and ceilings, paint inside and out, belfrey and bell, eight windows that admitted good light, wood stove, church benches, and map case. The Cherokees considered this one of the best black schools and the Vinita Colored School "one of the best schools in the nation." Lynch's Prairie school was also good. This twenty-five by forty-five foot frame house was wainscoted and had ceilings and linings. It was roomy and well lighted and had a platform and pulpit, wood stove, book case, long benches with backs, and a blackboard.[12]

Freedmen who lived near the schools apparently attended them well during the early years of freedman education, but attendance fell during the late 1870s and early 1880s. In 1876 the Tahlequah school had twenty-six students attending, and in 1884 it had an enrollment of forty-two but an average attendance of only twenty-four. In 1878 Grant had an average attendance of twenty-seven, and in 1884 the average attendance was thirty-seven out of an aggregate of fifty-one. In 1884 Flat Rock school had an average attendance of thirty-eight out of forty-seven, Big Creek had an average of thirty-six out of fifty-two, and Fort Gibson had an average of thirty out of sixty-five.[13]

These schools were rated first, second, or third class, according to the qualifications of the teachers. In 1878 three freedmen schools were first-class schools, and four were second. But the following year, six of the seven schools had third-class, or the most poorly qualified, teachers. The freedmen complained that the teachers for their schools were inferior to those in the Cherokee schools. During the 1870s they also complained that no blacks taught in the freedman schools. As late as 1883, only native, citizen, or white teachers were hired by the Cherokees. However, in 1884 there were some black teachers, who included Frank Vann of Illinois District and O. S. Fox, who taught at Goose Neck and later edited the *Afro-American Advocate* at Coffeyville, Kansas. By 1888 there were nine black native and five black noncitizen teachers.[14]

The curriculum was prescribed by the Cherokee board of education. The children of all grades in the second-class schools, for instance, studied reading, spelling, writing, numbers, drawing, plants, form, place, size, weight, objects, color, physical exercise, aesthetics, singing, conversation, and ethics. When a student advanced beyond his grade or level in any subject, he studied that subject with students of the next grade. Written examinations were required at least once a month, and the year closed with oral examinations. The board of education held training schools or institutes for teachers during vacation in order to aid them in carrying out the courses of study.[15]

As early as 1872, the freedmen spoke out against segregation and wanted to send their children to the schools in their own neighborhoods, whether the schools were for blacks or not. Although there was no law prescribing separate education, segregation by inference and by public opinion was a fact, although there had been one or two exceptions. The schools had been located so as to accommodate the most students, but a large number scattered throughout the Nation had not been provided for, although the people wanted to educate their children.[16] These particularly objected to segregated schools.

There were other public institutions, as well, from which the freedmen were excluded as a class. Until 1871 Cherokee orphans attending school were boarded in the neighborhood and clothed out of the orphan fund, which applied only to the indigent and destitute and excluded the freedmen altogether. The Cherokee Orphan Asylum was established in 1871, but there had been no provision for the freedmen. Early in 1873 the freedmen sought to gain a share of the Cherokee orphan fund for their orphans. The board of directors for the asylum denied having jurisdiction and turned the matter over to the National Council, which took no action. Appealing to the United States, the freedmen said that because of prejudice they did not ask that their orphans be taken into the asylum but simply that they be given their share of the fund according to their numbers.[17]

The orphan fund had been established by the Treaty of 1835 and expanded by the Treaty of 1866 to cover certain orphans who attended public schools. The Cherokees decided that the money could be better applied if a home were created. Established on November 25, 1871, the asylum went into operation in the spring of 1872. When asked by the Indian Office about the freedmen's charge, William P. Ross, who had become chief upon Lewis Downing's death in late 1872, denied that children were excluded by color; rather, he said, the asylum was established for orphans whose "condition" entitled them. The freedmen came to him near the end of the session of the National Council in 1872, complaining that the board had refused to admit some of their orphans, in whose behalf application had been made to the National Council without any action. Ross had not had time to confer with the board, of which he was a member, and claimed not to know the grounds on which the application had been denied. He believed the board would rectify any mistake that had been made when their attention was brought to it. However, he said that only a few orphans gained admittance to the asylum because of the limited facilities and stressed more than once that the public schools were open to the children of all races in the Nation and to the orphans who could not gain admittance to the national asylum. He denied that prejudice existed in the Nation. Nowhere, he said, had so little trouble occurred since the war in relation to color, and nowhere else had the freedmen been so "generously and munificently" provided for and so kindly treated "as an almost universal rule." Nowhere, as a class, were they better and more prosperous members of the community. Ross bitterly opposed the division of the orphan fund, claiming that division of funds among groups of citizens would result in a breakdown of the national institutions. However, that fall he went before the National Council and asked it to settle without delay the rights of the freedmen to benefit from the orphan fund and to carry out the provisions of the existing treaties, thereby removing all grounds for reasonable complaint by the freedman citizens.[18] No action was taken.

The freedmen were also denied access to the Male and Female seminaries, the Cherokees' equivalent of high schools. For a number of years, the freedmen agitated for a high school of their own. The Downing party made the establishment of such a school a part of its platform in the election of 1887. It failed to fulfill its promises at the National Council of 1887, but the council of the following year provided the proper legislation. A site was selected at Double Springs about five miles northwest of Tahlequah, where a three-story brick building large enough to board fifty boys and girls was constructed in 1889. Known as the Colored High School, it opened on January 1, 1890, under the supervision of freedman Nelson Lowrey, steward.[19]

The board for each student was set at five dollars per month, a price that was probably prohibitive for most of the freedmen. Consequently attendance at the Colored High School was poor, and there was talk of discontinuing it. The National Council of 1891 passed a bill, which stated that if the enrollment fell below twenty-five at the end of any month, the school would be discontinued. O. S. Fox of Ohio, principal teacher at the school and editor of the Coffeyville, Kansas, *Afro-American Advocate*, urged the freedmen to send their children to prevent its closure: "If you have to make a sacrifice make it and fill that school up. Your neighbors see to it they fill up their seminaries. They realize that to be anything the Indian must be educated." Fox traveled to the areas of freedman population, urging support. The school opened its spring term with only twenty students but had enrolled twenty-seven by the end of the month.[20]

The students at the high school organized singing clubs and literary societies. The boys formed a baseball team and regularly played the "town" boys of Tahlequah. The school also tried to minister to the spiritual needs of the students. A Sabbath school was organized, and religious services were held regularly. The boys were allowed to attend the public hangings in Tahlequah as a means of emphasizing the importance of right thinking and acting.[21]

The education that the students received was poor. There were not enough books for the courses offered, as was the case in some of the public schools for the freedmen. In 1895 the Cherokees created a primary department at the high school and admitted one boy and one girl from each freedman primary school in the Nation. The opening of the primary department allowed the institution to serve the poor and orphaned who could not otherwise acquire a basic education. But the school did not accomplish what it was established to do. Some students who were admitted to the high school had never attended school before. It was, for all practical purposes, a primary school. No course of study had ever been pre-

scribed. Therefore, in 1899 the Cherokee board of education established
a course and instituted an examination for admission to the freshman
class. The prescribed freshman program was practical arithmetic, grammar, physiology, United States history, spelling and composition, and
penmanship. The sophomore program was practical and mental arithmetic,
general history, grammar, bookkeeping, botany, and spelling and composition. Juniors took algebra, arithmetic, physics, rhetoric, general history,
higher arithmetic, geology, and American literature. Seniors studied astron-
omy, algebra, natural philosophy, psychology, literature, and physical
geography. The Cherokees tried to improve standards further in 1900 by
requiring all teachers at the school to be graduates of reputable colleges.
Attendance at the school was never large. In the fall term of 1901 only
thirty-four students attended the Colored High School in the primary,
intermediate, and high school grades, only twelve of whom were in the
latter.[22]

Along with the educational growth among the freedmen came religious
growth as well. Some of the Cherokee freedmen had been church members before the Civil War. One was the Reverend Fred Martin, born in
Georgia in 1826 and brought to the West by the Cherokees. Converted in
1848, Martin began preaching in 1853, organizing the first black Baptist
church in the Cherokee Nation. Located on Grand River, the church began
with only three members and became known as Island Ford Baptist
Church, from which sprang the other Baptist churches in the Nation. When
Martin died in 1891, black Christians of other denominations paid him
homage. Funeral services were conducted by the Reverend J. R. White of
the Vinita Baptist Church, assisted by the Reverend C. Hildebrand of the
same church, the Reverend R. McGhee of the AME Church at Fort Gibson, and the Reverend J. C. Richardson of the AME Church of Vinita.
(Other interesting facts about Martin were that he was survived by his
mother, who was 107 years old, and that he was a member of the Eastern
Star Lodge of Masons, No. 8, at Vinita.)[23]

Facts are sketchy regarding the Christianization of the freedmen in the
first two decades after the Civil War. Most religious activity took place in
the areas of greatest freedman population. In 1876 a Sunday school was
organized by Julia R. Gourd at the freedman school in Tahlequah, but
there were no regular church services. In 1877 a black church existed at
Webbers Falls, but it did not have a regular preacher; circuit preacher W. C.
Brodie preached there on the Saturday before the first Sunday of each

month. That same year Frank Vann, a licensed black preacher in the Baptist church, held services at the Four Mile Branch church the first Sunday of each month. The Reverend Dennis Barrows of Fort Gibson preached there every Thursday night and Sunday, except the second Sunday of each month, at which time he preached at Tahlequah. On that day, Brodie preached at Barrows' church in Fort Gibson. Barrows, a black who had come from the states as a missionary to the Cherokee freedmen, was acclaimed as a spiritual leader by those who heard him. The Cherokees praised him as well: "He deserves great credit for the interest he is taking in the cause of christianity among his people; and other colored divines should imitate his noble example." On his part, Barrows was impressed by the good relations between the freedmen and the Cherokees. Sent by the African Methodist Episcopal church, he established a Sabbath school with fifteen members in March 1877. By the following summer, his flock numbered sixty-five.[24]

Religious services did not always bring about the "peace that passeth all understanding." In fact they were often the scenes of violence. In 1877 a fight between two young men at the Tahlequah Sabbath school outraged a "young and accomplished white lady who had been good enough to lend her presence, influence and intelligence to the proceedings from motives of benevolence." It outraged as well "the better class of colored people" who felt that such conduct by any of their people was "not the right way to testify their appreciation of the blessings of freedom." A few months earlier, Willis Pettit, a black who became intoxicated, had insulted a preacher, disturbed a church service, and fired his pistol in the streets of Tahlequah. He was collared by High Sheriff Samuel Sixkiller and a guard. It was Pettit's second offense on the same charge, and the result was a sentence of one year in the national prison. Pettit was incorrigible. The Cherokees hanged him in 1882 for killing his mother-in-law.[25]

There were as well camp meetings that sometimes lasted a week and drew crowds of up to four hundred. The freedmen also met on the banks of nearby streams to hold services and to baptize the converts. But the work was slow. By 1888 there were only nineteen black churches, eight ordained black ministers, and 550 church members in the Cherokee Nation. Of those thirty-two belonged to the Methodist Episcopal church.[26]

There was apparently a flurry of religious activity among the blacks in the early 1890s, perhaps because of a great influx of noncitizen blacks.

The AME church at Redland, Sequoyah District, had been established in 1882, but the church had got off to a slow start, the building remaining unfinished. P. H. Hill was appointed pastor in November 1891; within two months the building had been completed, a parsonage had been built, fifty scholars attended the Sabbath school, an organ had been bought, a choir had been established, and a congregation of 150 to 200 attended Sunday services. In 1892 Vian had two black churches, a Baptist and an AME church, the latter established in late 1891 with eight members. The black Baptists organized the Cherokee Association, led by J. R. White (president), J. S. Smith (vice-president), F. K. Patterson (secretary), L. Farmer, C. Hildebrand, and M. E. Johnson. Also active was the Ministers and Deacons Union.[27]

The church or school was often the center of social life in the black communities. The schoolchildren, like their Cherokee counterparts, held May parties each spring, outings consisting of picnics on some local stream (the Illinois River was the favorite spot for the Tahlequah children), games, and the crowning of a little May queen. The schools also held "a Christmas tree" each year—a program, the enjoyment of a tree, a visit from Santa Claus, and gifts for the children. The children also celebrated Christmas by shooting firecrackers.[28]

Besides the picnics and barbecues that served as political rallies and conventions, the freedmen often held huge picnics, at which they took turns rowing up and down the streams. There were also grand fishing parties that were advertised for weeks in advance in the local newspapers and featured singing and preaching as well. In the winter the freedmen held festivals, dances, and dinners. They also attended and competed in the agricultural fairs held in the Indian Territory. In 1878 freedman John Drew, for instance, showed the best draft stallion at the Indian International Fair held at Muskogee.[29]

They attended minstrel shows given by such men as Eli Gentry, "the boss negro minstrel showman," who drew large crowds and presented a "laughable programme . . . not easily excelled by any country show." Some freedmen established local musical ensembles, such as the "Tahlequah Philharmonic Jubilee club and string band organization," formed in 1882, and an all-women group at Hickory Creek, advertised as "the only Afro-American brass band in the Territory."[30]

The Cherokee freedmen celebrated Emancipation Day on August 4. Neither the blacks nor the Cherokees were certain why that date was chosen; it was not the date of Lincoln's emancipation proclamation, the Cherokee proclamation, or the signing, ratification, or proclamation of the Treaty of 1866. It made no difference to the freedmen, however, said Thomas Mayfield, "a prominent member of the church and one of the best farmers in Saline District," at an Emancipation Day picnic in 1876: "The fact that the hand cuffs were broken and they stood before the world as free men, was a matter of joy, and this meeting was to rejoice over the fact."[31]

About five hundred people attended the Emancipation Day celebrations in Tahlequah in 1876. Preparations went on for several weeks. On the morning of the awaited day, the commanders and marshals of the day assembled horseback riders and people on foot at the freedman school for a parade through town. Sarah Pack, Emancipation Day queen elect, led the procession: "She was neatly dressed, looked like a queen sure enough, riding a fine horse, and with such grace as to attract general attention." The parade went to Hendrick's spring about one quarter of a mile north of town, where a large crowd had assembled. Barbecued beef was placed on a scaffold, and people came in wagons with boxes of delicacies. Prominent Cherokee politicians gave speeches, as did a number of the freedmen. The people picnicked until five in the afternoon and dispersed after the announcement of a dance in town that night.[32]

Not to be outdone by the freedmen of Tahlequah, those of Delaware and adjoining districts held a massive celebration in 1876 on the west side of Grand River near Hunt's mill. They billed it several days in advance as "a grand horseback tournament together with speaking and a barbecue," with Augustus Buffington as president, the Reverend Frederick Martin, chairman and general referee, and Rachel Adams and Linda Landrum as reigning queens. The meeting site was on the edge of a prairie in a grove of trees where a speaker's stand and seats for the audience had been set up. The men who had horses were organized into two battalions, with officers and color bearers, in preparation for the "tournament." First, however, speeches were announced by Joseph Rogers, marshal and herald of the day. Thomas Mayfield looked forward to a time when brotherhood would prevail in the Cherokee Nation. Arthur Bean urged his fellow freedmen to educate their children. Joseph Bean had too much stage fright to say much. Cherokee educator S. S. Stephens urged the freedmen to educate their children and to work hard. He expressed doubts that they would achieve their social and political goals in the Cherokee Nation and urged

Cherokee freedmen doing the "square dance." Courtesy of the Oklahoma Historical Society.

those who had returned too late to seek federal help in colonizing lands west of the ninety-sixth meridian. Arthur Williams spoke against colonization and encouraged the blacks to demand their birthright, and Joseph Rogers did the same. After the speeches, the battalions and the queens "marched and countermarched around a red piece of bunting set on a pretty knoll" five or six times to the tune of "John Brown's Body" and "Rally 'Round the Flag, Boys." Following that show was the barbecue.[33]

Emancipation Day festivities were held elsewhere in the Nation—Four Mile Branch, Fort Gibson, and Goose Neck Bend. By the 1890s, these celebrations sometimes lasted a week. By then, too, they had lost some of the air of thanksgiving: "Day and night, from one end of the camp to the other, can be heard the mule-odious voice of the lemonade vendor, the squeeking of the numerous fiddles and the twang of the banjoes and accompanied by the voice of the prompters on the many dance platforms, the hum of thousands of voices, and the call of the festive faker as he plies his vocation and rakes in the spare change of the unwary who sometimes bets his last nickel on the wrong card or number. People gather from forty miles around and seem to enjoy the din and confusion of the occasion."[34]

In the earlier years, the Cherokees were pleased to see how appreciative the blacks were of their freedom. They rode in their parades as if to say, "See the difference and be glad with us!" Other Cherokees sympathized with the freedmen and wished them "God-speed on the road to freedom." The Cherokees viewed the celebration in the same light as they viewed their own July 4 celebration, "not so much out of direct personal gratitude as out of sympathy with those who have occasion to feel grateful."[35]

The citizen freedmen had access to the political system of the Cherokee Nation and voted in local and national elections.[36] Politically they were caught between the Cherokee parties. It was not popular to advocate equality for the freedmen, and the Cherokee politicians were too shrewd to do so. Yet both major parties courted the freedmen for their votes.

From the beginning, some freedmen distrusted the Cherokee politicians. In 1876 Joseph Rogers told his fellow freedmen:

The leaders of both parties always told me next Council we will fix it, we almost got it through this time, just vote us in once more. Just so it is, next Council and next Council, like tomorrow, never comes, it is the delusive [sic] end of the rainbow, with its

sacks of gold always in sight, but never in reach, a receding tan-
talizing will-o'-the-wisp, leading you further into the morass of
disappointment. However much they may honey you with sweet
words and promises of citizenship, however much they may Mr.
Smith and Mr. Jones you, they are only giving you a pill, sugar
coated it may be, still only a pill to work you through the election. I don't believe there is anything to hope for from these
politicians.[37]

Despite such warnings, most of the freedmen allied themselves with
the Downing party and in the elections of 1883 and 1887 tried to vote
as a bloc, the only elections in which they attempted to do so, although
the Cherokees urged them to vote independently in an obvious effort
to split votes. In the election of 1883, some freedmen charged the ex-
Confederate Cherokees with intimidation. In 1890 the freedmen re-
nounced both parties for having failed to keep promises to them.[38]

The freedmen were not successful in their efforts to secure political
offices. In the election of 1875, Joseph Brown of Tahlequah District
became the first and only freedman elected to the National Council; he
served one term in the lower house and was then nominated by the National party of Tahlequah District as one of the Cherokee national representatives to the Grand Council of the Indian Territory, which by that
time had lost congressional support and was on the verge of disbanding.
W. P. Boudinot, the editor of the *Cherokee Advocate,* wrote, "The
Grand Council is not dead but sleepeth, and the political talents of Mr.
Brown will have a wide and grand field for display. . . . Let no one re-
mark that the colored element of Cherokee citizenship is not strong and
duly appreciated." But Boudinot was not amenable to the idea of black
officeholders in general. He wrote about two weeks later that it was not
"complimentary or just, to this or any other element, or to the whole
nation, to distinguish between the interest of that element and the rest
of the nation in filling representative offices, to instill the fatally mis-
chievous idea that the element has distinct rights to hold office in proportion to its numbers and irrespective of qualifications." In 1877 a
coalition of Cherokees and freedmen in Illinois District tried to elect
a black to the National Council. A list of nominees contained a blank
"to be filled by a name of a colored citizen to be selected by other
colored citizens." In 1881 at its nominating convention and barbe-

cue in the Greenleaf neighborhood, the Union party of Illinois District nominated William Thompson, a black, for the council. That same year, the National party convention held near Mackey's old saltworks nominated freedman Daniel Roach for council.[39]

Although they were not successful in the political arena, the freed-men held responsible positions in the community. They served as school directors, whose job it was to see that buildings were erected and maintained, and they also served as jurors, guards, guardians, and administrators of estates.[40]

While most of the freedmen were law-abiding citizens, some were not. The gossip and local news columns of Cherokee newspapers contain evidence that the Cherokee freedmen were involved in crimes of all sorts: stealing horses, selling whiskey, disrupting religious services, attempting rape, obtaining goods under false pretenses, and committing assault. There were as well reports of murder. The frequency of violent crimes among the blacks, however, seemed no greater, proportionally, than among the Cherokees. Nor is there evidence that punishment was meted out any differently for one group or another, despite charges from outside the Nation that black murderers were dealt with more harshly than were Cherokee killers. Neither were they always found guilty as some implied. There were acquittals, as in the case of Andy Sanders, tried before Judge J. T. Adair in 1877.[41]

The Cherokees and freedmen were in a similar plight in relation to the U. S. court at Fort Smith, Arkansas. The Cherokees protested when the freedmen were arrested without warrants by the marshals. When Dick Humphreys was arrested in such a manner in August 1872, the editor of the *Cherokee Advocate* wrote: "We would like to know what use Deputy Marshals have for warrants, if they can deprive any man of liberty and the pursuit of happiness without one." Some blacks, especially those who were not recognized as Cherokee citizens, used the Cherokee-United States conflict over legal jurisdiction to advantage, claiming citizenship in one place or the other as necessary. One such case was that of Jim Harris, accused in 1877 of attempting to rape an eight-year-old girl at Tahlequah. When Harris was brought before Judge J. B. Mayes, he denied being a Cherokee citizen and claimed citizenship in the United States. He was released by the judge. Wrote the editor of the *Cherokee Advocate*, "If this had happened in any other place than 'Oklahoma' the court would not have had a chance to ask, 'are you ready for trial,' but, as they say out West, there would have been 'a necktie festival.' "[42]

The freedmen, like the Cherokees, suffered from the inadequacies of the Cherokee judiciary before the adoption of the New Code in 1876. The trial of two freedmen, Sam Scales and Stephen Foreman, for the murder of freedman Wash Forrester over a card game in 1873 was used by Cherokee proponents for judicial reform to point out the weaknesses in the judicial system. Procedural matters were not prescribed by law and therefore rested with the discretion of the presiding judge. Two prospective jurors in Scales's case, which came to trial in Canadian District, had admitted that they held opinions which might prevent them from rendering an impartial verdict. Judge S. M. Taylor asked them if their opinions could not be changed by evidence. One said yes, and one said no. The judge thought both had said yes and kept them. When the truth came out, a new trial was ordered, but had both said yes, they still would not have been impartial jurors.[43]

During the second trial of Scales, who was subsequently convicted and hanged, freedman witness Pomp Thompson was asked if he had ever had "a difficulty" with Scales. The answer was "Difficulty? I never had a difficulty with Sam Scales in my life." Thompson, who apparently did not understand what "difficulty" meant, did not give the answer expected by the prosecution, and he was charged with perjury before he was dismissed. The editor of the *Advocate* took up Thompson's case. Cherokee law did not define legal perjury. The law regarding it was "a mere outline," left to the courts to fill out. Injustice in administering the law was not in the administrators but in the law and lawmakers, said the editor: "In the present case here is an ignorant uneducated freedman, compelled to give some sort of definition to the word 'difficulty' in order to answer a question he is bound to answer, and because his definition, after repeating the word in a way to show his hesitation, does not agree with the idea of another man, he is charged with swearing a lie. We don't know anything of the facts, but if the witness meant by difficulty a *fight* or a *combat,* he committed an error common to hundreds of both black and white men—and no greater error than very many western men and women fall into when they confound 'plunder' with personal goods and chattels!" The editor then postulated a case in which a western attorney asked "an intelligent witness" if he had any plunder, received a negative answer, and then found that the witness had "some dirty shirts, a pair of new boots and a change of apparel—all stowed away in a valise, and constituting

to the western eye, unquestionable and irrefragable proof of '*plunder*' —
why if the perjury law was no more definite than ours the intelligent
witness would stand an excellent chance to have to answer to false swearing, and the only security he would have would be in the intelligence of
the Bench."[44]

The case of Pomp Thompson demonstrated another weakness in the
judicial system. The Treaty of 1866 had said, for the protection of the
ex-Confederate Cherokees in Canadian District, that an indictment had
to be signed by the judge of the district in which the accused resided.
Thompson was a resident of Illinois District, and the perjury indictment
in Canadian District was quashed. The same was true of Stephen Foreman, accused with Scales of killing Forrester. Although evidence in the
Scales case had exonerated Foreman, he was held under arrest. The *Advocate* editor pointed to his detention as "a proof of the perversion to
which the law is liable from its incompleteness and of the necessity of
amending it to prevent abuses of this kind and other kinds in the future."
Once more, he argued, the problem was not with the judicial officers
but with "the poverty and insufficiency" of the criminal code.[45]

Such arguments prevailed, and the New Code went into effect on
August 1, 1876. The first person to be convicted of a capital crime
under the New Code was freedman Henry Scales, who was convicted of
the murder of freedman Seymour Thornton in Illinois District in the
court of supreme court justice Richard Fields. Scales argued that according to a recent decision by the Cherokee supreme court, he should
have been tried under the old laws since his crime was committed before
the New Code took effect. He appealed to Chief Charles Thompson to
intervene. Confrontation between Thompson and the supreme court a
few months earlier over a similar question had created a constitutional
crisis that had nearly subverted the New Code. However, Thompson did
not intervene this time, and Scales was hanged at the Illinois District
courthouse at Greenleaf on October 21, 1876. He mounted the scaffold
"without sign of fear," made a statement that exonerated an accused
woman named Nan of any complicity in the murder, and gave "good
advice" to bystanders. Wrote the editor of the *Advocate*, "He had ex-
perienced religion during his confinement since his sentence, and died
mentally happy. The rope somehow got too far back, and his bodily
sufferings were somewhat prolonged." Scales was tried under the New
Code by a fair and impartial jury, said the editor, and one of the merits

of the code was that it assured such a jury in all cases. And he concluded, "While therefore innocent men have no cause to apprehend injustice the guilty may expect justice according to the evidence and all should take warning accordingly."[46]

In the early years after the war, the Cherokees apparently viewed the freedmen as ignorant and superstitious people who had to prove that they deserved political and social consideration by becoming intelligent, industrious, and honest. Law had freed them, but law could not teach them to read or write. In 1876 Cherokee educator S. S. Stephens urged them to "lay aside internal discord and outside bickerings about equality and being as good as any body and go to work accumulating wealth and educating their youth." While Stephens denied that all men were created equal, he admitted that the door to respectability and power was open to all regardless of race. Echoing these sentiments, the editor of the *Advocate* wrote the following year, "As one people we have no use for different classes. Let the maxim be honor to whom honor is due, and not to 'class, color, or condition.' "[47]

Despite such statements, there was racism in the Cherokee Nation. Some Cherokees admitted to holding prejudices similar to those of the white South. They believed that the blacks were intellectually and morally inferior. These attitudes became more widespread as large numbers of noncitizen blacks flocked to the Nation, especially in the 1890s. When the Oklahoma lands were opened to settlement, blacks repeated on a minor scale the "Exodus" to Kansas of a decade earlier. To escape depressing economic conditions and the prevalence of lynch law, thousands of blacks left the South for Oklahoma, but got no farther than the Indian Territory, many stopping off in the Cherokee Nation. The Cherokees responded: *"STILL THEY COME.* The Nigger in the Woodpile is Sticking his Head Out Farther than Ever. And Even the Cloven Foot too Can be Easily Identified." In 1894 the editor of the *Cherokee Advocate* urged his fellow Cherokees to resist the tide of immigrants: "Be men, and fight off the barnacles that now infest our country in the shape of non-citizens, free Arkansas niggers and traitors."[48]

Still, it is little wonder that the blacks of the South looked at the Cherokee Nation as a haven. The Cherokees did not indulge in mob violence as the Southern whites often did. There is no record of a lynching in the Cherokee Nation. Freedmen there did not fear for their personal safety, and they were assured of a hearing before a properly constituted tribunal.

There were also economic advantages. O. S. Fox, editor of the Coffey-ville, Kansas, *Afro-American Advocate,* wrote in 1892, "The opportunities for our people in that country far surpassed any of the kind possessed by our people in the U. S." They could gain wealth and prominence and could improve all the land they wanted.[49]

But some freedmen were caught by the prospects of a more distant paradise—Liberia—and there were frequent attempts to organize baçk-to-Africa movements. In 1892 a man named Priestly and Prentiss H. Hill, the AME minister at Redland, led a number of blacks from Sequoyah District toward the promised land. Priestly, who was apparently a fraud, took their money and left the group stranded in New York City where there was no ship to carry them to Africa. Fox used the incident to warn the freedmen: "It is nonsense for any Afro-American to emigrate to Africa or anywhere else if he can make a living in the Indian Territory. Only indolence can keep him from being independent there."[50]

Most of the freedmen were nationalistic, however, and considered the Cherokee Nation as their homeland. In 1876 Joseph Rogers made this eloquent speech: "Born and raised among these people, I don't want to know any other. The green hills and blooming prairies of this Nation look like home to me. The rippling of its pebbly bottom brooks made a music that delighted my infancy, and in my ear it has not lost its sweet-ness. I look around and I see Cherokees who in the early days of my life were my playmates in youth and early manhood, my companions, and now as the decrepitude of age steals upon me, will you not let me lie down and die your fellow citizen?"[51]

Arthur Williams and Nathan Duffie made the following statement to the commissioner of Indian affairs during a trip to Washington, D.C., in 1879: "The Cherokee Nation is our own country; there we were born and reared; there are our homes, made by the sweat of our brows; there are our wives and children, whom we love as dearly as though they were born with red, instead of black skins. There we intend to live and defend our natural rights, as guaranteed by the treaties and laws of the United States, by every legitimate and lawful means."[52]

Despite whatever racist feelings they harbored, the Cherokees were aware that blacks received better treatment from them than they could expect from the whites. The Treaty of 1866 had asked the Cherokees to do something that the whites in the South had not been asked to do or were not able to do. In a satiric editorial in 1873, W. P. Boudinot of the

Cherokee Advocate pointed out that the Cherokees had an excellent opportunity to demonstrate the social principle of the strong's preying upon the weak. If the Cherokees were to be as civilized as the whites, they must learn to abuse the blacks, legislate against them, and administer the laws unequally. But, alas, the Cherokees were "greatly behind" the whites in advancement. Boudinot wrote: "We must acknowledge that since the Blacks, late slaves of theirs, have been made freemen and their equals, they have been treated like equals. They are encouraged to vote. They have opened farms and made themselves homes without interruption. They enjoy the full benefits of the Government without contributing a bit of its expense. They are protected, and not victimized by the Administration of the laws of the 'Nation.'"[53] Some Cherokees felt that the freedmen of the Nation owed nothing to the United States for their freedom. They were freed by an act of the Cherokee council, not by Lincoln's proclamation. In fact, the Cherokees believed that even if Lincoln had not issued the proclamation, there would have been no slavery in the Cherokee Nation.[54]

This belief that the freedmen owed their advantages in the Cherokee Nation to the Cherokees and to no one else formed one of the bases for Cherokee insistence upon autonomy over citizenship matters and determination of the rights of the freedmen to share in the tribal lands and funds. Since the Cherokees had freed the blacks and made them citizens, the Cherokees believed that they had the right to determine what conditions were placed on that citizenship. During the four decades following the Civil War, that belief brought the Cherokees into conflict with policies of the U. S. government.

NOTES

1. Census, 1867, National Archives Microfilm Publications, *Microcopy M234* (Records of the Office of Indian Affairs, Letters Received)-101, R183-67; *Summary of the Census of the Cherokee Nation, Taken by the Authority of the National Council and in Conformity to the Constitution in the Year of 1880* (Washington, D.C.: Gibson Brothers, Printers, 1881).

2. J. Gus Patton to J. George Wright, June 26, 1902, Indian Archives Division, Oklahoma Historical Society, *Dawes Commission–Cherokee.*

3. Reuben Sanders et al. to Secretary of the Interior, received November 16, 1874, *Microcopy M234*-107, S1598-74.

4. *Cherokee Advocate,* July 25, 1874, November 11, 1876, July 21, November 17, 1882; Patton to Wright, June 26, 1902, *Dawes Commission–Cherokee; Afro-American Advocate,* September 9, 1891, January 15, 22, 1892.

5. Census, 1867; John W. Wallace to T. J. Morgan, October 26, 1889, National Archives Record Group 75 (Records of the Bureau of Indian Affairs), *Letters Received,* 31054-89; D. M. Browning to James Dickson, February 10, 1897, *Letters Received,* 8545-1927 Cherokee Nation 175.2, pt. 4.

6. *Cherokee Advocate,* September 9, 1876.

7. *Laws of the Cherokee Nation Adopted by the Council at Various Periods* (Tahlequah, Cherokee Nation: Cherokee Advocate Office, 1852), [pt. 2], 59-61; *Constitution and Laws of the Cherokee Nation, Published by Authority of the National Council* (St. Louis: R & T. A. Ennis, 1875), 189-195.

8. Report of the Secretary of the Interior, 42d Cong., 2d sess., *House Executive Document 1,* pt. 5, 979; Report of the Secretary of the Interior, 43d Cong., 2d sess., *House Executive Document 1,* pt. 5, 379; *Annual Report of the Commissioner of Indian Affairs to the Secretary of the Interior for the Year 1876* (Washington, D.C.: Government Printing Office, 1876), 61; *Cherokee Advocate,* August 20, 1879, January 28, 1880, July 20, 1881; 49th Cong., 1st sess., *Senate Report 1278,* pt. 2, "Documents," 11-12; *Annual Report of the Commissioner of Indian Affairs to the Secretary of the Interior for the Year 1876* (Washington, D.C.: Government Printing Office, 1876), 61; *Cherokee Advocate,* August 20, 1879, January 28, 1880, July 20, 1881; 49th Cong., 1st sess., *Senate Report 1278,* pt. 2, "Documents," 11-12; *Annual Report of the Commissioner of Indian Affairs to the Secretary of the Interior for the Year 1887* (Washington, D.C.: Government Printing Office, 1887), 109; Browning to E. R. Rollins, November 24, 1894, National Archives Record Group 75, *Letters Sent,* Land Letter Book 232; "List of Primary Teachers Appointed for the Fall Term of 1893 and Cherokee National Fund, Term Beginning 10th February, 1897," Indian Archives Division, Oklahoma Historical Society, *Cherokee Schools–Miscellaneous (Tahlequah); Annual Report of the Commissioner of Indian Affairs to the Secretary of the Interior* (Washington, D.C.: Government Printing Office, 1892), 254; *Annual Reports of the Department of the Interior for the Fiscal Year Ended June 30, 1900* (Washington, D.C.: Government Printing Office, 1900), 167, 168; A. Claggett to the Dawes

Commission, January 13, 1900, *Dawes Commission–Cherokee.*

9. *Cherokee Advocate,* February 10, July 18, 1877, July 27, 1878, August 20, 1879, July 28, 1880; 49th Cong., 1st sess., *Senate Report 1278,* pt. 2, "Documents," 11-12; Benjamin S. Coppoch to John D. Benedict, April 4, May 1, 1901, *Dawes Commission–Cherokee.*

10. *Cherokee Advocate,* November 18, 1876; petitioners to Rutherford B. Hayes, February 20, 1878, National Archives Record Group 75, *Letters Received Relating to Cherokee Citizenship, 1875-89,* Union P131-78 (hereafter cited as *Cherokee Citizenship File).*

11. *Cherokee Advocate,* September 9, 1876.

12. Ibid., January 1, 1875, March 16, 1878; Edward Derrick to Secretary of the Interior, May 4, 1877, *Microcopy M234*-867, D195-77; Coppoch to Benedict, April 4, May 1, 1901, *Dawes Commission–Cherokee.*

13. *Cherokee Advocate,* September 16, 1876, April 6, 1878; 49th Cong., 1st sess., *Senate Report 1278,* pt. 2, "Documents," 11-12.

14. *Cherokee Advocate,* February 10, July 18, 1877, July 27, 1878, August 20, 1879; 49th Cong., 1st sess., *Senate Report 1278,* pt. 2, 3-43, 81-95, and "Documents," 11-12; Louis·Rough to U. S. Grant, February 8, 1872, *Microcopy M234*-105, R283-72; Henry Ward and Cyrus Beede to H. M. Teller, June 2, 1883, in Hiram Price to Secretary of the Interior, November 17, 1883, *Cherokee Citizenship File,* 21353-83; statement of George Nave, December 27, 1897, National Archives Record Group 48 (Records of the Department of the Interior, Office of the Secretary), Indian Territory Division, *Chickasaw Freedmen,* box 393 (60b), 4868-00, Exhibit L[1]; *Annual Report of the Commissioner of Indian Affairs* (Washington, D.C.: Government Printing Office, 1888), 119.

15. *Cherokee Advocate,* December 20, 1873, April 4, 1874, June 24, 1876.

16. Report of the Secretary of the Interior, 42d Cong., 2d sess., *House Executive Document 1,* pt. 5, 979.

17. John B. Jones to F. A. Walker, February 10, 1873, *Microcopy M234*-106, J457-73.

18. Will P. Ross to H. R. Clum, March 8, 1873, Clum to Ross, March 5, 1873, and Ross to National Council, November 14, 1873, Indian Archives Division, Oklahoma Historical Society, *Cherokee–Freedmen (Tahlequah);* 42d Cong., 3d sess. *House Report 98,* 281.

19. T. L. Ballenger, "The Colored High School of the Cherokee Nation," *The Chronicles of Oklahoma* 30 (Winter 1952-53): 454-455, 456-457; Senate to J. B. Mayes, December 7, 1888, letter of Building Committee,

November 22, 1889, and Mayes to Senate, December 27, 1889, Indian Archives Division, Oklahoma Historical Society, *Cherokee Schools— Colored High School (Tahlequah);* contract of R. D. Knight, 1889, Amended Act, November 17, 1890, Appropriations Act, December 22, 1891, *Cherokee Schools—Miscellaneous (Tahlequah).* Succeeding stewards included George Vann (1895-99), George F. Nave (1899-1901), Nelson Lowrey (1902-03), Frank P. Pack, John H. Harlin, and A. S. Wyly. Ballenger, 458; confirmation of George Vann, November 26, 1895, President of Senate to Principal Chief, November 12, 1897, and John E. Gunter to T. M. Buffington, November 18, 1897, *Cherokee Schools—Colored High School (Tahlequah).*

20. *Afro-American Advocate,* January 29, February 5, February 19, 26, 1892.

21. Ibid., March 4, 18, April 15, May 6, 1892.

22. Ibid., March 25, April 20, 1892; "Act to Amend School Law," December 6, 1895, and Joseph M. Thompson to Mayes, September 30, 1897, *Cherokee Schools—Colored High School (Tahlequah);* Ballenger, "Colored High School," 458-459, 460-461; "Attendance at Cherokee High Schools," September 12, 1901, *Dawes Commission—Cherokee.*

23. *Afro-American Advocate,* December 25, 1891.

24. *Cherokee Advocate,* April 1, 1876, April 11, May 16, 1877, July 11, August 3, 15, October 3, 1877.

25. Ibid., April 25, 1877, August 15, 29, 1877, May 12, 1882.

26. Ibid., September 16, 1876, August 29, 1877, November 2, 1878; *Annual Report, 1888,* 123.

27. *Afro-American Advocate,* January 15, March 18, April 15, 1892.

28. *Cherokee Advocate,* May 13, 1876, June 10, 1876, December 16, 1881, January 5, 1883.

29. Ibid., October 19, 1878, May 19, 1880, June 15, December 2, 1881; *Afro-American Advocate,* May 6, 1892.

30. *Cherokee Advocate,* October 6, 1880, July 21, 1882; *Afro-American Advocate,* September 2, 1891.

31. *Cherokee Advocate,* September 9, 1876.

32. Ibid., August 12, 1876.

33. Ibid., September 9, 1876.

34. Ibid., July 13, August 3, 1878; *Fort Smith Elevator,* August 12, 1892.

35. *Cherokee Advocate,* August 8, 1877.

36. J. B. Butler et al. to Price, June 1, 1883, *Letters Received* (case 48), 2425-83; 45th Cong., 3d sess., *Senate Report 744,* 591.

37. *Cherokee Advocate,* September 9, 1876.

38. William Brown to D. W. Bushyhead, April 27, 1883, *Cherokee–Freedmen (Tahlequah); Cherokee Advocate,* July 27, 1883; *Indian Chieftain,* July 27, 1887; Ward and Beede to Teller, June 2, 1883, in Price to Secretary of the Interior, November 17, 1883, *Cherokee Citizenship File;* "Rouge et Noir" (clipping), March 8, 1890, Oklahoma Historical Society Library, Fred S. Barde Collection.

39. *Cherokee Advocate,* March 14, 28, April 18, July 4, 1877, June 15, 1881, January 16, 1895.

40. Ibid., July 27, 1878; Butler et al. to Price, June 1, 1883, *Letters Received* (case 48), 2425-83; 30 *Court of Claims,* 144; Leo Bennett to Commissioner of Indian Affairs, January 16, 1891, *Letters Received,* 2094-91. In 1878, for instance, the school boards of directors were as follows: Lightning Creek—N. J. Tanner, M. W. Couch, and W. A. Adams; Fort Gibson—Jesse Ross, Andrew Tiner, and William Hudson; Four Mile Branch—Berry Mayes, Arch Carter, Sandy Johnson; Vann's Valley—Tuck Vann, Murrel Johnson, Fog Johnson; Tahlequah—Jerry Fields, Jack Pack, Dick Humphreys; Grant—Samuel Wofford, Joe Brown, Tom Harlin; and Greenleaf—William Thompson, Daniel Roach, and George Crossland.

41. *Cherokee Advocate,* May 4, 1872, May 23, September 13, 27, 1873, February 28, 1874, April 8, October 21, 1876, August 15, 22, 29, October 3, 1877, April 6, 1883.

42. Ibid., August 24, 1872, August 22, September 26, October 3, 1877.

43. Ibid., September 19, 27, 1873.

44. Ibid., October 11, 1873.

45. Ibid.

46. Ibid., October 21, 28, November 4, 11, 1876.

47. Ibid., August 25, 1876, August 8, 1877.

48. *Afro-American Advocate,* May 6, 1892; *Cherokee Advocate,* June 6, 1874, August 26, 1893, October 17, 1894.

49. *Afro-American Advocate,* February 19, 1892.

50. Edwin S. Redkey, *Black Exodus: Black Nationalist and Back-to-Africa Movements, 1890-1910* (New Haven: Yale University Press, 1969), 102-105; *Afro-American Advocate,* March 18, 1892.

51. *Cherokee Advocate,* September 9, 1876.

52. Ibid., March 26, 1879.

53. Ibid., September 13, 1873.

54. Ibid., August 8, 1877.

FREEDMAN CITIZENSHIP AND NATIONAL

chapter 5   INTEGRITY

In the hard years following the Civil War, internal political problems and the business of rebuilding a destroyed nation had occupied the Cherokees' time, and they gave little attention to the freedmen. No doubt they felt that the Treaty of 1866 spoke clearly enough: blacks who had formerly belonged to the Nation and had returned within the six-months' limitation were citizens, and those who had not were not. But the facts were not that simple. As years passed and more and more blacks straggled back into the Cherokee Nation and took up residence, the Cherokees faced the difficult task of deciding which freedmen had a legitimate right to citizenship in the Nation and which ones were intruders who should be removed. During the 1870s and 1880s Cherokee policies regarding citizenship ran counter to U. S. policy, and like the railroads and the territorial bills, governmental interference in citizenship matters represented a danger to Cherokee national autonomy and a threat to the Nation's existence. For more than a decade, government officials insisted on reviewing Cherokee citizenship cases, while the Cherokees denied their right to do so. In the meanwhile the intruder problem grew worse, and the freedmen who had claims to citizenship languished in uncertainty. Their very existence as a nation assailed on several fronts, the Cherokees devoted much valuable time and energy to this problem, and all for naught. After a decade of wrangling, the two sides were still at an impasse.

The Cherokees began to take steps to deal with the freedmen who had claims to citizenship with the census of 1870, which listed the classes of residents: citizens, including freedmen, and those whose citizenship was questioned. An act of council of December 3, 1869, required all persons whose rights were questioned by the census takers to appear before the

supreme court of the Nation in December 1870 to establish their rights
to citizenship. The act made the supreme court a court of commissioners
on citizenship, whose judgment was final.[1] This was the first of such
special courts that the Cherokees established during the next several years
to deal with the matter of citizenship. Some Cherokees felt a moral obligation to the freedmen who had returned too late, but most wanted
them and all others not entitled to rights removed from the Nation.

Agent John N. Craig took a census of his own in 1870. His returns
list 1,545 Cherokee citizens of African descent, who constituted only an
estimated two-thirds of the former Cherokee slaves and free blacks and
their descendants. Cherokee returns from all but two districts show, as
well, over 700 black intruders, most of whom were not entitled to citizenship by virtue of having returned to the Nation too late. The fewest black
citizens resided in Going Snake District; the largest number were in Illinois District. The fewest black intruders were also in Going Snake District, and the most were in Delaware District. This census formed the
basis of Cherokee attempts during the next several years to expel from
their nation the freedmen whom they did not recognize as citizens. Cherokee authorities furnished Craig with lists of those known not to be entitled to citizenship and of those whose status was doubtful. The former
were subject to immediate removal, and the latter were to have their
cases heard by the supreme court during the next winter. If judgment
went against them, they, too, were subject to removal.[2]

Because of questions asked by the Cherokee census takers, many of
the freedmen who had returned too late became anxious and asked Craig
to clarify the law regarding their rights to citizenship. Was their ignorance
of the treaty provisions to bar them from rights in the land where they
had been born? Were they to be denied citizenship because they could
not return within six months from Missouri, Kansas, Arkansas, Texas,
and the other Indian nations? Were they to blame because their former
masters had taken them against their will to areas distant from the Nation
and in some cases held them there until it was too late? They were still
straggling back in 1870; one group returned that year from California,
where they had been taken during the war, and were surprised to find
that they were barred from the land they considered their home.[3]

There was talk of a supplemental treaty to deal with the freedmen
and the possibility of an act by the National Council to admit all blacks
and their descendants who had been residents in the Nation at the out-

break of the war. Meanwhile the freedmen who had returned too late continued to farm and make improvements on the public domain. The position of the Indian Office officials was that the six-months' clause was explicit enough and that there was nothing the department could do for them. The officials recognized the authority of the Cherokee National Council in those freedman cases. Unless the council took some action regarding them, Craig was directed to consider them intruders and to deal with them accordingly. Even some of those freedmen who had been granted citizenship rights felt dissatisfied. Their leaders wanted a country set apart where they could own their land individually. While the Cherokees themselves did not want to give up their communal owner-ship of the land, Craig felt that they might agree to a reservation where each freedman head of family could take 160 acres of his own.[4]

Recourse for the excluded freedmen rested with the Cherokee supreme court before which, convened as a court of commissioners on citizen-ship, the blacks filed their claims to citizenship in December 1870. The cases were heard during the succeeding months. In its final report in the summer of 1871, the supreme court admitted 5 freedmen and their families to citizenship and rejected 131 cases, 93 of them because they had not returned within the six-months' limitation. Henry Johnson, Lee Cooper, Henry Bird, William Madden, and Alonzo Cullen (Manley) of Tahlequah District and Soloman Foster and William Hudson of Illinois District were rejected although they had married Cherokee freedwomen. The court ruled that there was no law for the court to follow since the intermarriage laws applied only to white men and Cherokee women or white women and Cherokee men, not to freedmen. The Cherokees believed that the freedmen had had ample opportunity to prove their claims. The census takers had clearly indicated those who, they believed without doubt, had returned too late. Those about whom they were uncertain had been sent to the supreme court.[5]

The excluded freedmen were dismayed. They had struggled to get back home, had established farms, and had built houses, assuming that they were on an equal footing with the other freedmen of the Nation. If the dictates of the court were carried out, all of those not admitted were subject to expulsion from their native land, homes, farms, family, and friends and to the loss of years of labor. They had a stake in the Cherokee Nation. They had toiled without pay during slavery to build the Nation. The former Confederate Cherokees, whom the freedmen considered their greatest enemies, owed to slave labor the very education that enabled them to hold power.[6] Because of ignorance, some of the freedmen had been unable to prove to the satisfaction of the supreme court that they had returned within the six-months' limit. Others had married Cherokee freedwomen under the impression that the laws of the Nation regarding marriage with noncitizens applied to them as well as to whites. Officers of the Cherokee courts for some time interpreted the law that way, taking fees and issuing licenses. Now those freedmen faced the possibility of having to leave their wives and children or of asking the latter to give up their rights as Cherokee citizens. The excluded freedmen had petitioned the National Council for relief from time to time, but sometimes their petitions had not been read.[7]

In the annual National Councils of 1870 and 1871, Chief Lewis Downing vainly sought passage of an act to adopt the freedmen. The freedmen blamed Downing's failure on the former Confederate Cherokees, who had "succeeded in working upon the prejudice of the Councillors." The Cherokees instead asked for removal of the freedmen and other intruders. In compliance Cherokee Agent John B. Jones issued a notice on February 2, 1872, giving the intruders who did not have permits thirty days to leave the Cherokee country. When the freedmen who had returned to the Nation too late found that the order applied to them, they persuaded Jones to suspend action against them until they could appeal to the U. S. government. As a result, Jones's superiors directed him to leave them alone but to remove all other intruders, hoping that the Cherokees would soon make some arrangements by which the freedmen would be allowed to remain legally in the Nation.[8] This act was the government's first intervention in the matter of Cherokee citizenship, and it set a precedent for decades to come.

The Cherokees were divided concerning what course justice, humanity, and expediency required concerning the freedmen. Downing and his political rival William P. Ross favored adoption. They were opposed by men such as William P. Boudinot, who edited the *Cherokee Advocate,* the national newspaper, and Chief Justice James Vann of the supreme court, who led those who claimed that adoption would be unfair to the Cherokees. Granting lands and money to the blacks, they said, would diminish the land and money remaining to the common heritage of the Cherokees. Agent Jones agreed with the freedmen's charges that the educated class was the most influential and the loudest in opposing adoption. He recommended that if the Cherokees did not make some arrangements for the blacks, they be given a tract of land west of the ninety-sixth meridian in repayment for the improvements they would have to give up in the Cherokee Nation. The five hundred to eight hundred freedmen in question were certain to lose everything if they were ejected. Yet Jones understood the Cherokee position; they treated the blacks well but were anxious to have the matter settled and, if the blacks were intruders, to have them removed. After the council of 1871 failed to adopt the blacks, Jones became convinced that future councils would not likely do so.[9]

In February 1873 Woodson Lowe, Stephen Little, Nelson Webber, and others of Snow Creek, near Parker, Kansas, were notified by order of the National Council that they were trespassing and must leave the farms they had established after the war. They were told not to plow, plant, or sow in the coming spring. "Rebel Cherokees," the freedmen said, claimed their improvements. They appealed to the Interior Department to save their homes and the schools they had organized and staffed. The department once more countermanded the orders of the National Council until Jones could investigate. In his report on November 25, 1873, Jones concluded that Lowe, Little, William Love, and Anthony Rogers were intruders and ordered their removal. Lowe was apparently a fugitive slave from Tennessee who had come to the Cherokee Nation in 1859. His owners had found him and were trying to recover him when the war broke out. He had gone to Kansas with the loyal Indians. In attempting to establish Cherokee rights, he now claimed that he had been owned by the Eli Murphy family, who supposedly held no slaves. Stephen Little, from Missouri, claimed rights through his wife, who, he alleged variously, had belonged to the Foreman family and to the Reverend Samuel A. Worcester, a missionary who had never been a slaveholder. It was learned that she had been sold by her Cherokee master some time before the war to a man in Van Buren, Arkansas. Little also claimed citizenship rights on the basis of having voted in the general elections in the Cherokee Nation. William Love, who had settled on the Verdigris River in 1866, claimed Cherokee blood, but he had been sold as an infant and had been a slave in Missouri. Agent Jones found, however, that Love's two daughters, Ellen and Martha, had been owned by Mansfield Seamore, a white man who had married a Cherokee. Anthony Rogers had been owned by

a man named Rogers at Fort Smith, Arkansas, and there was evidence
that he had been freed by the Cherokees. Henry Clay, who was from the
United States and had married a Cherokee freedwoman, was allowed to
remain unless his presence in the Cherokee Nation was likely in some
way to be detrimental to the relations between U. S. officials and the
Cherokees. Nelson Webber was found to be entitled to rights of citizenship and was allowed to remain.[10]

These cases reflect the Cherokee determination to rid the Nation of
blacks who had no legal claim to rights in it. William Love had died while
Jones was conducting his investigation, and Cherokees tried to eject
Love's family, whose affidavits show how weak some of the freedman
claims were. John Holt, Matilda Love, and Mary Washington—all relatives
of Love—claimed to have settled on and cultivated lands in the Cherokee
Nation by permission of Cherokee authorities. John Holt, from the United
States, had married Martha Love, William's daughter, who at the age of
five had been purchased by a Cherokee citizen and held until emancipation.
They had married by authority of the Cherokee officials and had opened
a farm on the Verdigris. Matilda Love was William's widow, and Mary
Washington was her daughter and the wife of George Washington. Martha
Love Holt had died in October 1868, and when William Love died, Chero-
kees moved in, took possession of his farm, and began cutting timber.
The blacks, who claimed to have been regarded previously as citizens,
were now regarded as trespassers; unable to secure protection for their
property from the Cherokee Nation, they turned to the United States.
Jones was asked to report, but he never did, probably because he considered the matter closed with his report on Love.[11] The case was typical.
The only tie the group had to the Cherokee Nation came through Martha
Love Holt, who had been a slave in the Cherokee Nation. After her death,
the Cherokees had apparently left the freedmen alone out of deference
to her father, William Love. When he died, all blood ties with the Nation
had been severed, and the Cherokees moved in.

Chief Lewis Downing died in office, and William P. Ross was elected
to fill his unexpired term. On November 5, 1873, Ross asked the National
Council to recognize the rights of those freedmen who were citizens and
to adopt those who had returned too late, "as a measure humane in its
spirit, liberal in character and expedient in result." He asked as well for
repeal of any statutes that might bear unequally upon the freedmen,
thus bringing the Nation into full compliance with the spirit as well as

the letter of the treaty.[12] Ross apparently viewed the freedmen with more foresight than did his less enlightened tribesmen. Had they followed his suggestion, the direction of Cherokee affairs during the next three decades would have been vastly different from what it was.

In 1874 the Interior Department put the affairs of the Five Civilized Tribes under the management of the newly created Union Agency at Muskogee, Creek Nation. Agent G. W. Ingalls was at first active in trying to remove trespassers reported by the Cherokees, who became more determined as time passed to have the intruders removed. In late October Ingalls requested and received approval for the removal of a number of trespassers, including the blacks Charles Cooper, Lee Cooper, and Alonzo Cullen of Tahlequah District and Jemima and her family of Sequoyah District, who were notified that if they did not leave within thirty days, their names would be turned over to military and civil authorities for removal by force.[13]

Faced with the possibility of the same fate, a group of "too late" freedmen—composed of Reuben Sanders, Alford Bell, Michael Sanders, Peter Meigs, Daniel Sanders, David Mayes, and Maryland Beck—petitioned the secretary of the interior concerning their treatment by the Cherokees. Their story had been told many times before. It had been impossible, they said, to return within six months after the treaty; they had had no clothing, money, horses, or wagons. Pressure to remove them, they felt, was the design of certain Cherokee officials and senators who had been Confederate officers. They pleaded for intercession because they had built comfortable houses and had from fifteen to seventy-five acres under cultivation. They could make a good living if left alone, they argued. Ingalls was ordered to investigate and to assist the freedmen in obtaining their rights. He asked Chief Ross to secure legislation by the council in behalf of the freedmen and to lay the petition of Reuben Sanders and the others before the council for action. Ross made the freedmen the subject of a special message to the council, in which he said that there could be no doubt about the legal status of the "too late" freedmen. Yet he wanted to give citizenship to that class of freedmen and asked for favorable legislation. A bill for adoption was introduced in the Cherokee senate. On the day it was read, a group of freedmen presented the National Council a petition, drafted at Four Mile Branch in Tahlequah District, in behalf of those "too late" freedmen named in the senate bill. The bill failed. Instead the council passed one that had a profound adverse effect upon some of the freedmen. Approved on December 4, 1874, it authorized the district sheriffs to sell at public auction, after fifteen days' public notice, the improvements of noncitizens.[14]

Meanwhile Agent G. W. Ingalls had asked for authority to exclude the freedmen from his earlier order for the removal of intruders and to protect them until their claims could be properly acted upon by the Cherokee courts or council. In response, Commissioner E. P. Smith directed him to keep separate lists of three classes of residents: those about whom there was no doubt; the freedmen; and North Carolina Cherokees who had come west after the war to join their tribesmen and who claimed a right to remain. Ingalls was to send the lists to the department and to allow the residents to remain undisturbed until their cases were finally decided. Notwithstanding these instructions, the Cherokees continued to press for the removal of all intruders. In Washington, their delegates asked for cavalry and a posse of Cherokee police to expel intruders. Indian Office officials refused the latter suggestion as a dangerous one, for if the Cherokees aided in ejecting the intruders, it would likely lead to conflict and bloodshed. The Cherokees got no troops, either, for at the time, none were available.[15]

Because grasshoppers and chinch bugs had destroyed crops in 1874, the following spring the Cherokees made a per-capita payment of "bread money" to all Cherokee citizens out of funds received for land on which the Osages had been located west of the ninety-sixth meridian. Over four hundred freedmen and many others claiming Cherokee citizenship rights were excluded from the payment. Ingalls tried to stop the payment because he estimated that one-third of the excluded freedmen were entitled to draw money as citizens. The commissioner of Indian affairs would not do as he requested, but he advised Ingalls to warn the Cherokee Nation that no person on account of temporary absence should be deprived of his right to collect money.[16]

In June Ingalls refused to remove a white family named Watts on the basis of his earlier orders to make separate lists of intruders for review by the department. Always sensitive to outside encroachments upon their authority, the Cherokees responded as might have been expected. In protest Chief William Ross refused to accept the department's right to review citizenship cases. The National Council had ordered the removal of the Watts family; to refuse would be to suspend the constitution. The Cherokee delegation in Washington asserted the National Council's "unequivocal right" to pass and enforce acts against intruders. Secretary Columbus Delano ordered the commissioner to investigate the rights of the freedmen in light of the Cherokees' stand on the matter of intruders and, if they were found intruders, to suggest measures for their removal, and the agent was again instructed to maintain separate lists of black, white, and Indian intruders.[17]

As Ingalls looked into the complaints of some of the blacks whom the Cherokees considered intruders, he became aware of special cases among them, such as those of John and Cynthia Morgan. John had belonged to Peggy Morgan and Cynthia to Chief John Ross. In 1862 Ross had taken them to Philadelphia. In August 1866 they had learned of the treaty and asked Ross to send them back to the Indian Territory. Ross, who was ill, had told them that being employed by the chief of the Nation was equivalent to being in the Nation and promised to take them back as soon as he could travel. However, he died, and they did not get back until June 1867. There were also the cases of Posey Gibson, Esau Fox, and many others who had settled on the Cherokee Neutral Lands in Kansas, which had been ceded to the United States. When the freedmen were forced to leave the land, the Cherokees would not recognize them as citizens even though, technically, they had been on Cherokee soil at the time that the treaty was made. Gibson, a farmer on the Verdigris River, had resided in the Cherokee Nation as a free person. He had purchased his wife, Emerrilla, but their two minor sons, James and Lewis, had been slaves when the war began. They fled to Kansas in 1862, returned to the Neutral Lands in January 1866, and moved to the Verdigris on August 20, 1867. Ingalls and Enoch Hoag, the superintendent of the Southern superintendency, were convinced that many similar cases existed and promised a formal investigation of these and others as soon as the "intense excitement" concerning the election of 1875 subsided.[18]

The election was a hotly contested one, with several politically related murders and disturbances at Pryor Creek, Vinita, and Tahlequah. Ingalls postponed the freedman cases, although Downing party men urged him to begin the investigations at once, apparently to influence the citizen freedmen to vote the Downing ticket. Ingalls refused, but at the height of the excitement he offered his services in calling the leaders of the parties together in a convention to work out their differences and to stop the frequent murders. Ross declined the offer, denying that there was any trouble in the Nation other than "a few old personal feuds." Downing party candidate Charles Thompson (Oochalata) won the election.[19] A conservative representative of the full-blood class of citizens, Thompson was the only chief of full or nearly full Cherokee blood to be elected after the war.

With the election over, Ingalls set about his investigations, estimating that there were at least five hundred freedmen who had either citizenship or per-capita payment claims. Since Ross had not cooperated with him earlier on the matter of keeping separate lists of intruders, Ingalls took it upon himself to create his own list of residents who, in his opinion, had a claim to Cherokee citizenship. He published notices in the newspapers, saying that he would hear complaints of Indians and freedmen who had claims.[20]

Among the first to apply to Ingalls for aid were freedmen Sam Starr, Allen Wilson, and Henry West. Starr, of Sequoyah District, had been taken as a slave to the Red River during the war and had returned to the Cherokee Nation in February 1866. He had been recognized as a citizen of the Nation, he claimed, voting in all elections as a staunch Downing man. Yet he was refused a per-capita payment in May 1875. Among Starr's witnesses was J. F. Berthel, a Cherokee who had taken the census in Sequoyah District in 1870. Wilson, whose story was much the same, had been owned by various Cherokees in the Old Nation and in the West since he was twelve years old and, at the beginning of the war, had been taken to Fort Towson on the Red River. Wilson's family were very ill at the end of the war, and he had awaited their recovery to start for the Cherokee Nation, arriving there in December 1867. He began farming in Tahlequah District and was considered a citizen until the per-capita payment of 1875. West, however, told a different story. He had come west with the Cherokees, married, and had a large family. For thirty years he was the property of Walker Mayfield, a Cherokee who had gone south during the war, taking West and his family with him to Russell County, Texas. West returned to the Cherokee Nation on April 1, 1871, and made a place on Camp Creek, about seven miles from Fort Smith, Arkansas. In 1871 he had talked with Samuel Houston Benge, a prominent Cherokee senator, who had told West that he was safe in his improvements. Benge had given him a letter to the agent, who in turn had told West to continue working and to report anyone who bothered him. All went well until July 1875, when his improvements were sold to the highest bidder at the Sequoyah District courthouse.

West had received no news of the sale until the man who had bought his property came and told him. When West made his deposition to Ingalls, the buyer was offering for resale, at several hundred dollars, the improvements he had bought at auction for the incredible price of six dollars. One of West's witnesses was Walker Mayfield, his former owner, who believed that West was entitled to citizenship because he was not aware of the treaty and had been advised by the agent and others to continue to work on his improvements.[21]

Outraged by such accounts, Ingalls was convinced that a number of the freedmen had been unjustly treated by the Cherokees and gave them letters directing the Cherokee authorities to refrain from removing them and selling their improvements until the cases were reviewed by the department. He believed that in exercising their right to determine Cherokee citizenship, the Cherokees had deprived hundreds of North Carolina Cherokees, citizens by marriage, and freedmen of their right of franchise, of their share in breadstuff funds, and of their property in the sale of their improvements. He accused the Cherokees of partiality in determining citizenship, of the frequent intentional destruction of papers of claimants by members of the National Council, of unnecessary delay in examining cases, and of selling improvements at a nominal price for resale later at much higher prices. To Ingalls, interference by Congress was necessary to remedy the situation.[22]

The Cherokees were outraged by Ingalls's advertising for and taking depositions from the freedmen and others. His action had exceeded his authority in the matter of citizenship, they claimed, and it would lead to "endless difficulty and confusion" because it would invite "all malcontents" to make claims, even without foundation. Always on guard against encroachments upon their autonomy, the Cherokees insisted that the Treaty of 1866 gave them alone the right to determine citizenship. Review of an act of council by authority other than Cherokee implied the right to reverse such action. Those who had been refused a share of the per-capita payment by mistake had recourse in the National Council. Therefore the Cherokees asked the secretary of the interior to instruct Ingalls to stop his investigations and to cooperate with Cherokee authorities in removing all intruders named by the National Council, using military force if necessary. Despite these Cherokee protests, affidavits of freedman residents concerning their rights to citizenship continued to be forwarded to the Indian Office. Groups of affidavits were sent in July,

August, October, November, and December 1875, and several subsequently proved to be good test cases. More were filed in January 1876.[23]

By midsummer 1875, Secretary Zachariah Chandler had become convinced that Congress must intervene to resolve the freedman matter. When
E. C. Watkins was sent to the Cherokee Nation to investigate, he agreed
essentially with Ingalls's assessment. He found a large proportion of those
whose cases were referred to him to be "clearly entitled" to Cherokee
citizenship, including eleven whose affidavits had been referred to the department. Watkins also named four others who had returned under the
six-months' limitation of the treaty but had been denied their rights. Most
of these claimants, he found, had applied to the courts and National Council, but no action had been taken. Watkins did not believe that the political
views of the applicants as a rule affected the question of citizenship. The
political parties were nearly evenly matched, and the National Council was
controlled by the Downing party, to which many of the freedmen belonged. Watkins believed that the per-capita payment had been the cause
of excluding a large number and naming them as intruders and that the National Council had been negligent in acting on applications, allowing some
to come for years before successive councils. Some freedmen, Watkins
found, had returned to the Cherokee Nation too late to come under the
treaty, and some, such as Henry West, John Landrum, John Davis, and
Soloman Nave, had lived in the country unmolested for years before
being placed on the intruder list. Although they had not returned under
the limitations of the treaty, Watkins felt that they were "equitably entitled" to citizenship and suggested that legislation be enacted to secure
their privileges.[24]

Charles Thompson assumed office as chief of the Nation in December
1875. Under his leadership, the Cherokees began to take a harder line on
the freedman issue. Early in 1876 he protested the freedmen's taking
their cases directly to the government and causing the subsequent investigations by Ingalls, whom former Chief Ross had charged with interference in the political concerns of the Cherokee Nation. Cherokee accusations had resulted in official charges against Ingalls in December 1875,
and in defense, Ingalls insisted that he had made no investigations except
those ordered by the department.[25]

Watkins's investigation spawned a number of affidavits from the freedmen. Between the time of his report in February 1876 and the following
November, no fewer than seventy-two affidavits were filed through Indian

superintendent William Nicholson. In February and March, Nicholson endorsed and forwarded the sworn affidavits of fifty-one freedmen, mostly heads of families, who had applied to the Cherokee courts and had been denied a hearing. On May 9 he filed a list of twenty-nine freedman children whose parents claimed citizenship rights but who were denied school privileges and the benefit of school funds.

The Cherokees, however, persisted in demanding the removal of intruders, both white and black. In November thirty-four citizens of Cooweescoowee District, including freedman Charles Rogers, petitioned the chief, complaining of intruders, including whites, freedmen who had not returned under the limitations of the treaty, and freedmen from the United States who had never resided in the Cherokee Nation before the war. In his annual message of 1876, Charles Thompson said that it had been the policy of former administrations to recommend the adoption of those who had been excluded by the treaty but that no action had been taken. He asked the council to take some final action—either to reject the freedmen or to adopt them.[26] Meanwhile Thompson had transmitted the complaint of the Cooweescoowee citizens directly to the President.

The new commissioner of Indian affairs, John Q. Smith, evidently angered by Thompson's having gone over the department's head, wrote Thompson early in December. This letter was extremely important, for it set the departmental policy in the matter of Cherokee citizenship for years to come. Following Inspector Watkins's cue, Smith charged that many freedmen who had repeatedly applied to the Cherokee authorities had prima facie evidence of their rights as citizens, that many others had been recognized as citizens at one time or another, but that the Cherokees had fixed no rules of law or procedures by which rights could be tried, determined, or protected by the courts and council. In fact, said Smith, there had been practically an entire disregard by the courts and council for the rights of the Cherokee freedmen, whereas more justice had been shown other classes of claimants. Therefore, Smith said, the department would not permit the removal of any persons theretofore reported until the Cherokee council devised some uniform and just system of rules by which the Cherokee courts could impartially hear and finally determine their rights. Smith suggested an act of council by which the jurisdiction to hear all cases of citizenship would be vested in the circuit courts of the Cherokee Nation, operating under rules approved by the secretary of the interior. Cases could be heard on petition of the claimant or upon notice served to the doubtful citizen, who had sixty days to prepare. Failure to appear would be deemed a confession of lack of evidence. All adverse judgments with the evidence in the cases were to be forwarded to the secretary of the interior for review. Judgments affirming citizenship were to be final.[27]

Thompson wrote Smith a 139-page reply, a mixture of protests and constitutional arguments against infringements upon Cherokee autonomy in citizenship matters. Thompson claimed that the freedmen had had every opportunity to prove their rights. Since 1870 the supreme court had decided doubtful cases. This, he said, disproved Smith's contention that the freedmen had no law by which they could prove their citizenship. He also defended the census takers of 1870, who generally took the word of the freedmen unless it was disputed by someone. In that case, and when evidence was clear and showed that the freedman did not return within the six-months' limit, he was put on the doubtful list. Thompson was clearly biased against the freedmen, who he said were the "most numerous but least deserving" class of noncitizen. Those who had never been owned by Cherokees and those who did not return in time were the loudest, and Thompson protested against their being forced upon the Cherokees. Finally he rejected the commissioner's suggestion that intruders be given sixty days' notice to prove their rights.[28]

The Cherokee delegation, too, insisted that action had been taken to determine the rights of most of the claimants whose affidavits had been forwarded to the department. However, Smith believed that if action had been taken, it was entirely ex parte and therefore should not be conclusive of the rights of individuals. Many deserved to be ousted, he admitted, but to remove all of those the Cherokee authorities wanted removed would do great injustice, to which the U. S. government would be a part. The delegation had also defended Cherokee autonomy in the matter of citizenship, which Smith denied. As time passed, he became more convinced that the freedmen should be protected, that none should be removed before the matter of jurisdiction was determined and a uniform method of deciding their rights was adopted. Smith realized that his letter to Thompson might result in Cherokee legislation that would make the matter only more confusing; therefore in early February 1877 he recommended that the department authorize the immediate removal of all persons reported by the Cherokees as intruders who could not, upon an investigation by the agent, present evidence of their right to citizenship. He wanted those with such evidence held for future consideration and action in the manner suggested in his letter to Thompson.[29]

Meanwhile the Cherokee delegation, supported by their counterparts from the Creek Nation, had written to President Grant, asserting their rights to determine citizenship in their nations. Grant referred the matter to Secretary of the Interior Carl Schurz, who took the position that while the government of the United States recognized the rights of the Cherokees under the treaty stipulations, it reserved the right "to determine the question as to who are and who are not intruders under the law." He directed Commissioner Smith to remove all those who could not, in an investigation by the agent, present evidence that they were entitled to citizenship by adoption, blood, or treaty. Those who could present such cases would be allowed to remain until their cases could be disposed of in the manner suggested by the commissioner in his letter to Thompson on December 8, 1876. Smith, in turn, asked the Cherokees and Creeks to furnish Union Agent S. W. Marston lists of those they considered intruders, whom Marston was to notify to show proof in the form of affidavits, witnessed by at least one disinterested person. Smith sent Marston the names of eighty-four Cherokee freedmen who had already presented prima facie cases.[30]

In August 1877 Chief Thompson submitted a list of intruders from seven districts, demanding their removal and stressing that no Cherokee law provided for the intermarriage of noncitizen blacks with Cherokee freedpeople. In 1871 the supreme court of the Nation had held such marriages illegal, and those who had intermarried were considered intruders. Thompson did not deny that many freedmen on the lists had been formerly owned by citizens of the Cherokee Nation, but they had failed to prove their rights even though the Cherokees had given them ample opportunity to do so. Thompson listed twenty-five black and fifty-eight white intruder families in Sequoyah District. Of the blacks, four were cases of intermarriage with recognized freedwomen, five (including Henry West) had returned too late, and four had been sold out of the Nation before the war. Canadian District, which had been settled after the war by Cherokees who had fought for the South, had only one black listed—Jim Caloway—but thirty-four white intruder families. Illinois District had thirty-nine white and four black families listed—Taylor Goin and Jack Hawkins at the mouth of the Illinois and John Wheat and a family named Hall at Greenleaf Bend. In Tahlequah District there were twenty-five white and twenty-six black families, including that of Charles Cooper who had married a Cherokee freedwoman. Two blacks were listed as intruders in Flint District. By far the greatest number were in Cooweescoowee District— forty-eight at Big Creek, five at Cedar Creek, four at Lightning Creek, and thirteen at Cabin Creek, all of whom returned "long after" the deadline. Two on Cabin Creek allegedly had not lived in the Nation before the war.[31]

The list clearly reveals the nature of the problem facing the government. To remove those declared intruders by the Cherokees would mean breaking up homes, forcing one parent to leave his children or to remove them and deprive them of their rights as Cherokee citizens. And then there were those who had been born and reared as slaves in the Cherokee Nation. Their families were there, their dead were buried in Cherokee soil, and they knew no other home. However, because of postwar circumstances, they had been unable to return within the time allotted. As directed, Agent Marston sent them notices to show proof, and in the fall, a number of affidavits were filed.[32] The new commissioner, E. A. Hayt, continued Smith's policies. He wrote to delegates W. P. Ross and H. T. Landrum on November 7, 1877, reiterating the stand Smith had taken the year before: "While the department reserves to itself the right to finally determine who are and who are not intruders under the law, it expects the Cherokee National Council to enact some general and uniform law by which the Cherokee courts shall hear and determine the rights of claimants to citizenship, subject to only the reversion of the Secretary of the Interior after a final adjudication has been reached in each case in accordance with said law."[33] In other words, the department still insisted on control in the matter.

In an attempt to head off a usurpation of Cherokee power, the National Council passed an act, approved December 5, 1877, establishing a court of commissioners to decide citizenship cases. Known as the Chambers court, it consisted of John Chambers, O. P. Brewer, and George Downing.[34] Its creation had come after years of frustration for all involved—the freedmen, the Cherokees, and officials of the Department of the Interior. If the Cherokees hoped that the new court would form a bulwark against erosion of their authority and would finally dispose of the freedman cases, they were to be disappointed. The narrowness of vision of officials in the Interior Department persisted for a number of years as they insisted on review of rejected cases. In fact the legal struggle to define the rights of the freedmen had just begun.

The court of commissioners set about its task early in 1878, and its work soon resulted in another clash with the commissioner of Indian affairs. The commissioners defined *citizen* according to article 3 of the Cherokee constitution: "All native-born Cherokees, all Indians and whites, legally members of the nation by adoption, and freemen who have been liberated by voluntary act of their former owners or by law, as well as free colored persons who were in the country at the commencement of the rebellion, and are now resident therein, or who may return within six months from the 19th day of July, 1866, and their descendants who reside within the limits of the Cherokee Nation." The commission had jurisdiction over citizenship cases that the supreme court or the National Council had failed to adjudicate; that the National Council had decided adversely and the claimant had appealed to the United States; that had been taken directly to the United States; that had involved fraud in gaining citizenship; and that had not yet been decided. At meetings publicly announced at Tahlequah and Fort Gibson, the commissioners accepted, with an attorney's assistance, oral testimony of witnesses under oath, the records or certified copies of records of the council and supreme court, or affidavits taken in any court of record in the United States. All persons who refused or failed to bring their cases before the commission for adjudication would be considered intruders, whom the principal chief would report for removal. Results of the hearings were to be announced at the annual meeting of the National Council the next fall.[35]

The freedmen distrusted these activities. A petition signed by sixty-three blacks charged that no person of African descent could receive justice at the hands of the Cherokees. They claimed that a number of freedmen had been murdered and that their Cherokee killers had not been punished. Finally they accused Agent S. W. Marston and his clerk of being their "most dangerous enemies." Marston, they said, had issued an order to have freedman Moses Hardwick removed and his improvements turned over to James McCamish, a white man. Although the orders were not carried out, they set what the freedmen viewed as a dangerous precedent regarding them. Among the signers of the petition to President Hayes were Hardwick, Isaac Rogers, and a number of the Vanns, Martins, Beans, and Downings, whose cases the Cherokees had consistently rejected. The freedmen considered the three Cherokee commissioners their enemies, and their belief that the Cherokees were determined to "crush" them was supported by Daniel C. Finn, a white attorney who had represented many of the freedmen in presenting their evidence and who was ordered removed from the Cherokee Nation as an intruder on March 13, 1878.[36] It is likely but uncertain that his removal was politically motivated.

C. W. Holcomb, the new commissioner of Indian affairs, refused to recognize the citizenship court or to cooperate with the Cherokees in the matter of intruders. Since Watkins had been ordered to investigate the matter in 1875, the Cherokees had submitted between five hundred and six hundred names of intruders, most of whom claimed rights under the Treaty of 1866. In Holcomb's view, the fact that the secretary of the interior was asked to remove them implied his right to review intruder cases. The Cherokees, of course, rejected this right, as well as the right of the secretary to require the Cherokees to submit their laws regarding citizenship for his approval. In reply, Holcomb said, "You are shutting the door and rendering it impossible to expel these men, because you are not willing to make a law that will be considered fair among men." Cherokee delegate W. P. Adair argued that there were no fewer than twenty-five hundred people who were in the Cherokee Nation illegally. Said Holcomb, "You are keeping them there." It was a stalemate, but the Cherokees agreed to submit, *without obligation,* the draft of a law to the secretary for his opinion.[37]

Despite the commissioner's refusal to recognize their commission, the Cherokees continued, during the next few months, to summon freedmen to appear, with attorney, before them. The freedmen had to hire their own attorneys while the commission employed two lawyers at national expense to defend the Nation. Some became discouraged and tried to sell their homes for what they could get; most became afraid that they were going to lose the property they had worked for during the past several years because they could not afford a lawyer. A group from Big Creek, including Reuben and Daniel Sanders, Peter and George Meigs, and William Tower, asked to send one or two representatives to state their case before the next Congress, but Acting Commissioner William M. Leeds refused permission. Other freedmen complained of being put on the doubtful lists.[38]

Most freedmen who appeared before the commission did not fare well. Louis Carter, for example, was a freedman from the United States who had married Julia Reese, who he claimed was a former slave of Judge H. D. Reese, clerk of the Cherokee supreme court. Carter produced a copy of the marriage license, which showed that the ceremony had been performed in 1873 by Judge T. M. Walker of the middle circuit court. Nevertheless the commission rejected Carter's claim on the grounds that Julia Reese had not been a slave at the beginning of the war. A similar case was that of William Hudson of Fort Gibson, who claimed to have returned to the Nation and married a Cherokee freedwoman. He was acknowledged a citizen until 1870, when he was placed on the doubtful list. He said he had placed his testimony before the courts, which failed to act. When he asked for the return of his legal papers, he was told that they had been lost. He asked Dobson Reese, clerk of the supreme court, for a duplicate of his marriage license. When he presented it as proof before the citizenship court, the judges told him that it had not been procured from a legal authority.[39]

At the August session of the citizenship court, several freedmen were denied citizenship by default for failure to appear. Among them were the following, which exemplify the kinds of claims with which the commission had to deal. Harriet Ward of Big Creek, widow of Berry Ward, had five minor children. She claimed to have been the slave of George Ward at the beginning of the war, to have fled to Kansas, and to have returned to the Cherokee Nation on August 25, 1866. Visey Foreman of Cedar Creek, the widow of William Foreman, said that she and her husband had been slaves of Johnson Foreman at the beginning of the war, that they had fled to Kansas during the war, and that they had returned to the Cherokee Nation on August 25, 1866. Peter Hudson of Big Creek claimed that he had been the slave of Susan Hudson, that his wife, Charity, had been owned by Thomas Hudson, and that he had fled to Kansas, returning to the Cherokee Nation on July 19, 1866. Zelfrey Holt of Big Creek stated that she and her two daughters, Wannah and Rebecca, had been slaves of William Holt at the start of the war and that her mother, Wannah Thompson, had been the slave of William Thompson. They had fled to Kansas together, returning to the Cherokee Nation on December 13, 1866. Jack Nelson, who lived on Grand River in Saline District, asserted that he had been a slave of Joseph Martin when the war began and had fled to Kansas where on June 16, 1863, he enlisted in Company H, Seventy-ninth United States Colored Troops, from which he was discharged at Pine Bluff, Arkansas, on October 1, 1865. He said he returned to the Cherokee Nation on September 6, 1866. Caesar Smith of Cooweescoowee District maintained that he had been the slave of Ned Smith when the war began, that he went to Kansas in 1864, and that he returned in 1866. Polly Ann Whitmire of Salt Creek, Cooweescoowee District, claimed to have been the slave of George Whitmire and to have resided in the Nation until July 6, 1866, when she went to Kansas, returning on December 21, 1866. Johnson Webber of Coowee-

scoowee District had been the slave of Aka Webber at the beginning of
the war, he said; he fled to Kansas during the war, returned in December
1866 with his father, Sam Webber, and made a place, returned to Kansas,
and came finally to the Cherokee Nation in the summer of 1867. Santa
Anna Nevins of Big Creek claimed to have been a slave of Moses Nevins,
and his wife, Elga, claimed to have been a slave of Johnson Whitmire and
to have gone to Kansas in 1862 and returned on August 25, 1866. Also
denied citizenship on August 20, 1878, were George and Peter Meigs of
Big Creek.[40]

These freedmen had been rejected for failure to appear. But why had
they gone to the trouble to make affidavits and then had not appeared
before the commission? The reason may have been a letter from Acting
Commissioner W. M. Leeds to some of the freedmen on July 16, 1878,
in which he told them that the department had never recognized the
authority of the Cherokees to decide who were and were not citizens of
the Nation and that until such recognition was given, it was not necessary
for the freedmen to attend meetings of the court of commissioners. No
plan would be adopted for deciding doubtful cases, Leeds said, that did
not provide for a fair and impartial trial of the freedman cases. The department was determined, he said, "to protect to the last extremity all
parties who are by treaty or law entitled to citizenship in the nation."[41]

In the early fall of 1878, Commissioner E. A. Hayt requested Chief
Thompson to permit no enforcements of decisions by the Cherokee commission until the questions involved were determined by the department.
Thompson remained firm, insisting on the Cherokees' authority to deter-
mine the rights to citizenship and asked the department not to interfere.
Once more, he went over the commissioner's head, this time to the at-
torney general of the United States and to President Hayes, asserting that
Cherokee jurisdiction over its own citizens was "an inherent national
right that has been uniformly recognized by the Supreme Court of the
United States and by treaty stipulations."[42]

Complaints from both Indians and freedmen resulted in an investigation of the intruder and citizenship questions by a subcommittee of the
Senate Committee on Territories who were in the Indian Territory to
find the sentiments of the Indians regarding the establishment of a territorial government for the Indian Territory and regarding allotment of
lands in severalty. The Cherokees' key witness was Jesse Ross of Illinois
District, the only Cherokee freedman interviewed by the subcommittee.

According to Ross, the three schools in his district were adequate at the
time for the educational needs of the freedman children. He said that
the black citizens of his district were well satisfied with their condition,
and that they had the same rights as Cherokees: voting, sitting on juries,
and cultivating as much land as they were able. According to Ross, there
were no freedmen in his district on the doubtful list, none of them had
gone before the citizenship court to prove their rights, and none had been
denied their share of the bread money in 1875.[43] Perhaps Ross was ignorant of freedman affairs in the Nation, but his answers were the kind
the Cherokees wanted given to the subcommittee. The only other witnesses questioned concerning citizenship matters were John F. Lyons,
attorney for the citizenship court, and George Downing, one of the
judges.

At the November session of the citizenship court, other cases went
by default because the freedmen failed to appear. The Chambers court
filed its report on November 18, and on December 3, Chief Thompson
sent President Hayes the names of 185 applicants, including those the
Chambers court had tried and rejected, among whom were 14 freedmen
households in Saline District, 5 in Flint District, and 52 in Cooweescoowee
District. Many of those listed had been rejected by default.[44]

On December 5, 1878, the National Council extended the jurisdiction
of the citizenship court to the cases of all claimants to rights of citizenship who at the time of the bill's passage were residing in the Cherokee
Nation and directed the commission to sit without adjournment from
the time of its first session until June 30, 1879.[45]

Early in 1879, the Cherokees worked toward a compromise with the
United States. In a memorial, the Cherokee delegation proposed, first,
to suspend confiscation of the property of alleged intruders until their
rights to citizenship had been decided. Second, the Cherokee court of
citizenship would hear all claims to Cherokee citizenship, their rulings
in the case of freedmen subject to revision by the department. Third, the
status of freedmen who had not returned within the six-months' limit
was subject to such an arrangement as the United States and the Cherokee
council might agree upon. Finally, all other persons, except the freedmen
referred to, who had presented claims and were in the Nation without
authority were to be removed immediately.[46]

In reply Commissioner E. A. Hayt proposed a joint commission of
four—two appointed by the secretary of the interior and two by the

Cherokees—to act on all claims of persons whom the Cherokees considered intruders or noncitizens. A unanimous decision of the commission would be final and would fix the status of the party concerned.
Those ruled intruders would have thirty days after notification to sell
their improvements and to leave the Nation. If the commission divided
in opinion, testimony was to be forwarded to the Office of Indian Affairs for final disposition. What Hayt was saying, in effect, was that the
Cherokees' right to exist as a nation did not include the right to determine their own citizenship.[47] His plan was obviously a departure from
former departmental decisions, which had recognized the Cherokee circuit courts as the proper tribunal to give preliminary hearings to citizenship cases. However, its purpose was ultimately the same. Hayt's hasty
answer, on the same day of the Cherokees' memorial, failed to recognize
the Cherokee concessions and their willingness to negotiate. Here was a
missed opportunity to work toward a solution to the difficult problem
that was to drag on for almost another decade. More important was
the forecast of serious inroads the government would make on Cherokee
autonomy before the end of the century.

The Cherokees were clearly disappointed, for the concessions they had
offered showed their willingness to dispose of the citizenship question.
Their propositions in regard to the freedmen showed that they would
deal justly with the legal claimants and liberally with the illegal ones.
They therefore rejected Hayt's idea of a joint commission and retreated
to their former position that the right to settle citizenship matters lay
solely with the Cherokee Nation. They maintained that the National
Council was well within its rights to create the court of commissioners.
To deny the court would be to relinquish legislative functions and surrender all legislative freedom. Since no agreement was likely to be
reached, the Cherokees wanted the matter referred to the attorney general
for an opinion.[48]

The Cherokee delegation felt that Hayt's reply had been created, in
part, by misrepresentations to the Indian Office "by evil disposed persons,"
both citizen and noncitizen, who accused the commission on citizenship
and the Cherokee authorities of failing to do justice to the freedmen. The
"evil disposed persons" they had in mind were probably the representatives, then in Washington, of a number of freedmen in Cooweescoowee
District. In February 1879 W. S. Watkins, Nathaniel Duffie, R. N. Sanders,

H. C. Hayden, Arthur Williams, and Isaac Rogers formally presented their grievances to the secretary of the interior. They said that some had received notices that their improvements would be confiscated in ninety days, that they had been summoned to appear before the court, but that the Indian Office had informed them by letter that the court had no authority. Therefore they had not appeared and were pronounced intruders by the court. Of course, they referred to the letter of Acting Secretary Leeds to Daniel Landrum and W. M. Davis during the preceding summer. On the one hand, he had told the freedmen that until the department recognized the authority of the Cherokee citizenship court, there was no need for them to appear before the commission, assuring them that the department would see that their cases were adjudicated impartially and fairly. Yet Leeds told them that those who had not conformed to the ninth article of the Treaty of 1866 would be forcibly removed.[49] It is little wonder that the freedmen were confused, for there was certainly something contradictory in this expression of policy. Evidently the freedmen took up as a directive only that part which they wanted.

Williams, Watkins, and Duffie presented a petition to the commissioner of Indian affairs, asking that he interpose to guarantee their access to the public schools, the orphan fund, the seminaries, and the insane asylum of the Cherokee Nation and to prevent the confiscation of their property. Williams and Duffie, accompanied by Oliver C. Black, a black attorney from Washington, met with the commissioner on February 25, the day Hayt rejected the Cherokee memorial proposing the compromise regarding the settlement of citizenship cases. Williams and Duffie charged that "under cover of an illegal construction of a clause of the treaty, the Council of the Cherokees had begun a system of confiscation which threatens the ruin of the negro population." In case of confiscation, they said, property and improvements of the three hundred families (an exaggeration) could be bought by Cherokee citizens for nominal sums. A farm of 160 acres that had been improved for ten years could be bought for ten or fifteen dollars, they said, and "the colored farmer and his family turned out of doors homeless, penniless, and without any tribunal to appeal to for protection." Duffie claimed that the freedmen were in worse condition than they had been under slavery, and he threatened that if confiscation orders were enforced, the freedmen of the entire Nation would be forced to fight to protect their rights, for freedmen in all nine districts

were threatened with the fate of those in Cooweescoowee. They
wanted a black agent appointed to look after the interests of the estimated
fifteen thousand freedmen in the Indian Territory. The secretary and commissioner assured them that steps would be taken to save their property,
and they took under consideration the matter of an agent, an idea that
never fructified. The freedman delegation, destitute, applied in early
March for departmental funds to meet expenses they had incurred in
Washington and to return home.[50]

No doubt the entreaties of these freedmen influenced the commissioner
in taking his hard-line stand of February 25. Perhaps more significant was
the case of Allen Wilson, which came to his attention at about the same
time. Wilson, about sixty, had been born a slave in the old Cherokee Nation and had moved to the West with the Cherokees. He had been taken
to the Choctaw Nation by his master during the war and afterward had
been unable to return to the Cherokee Nation because his master had
died. Wilson had a large family and therefore had to make a crop and
dispose of it in order to obtain enough money to return to the Nation
His first crop failed, so he had to make another. Thus, he did not return
to the Nation until the fall of 1867. He went to the chief and leading men
who told him to go to work and open a farm. He built his house about nine
miles east of Fort Gibson and opened a sixty-acre farm. He planted an orchar
and nursery, and in 1879 he had 350 bearing apple trees and over 1,000
peach trees. He also had twelve acres planted in wheat.[51]

When Wilson appeared before the commission on citizenship, he was
rejected. As a result, on January 25, 1879, the *Cherokee Advocate* published a notice of the sale, in fifteen days, of Wilson's property. Wilson
estimated his property's value at two thousand dollars, but it would
bring only a fraction of that at public auction. Some Cherokee citizens
offered to buy his improvements and to let him work for them, but to
Wilson, that was not freedom. He would rather have sold his improvements
and moved out of the Nation. Wilson's attorney was W. P. Boudinot, a
Cherokee of Fort Gibson who had defended many of the freedmen before
the Cherokee commission. Many of these people, Boudinot said, were "patterns of industry" who had made excellent improvements in desirable locations. Wilson was especially industrious, prosperous, and respected. Boudinot
appealed to the secretary to intercede in Wilson's behalf. The sale was too hasty
The Cherokee commission would sit until the end of June, and applica-

tions for copies of evidence taken by it were refused until it was forwarded to the chief's office. By the time the department could request it and review the case, Wilson's property would be sold. The acting commissioner talked to Charles Thompson, who was in Washington with the delegation. Thompson sent a telegram through the commissioner's office, requesting the sheriff of Tahlequah District to suspend the sale of the improvements of Wilson and those of Green Goff and to await further orders.[52]

Wilson's case was just one of several. In his defense of the freedman claims, Boudinot had operated under the commissioner's directive of December 8, 1876, and had told his clients that all adverse decisions would be referred to the department for final decision. However, the *Cherokee Advocate* published a long list of those rejected and named as intruders. Among them were several of Boudinot's clients. In an attempt to clarify the matter, the principal chief ordered the suspension of the sales of intruder improvements, and the Cherokee delegation asked Secretary Carl Schurz to submit to the attorney general a request for clarification of three points: (1) Did the Cherokee Nation have the right to determine citizenship; (2) did the freedmen have any claim to participation in lands, property, and moneys under the Treaty of 1866; and (3) was it the duty of the government to protect the Cherokee Nation from intruders?[53] While the decision was pending, Attorney General Charles Devins gave the Cherokee delegation and their special agent W. A. Phillips every opportunity to present their arguments to him.

The decision was not rendered until late that year, but six or seven weeks after the questions had been submitted, Phillips had seen an opinion in Schurz's office. Phillips assured the Cherokees that in the decision, Devins had upheld the Cherokee Nation and had dissented from the former opinions of the department. It recognized, he claimed, the Cherokees' right to decide matters of citizenship in their tribunals and to have intruders expelled by the government. The Cherokees hailed the decision. They hoped at last to be able to cope with the rapidly growing number of intruders; there were now so many that the land speculators were using them in their pleas before Congress as a reason for opening the Indian Territory and organizing it under a territorial government. Equally important to the Cherokees was the belief that the opinion allowed them to deal specifically with the freedmen who claimed citizenship but who had not been recognized as bona fide citizens by Cherokee authorities.

To this class were added those who had been unable to return within the six-months' limit and those who had wandered back at leisure, bringing with them numbers of blacks from the states. The Cherokee delegation believed that the attorney general had ruled that the Nation must render impartial justice to the bona fide citizens. Failing such, the United States was obligated to see that it was done. The opinion intimated that this latter could be done voluntarily by the Nation or concurrently with the government. It was up to the Cherokees to settle the status of the freedmen by adoption or by negotiation. The Cherokees read in the decision a recognition of their commission on citizenship and fully expected the acceptance of its decrees in all but "exceptional cases of certain colored persons."[54]

The freedmen did not receive well the news of the opinion. Confiscation of property had been resumed. There was the case of Maryland Beck of Vinita, for instance, who had already put his crop in when his improvements were confiscated and sold. Some freedmen, including those who had gone to Washington earlier that year, held meetings to discuss their dilemma; others appealed for a guarantee·of their rights and for an investigation.[55]

Under the assumption that the opinion had gone in their favor, the Cherokee delegation called Hayt's attention to their various letters concerning the freedmen during the past two or three years. They reasserted their desire to deal fairly with those people and asked Hayt to submit to the National Council in November any proposition he thought would settle all difficulties "by negotiation or otherwise" between the Cherokees and the United States. Meanwhile they recommended to Chief Thompson that he suspend the sales of intruder freedmen's improvements until the matter was finally settled. In response, on July 25, 1879, the commissioner again proposed to the principal chief the establishment of a joint commission to decide the cases of citizenship claimants. But Thompson took no action, perhaps because he was about to leave office. In the summer elections of 1879, National party candidate Dennis Wolfe Bushyhead had been elected principal chief. At the polls, some freedmen who claimed citizenship but had not proved it had been challenged. Election clerks and judges took down the names of candidates for whom the freedmen would have voted so that if the need arose, the votes could be tallied.[56]

When the National Council met in November, the Cherokee delegation reported the decision by the attorney general. In his first annual message on November 10, Chief Bushyhead made a special plea for the freedmen. To those who had been enfranchised and adopted into the body politic, he gave assurance that they would be treated justly. He asked the council to give them all of their rights under the treaty, just as the Cherokees would hope to have their treaties with the United States respected: "Let them feel that they live under the shadow and protection of our and their own laws." Bushyhead also reported on the citizenship commission. It had been in session for nearly two years at a cost of $14,905.95 to the Nation. It had disposed of 416 applications. Citizenship had been given in 67 cases and rejected in 338. Five had been withdrawn and 6 declined for want of jurisdiction.[57]

The National Council created a new citizenship commission. Consisting of three men appointed by the chief and confirmed by the Cherokee senate, it was to be "a tribunal of last resort." It was to try, among others, all cases not resolved by the late commission, those presented to the National Council before the act, all cases that were adjudicated adversely by the National Council and appealed to the United States, all cases where claimants had ignored the Cherokee authorities and appealed directly to the United States, and all cases of Africans who claimed to have complied with the treaty, had had no adverse decision by a Cherokee tribunal, but had not yet been recognized as citizens. Operating under the same rules as the former commission, it was to meet twice a year in month-long sessions at which it could compel witnesses to appear. Bushyhead appointed Roach Young, G. W. Mayes, and William Harnage to the commisison. Still under the assumption that the attorney general's opinion was in their favor, the National Council also passed an act empowering the delegates to Washington to "make arrangements by negotiation or otherwise" with the United States to settle "all existing difficulties and embarrassments" between the two nations regarding the status of the freedmen.[58]

During this time, the Cherokees had not received a copy of the opinion Phillips had seen in the secretary's office although they had requested it repeatedly. When it finally came, it was not what the Cherokees had expected. It was instead an opinion answering the three questions of the Cherokees and two submitted by the commissioner. Rendered on December 12, the decision clearly upheld the department's position regarding the freedmen: "I reply that it is quite plain that in executing such treaties

the United States are not bound to regard simply the Cherokee law, and
its construction by the council of the Nation, but that any Department
required to remove alleged intruders must determine for itself, under the
general law of the land, the existence and extent of the exigency upon
which such requisition is founded." The opinion meant that any intruder
reported by the Cherokees must be found to be an intruder by the department. If it lacked confidence in the Cherokee authorities in the matter,
it had the right to investigate. If the alleged intruder could present merely
a prima facie case, he would not be removed until his case could be disposed of.
The commissioner, apparently exploring other possible ways to solve the
difficult problem of citizenship, had asked if the matter of jurisdiction
might not be determined by the U. S. courts, but Devins had carefully
avoided answering.[59]

Throughout the preceding months, the Cherokees had proceeded,
under a false assumption, as if their complete authority in the matter
had been supported by Devins's opinion. During that time, the freedmen found little sympathy and a good bit of prejudice among the
Cherokees. George W. Johnson, editor of the *Cherokee Advocate,*
spoke out against them. He said that no Cherokee would deny a freedman his treaty rights. But, Johnson said, "If that instrument is not in
their favor, there is no help for them; they cannot live in this Nation
as citizens." Those who had been slaves before the war but had failed
to return in six months could not be legally admitted as citizens. "We
admit," Johnson wrote, "their case is a hard one; but it is not our fault."
He said of the citizen freedmen: "As an individual, we shall at all times
object to having our colored citizens sitting in our Council to legislate
for us. Our principal reason is, we know of none that has the capacity
to make laws for us, and as to voting on bills, we know from the past,
that their votes would be cast according to the dictation of others. We
believe that we have Cherokees in sufficient numbers, and of ability, to
legislate for us."[60]

By the time Bushyhead took office as chief, the Cherokees were no
closer to settling the matter of freedman citizenship than they had been
when they started. The special sense of obligation to the Cherokee freedmen on the part of U. S. officials had resulted in their refusal to recognize
the authority of the Cherokee commissions on citizenship; thus they had
denied that the Cherokees had control over that part of their internal

affairs. This deliberate action by Indian Office officials was perhaps the most profound inroad on Cherokee autonomy in the post-Civil War period. It made it virtually impossible for the Nation to rid itself of the people who had no claim to Cherokee citizenship, and it opened the door to another decade of wrangling over the question of ultimate authority in the matter, a time when the Cherokee Nation—indeed, the Indian Territory—was overrun by intruders.

NOTES

1. Act of December 3, 1869, National Archives Record Group 75 (Records of the Bureau of Indian Affairs), *Irregularly Shaped Papers,* shelf 6, and *Letters Received Relating to Cherokee Citizenship,* 12339-83 (hereafter cited as *Cherokee Citizenship File*).

2. 42d Cong., 3d sess., *House Report 98,* 470; W. L. G. Miller and Maxwell Chambers to James Vann, July 26, 1870, and John N. Craig to Commissioner of Indian Affairs, October 26, 1870, National Archives Microfilm Publications, *Microcopy M234* (Records of the Office of Indian Affairs, Letters Received)-103, C1576-70, C1885-70; F. E. Foster to Commissioner, December 28, 1871, *Microcopy M234*-104, F785-71; Report of the Secretary of the Interior, 41st Cong., 3d sess., *House Executive Document 1,* pt. 4, 747. Cherokee returns listed citizen freedmen by districts as follows: 70 in Sequoyah, 3 in Going Snake, 274 in Tahlequah, 36 in Delaware, 143 in Cooweescoowee, 79 in Canadian, and 430 in Illinois.

3. Craig to Commissioner, July 27, 1870, *Microcopy M234*-103, C1521-70; Report of the Secretary of the Interior, 41st Cong., 3d sess., pt. 4, 747-748.

4. Report of the Secretary of the Interior, 41st Cong., 3d sess., pt. 4, 747-748, 753; W. F. Cady to Craig, September 8, 1870, National Archives Microfilm Publications, *Microcopy M21* (Records of the Office of Indian Affairs, Letters Sent)-98, 55.

5. "Colored Persons Admitted to Cherokee Rights and Citizenship by the Supreme Court," June 21, 1871, and "Applicants for Citizenship: Supreme Court Cases, Admitted, 1871," Indian Archives Division, Oklahoma Historical Society, *Cherokee--Citizenship (Tahlequah);* Charles Thompson to S. W. Marston, August 30, 1877, *Cherokee Citizenship File,*

U208-77. Admitted from Cooweescoowee District were Sam and Johnson Webber, Charles Campbell, John Rogers, Harry Still, Armstead Nave, and Joseph Wolfe; from Tahlequah District, Eli and Jonas Keys, Hardy Thompson, Russell Vann, Feeling Evans, and Josh Whitmire; from Saline District, William Lynch, Charles Nave, Butler McNair, Delilah Vann, and the children of Bill Vann; from Illinois District, Mike, Ony, William and Abraham Fields, Nancy and Polly Alberty, Cobb Vann, Sally Vann, her children and grandchildren, and Eli Gentry; from Canadian District, Allen Latta. "Colored Persons Rejected, June 21, 1871," Indian Archives Division, Oklahoma Historical Society, *Cherokee–Freedmen (Tahlequah);* "List of Coloreds Who Were Rejected by the Supreme Court," *Cherokee Citizenship File,* Union I348-77.

6. Report of the Secretary of the Interior, 42d Cong., 2d sess., *House Executive Document 1,* pt. 5, 984; petition to U. S. Grant and Senate and House, February 1872, *Microcopy M234*-105, I1216-72.

7. Report of the Secretary of the Interior, 42d Cong., 3d sess., *House Executive Document 1,* pt. 5, 617.

8. *House Report 98,* 461, 471; Hanna R. Warren, "Reconstruction in the Cherokee Nation," *The Chronicles of Oklahoma* 45 (Winter 1967-68): 185; Report of the Secretary of the Interior, 42d Cong., 3d sess., pt. 5, 617; F. A. Walker to John B. Jones, March 9, 1872, *Microcopy M21*-106, 206. Those freedmen who petitioned Jones and the President were William S. Madden, George Martin, Jackson Davis, Caroline Davis, John Bean, Jordan Thompson, Clarenda Bean, George Bryant, Nancy Bryant, Tobias Bean, Margaret Bean, Arthur Bean, George Adams, Clarrie Adams, Thomas Mayfield, Nicey Mayfield, George Bean, Sandy Bean, William Vann, Rachel Bean, Nancy Vann, Nelson Martin, Joseph Rogers, Sarah Rogers, Albert Nelson, Henrietta Martin, George Landrum, Caroline Landrum, Jacob Bean, Thomas Moore, Rose Moore, Samuel Roberts, Ellen Roberts, Joe Lynch, Sophie Lynch, John Nelson, Jerry Lane, Rachel Lane. William S. Madden et al. to Jones, February 1872, notice, February 2, 1872, and petition to U. S. Grant and Senate and House, February 1872, *Microcopy M234*-105, I1216-72.

9. Jones to Walker, February 21, 1872, *Microcopy M234*-105, I1216-72; *House Report 98,* 471-472.

10. Woodson Lowe to Secretary of the Interior, February 5, 1873, and Jones to Smith, November 25, 1873, *Microcopy M234*-106, L217-73, J949-73; H. R. Clum to Lowe, February 14; 1873, and Clum to Jones, February 14, 17, 1873, *Microcopy M21*-110, 407, 406, 416; E. P. Smith to Jones, April 28, 1874, *Microcopy M21*-118, 99; Smith to Secretary of the Interior, May 17, 1875, National Archives Microfilm Publications, *Microcopy M348* (Records of the Office of Indian Affairs, Report Books)- 26, 214.

11. John Holt to Secretary of the Interior, December 24, 1873, and Matilda Love to Secretary of the Interior, December 24, 1873, *Microcopy M234*-106, H26-73; Smith to Jones, January 16, 1874, *Microcopy M21*-116, 128; Smith to Secretary of the Interior, May 17, 1875, *Microcopy M348*-26, 214.

12. Mrs. William P. Ross, comp., *The Life and Times of William P. Ross* (Fort Smith, Ark.: Weldon & Williams, Printers, 1893), 73.

13. G. W. Ingalls to Smith, October 28, 1874, *Microcopy M234*-107, I1243-74; Smith to Secretary of the Interior, May 17, 1875, *Microcopy M348*-26, 214; C. Delano to Commissioner of Indian Affairs, November 3, 1874, National Archives Microfilm Publications, *Microcopy M606* (Letters Sent by the Secretary of the Interior)-13, 209.

14. Reuben Sanders et al. to Secretary of Interior, received November 16, 1874, *Microcopy M234*-107, S1598-74; Smith to Ingalls, November 23, 1874, *Microcopy M21*-120, 556; Ingalls to Ross, November 22, 1874, National Archives Record Group 48 (Records of the Department of the Interior, Office of the Secretary), Indian Territory Division, *Chickasaw Freedmen,* Box 393 (60b), Cherokee I106-75 (this file, hereafter cited as *Freedmen File,* is misnamed, for most of the documents in it relate to the Cherokee freedmen); Ross to the National Council, November 27, 1874, and Act of December 4, 1874, *Cherokee Citizenship File,* I106-75, I348-77; Smith to Secretary of the Interior, October 27, 1875, *Microcopy M348*-27, 62; Senate Bill No. 7, October 31, 1874, *Cherokee–Freedmen (Tahlequah).* Besides Daniels, others who signed the petition to the council were Sandy Johnson, Barney Brady, H. W. Scales, Andy Brewer, Seymour Matthew, Edward Blackburn, Alec Nevens, Erven Vann, Luster Foreman, Sank Vann, George Johnson, George Landrum, Johnson Ragville, Edward Alberty, Gilbert Vann, Isaac Wilson, Washington Shepherd, Russel Vann, Bartlet Thompson, Fred Scrimpsure, Jack McKay, Nelson Carter, and L. Vann.

15. Ingalls to Smith, January 22, 1875, *Freedmen File,* I106-75; Smith to Secretary of the Interior, May 17, 1875, *Microcopy M348*-26, 214; Smith to Ingalls, January 30, 1875, *Microcopy M21*-122, 259, *Microcopy M234*-108, 1310½-76; Ingalls to Ross, June 28, 1875, in Delano to Commissioner, July 13, 1875, *Cherokee Citizenship File,* I1465-75; Delano to Secretary of War, April 27, 1875, *Microcopy M606*-16, 83.

16. W. A. Phillips to Delano, September 13, 1875, and D. H. Ross and W. P. Adair to Delano, September 24, 1875, *Cherokee Citizenship File,* P454-75, R422-75; Ingalls to Smith, May 22, 1875, *Microcopy M234*-108, I672-75; Smith to Ingalls, May 28, 1875, *Microcopy M21*-125, 333.

17. Delano to Commissioner, July 13, 1875, with enclosures, *Cherokee Citizenship File,* I1465-75.

18. Statement of David Ross, August 12, 1875, Enoch Hoag to Smith,

July 17, 1875, statement of Posey Gibson, June 26, 1875, and Ingalls to Smith, August 3, 1875, *Microcopy M234*-108, H1129-75, H982-75, I1012-75; Clum to Ingalls, August 24, 1875, *Microcopy M21*-126, 188.

19. Ingalls to Smith, June 9, 1875, and Ingalls to Zachariah Chandler, January 12, 1876, *Microcopy M234*-108, I738-75, 1310½-75; John Bartlett Meserve, "Chief Lewis Downing and Chief Charles Thompson (Oochalata)," *The Chronicles of Oklahoma* 16 (September 1938): 324.

20. Ingalls to Smith, August 2, 1875, *Microcopy M234*-108, I1006-75; Phillips to Delano, September 13, 1875, *Cherokee Citizenship File,* P454-75.

21. Ingalls to Smith, August 25, 1875, *Cherokee Citizenship File,* I1131-75; Smith to Secretary of the Interior, October 27, 1875, *Microcopy M348*-27, 62.

22. Ingalls to Smith, August 25, 1875, *Cherokee Citizenship File,* I1131-75.

23. Phillips to Delano, September 13, 1875, and Ross and Adair to Delano, September 24, 1875, *Cherokee Citizenship File,* P454-75, R422-75.

In 1875 affidavits were made by Polly Sanders, Colbert Mayhew, Andrew Daugherty, and John Davis. In late November, Superintendent Enoch Hoag sent the claims of Zelfrey Holt, Caesar Smith, Washington Melton, Soloman Nave, David Sanders, Vicy Foreman, Polly Sanders, Reuben Sanders, Harriet Ward, William Towers, Abraham Foreman, Peter Meigs, and George Meigs. Hoag to Smith, November 22, 1875, *Cherokee Citizenship File,* H1556-75; affidavits of Polly Sanders, Colbert Mayhew, Andrew Daugherty, John Davis, John Landrum, Eby Shaw, October, November, December 1875, *Cherokee—Freedmen (Tahlequah).* In January 1876 Hoag forwarded affidavits of John Davis, Virgil W. Vinson, Benjamin Bean, John Landrum, Andrew Daugherty, Santaan Nevens, David Mayers, and Colbert Mayhew. Some of these affidavits were sent for investigation to E. C. Watkins, an Indian inspector who, by that time, had been sent to the Indian Territory. Hoag to Smith, January 11, 1876, *Microcopy M234*-110, H68-76.

24. Smith to Secretary of the Interior, October 27, 1875, *Microcopy M348*-27, 62; Chandler to Commissioner, November 6, 1875, *Microcopy M606*-13, 477; E. C. Watkins to Commissioner, February 15, 1876, in C. Schurz to Commissioner, April 21, 1877, *Cherokee Citizenship File,* I347-77; *Cherokee Advocate,* June 30, 1882.

25. Charles Thompson to J. J. Upham, February 16, 1876, and Upham to Smith, February 24, 1876, in Schurz to Commissioner, April 21,

1877, *Cherokee Citizenship File,* 1348-77; Upham to Thompson, February 24, 1876, *Cherokee–Freedmen (Tahlequah);* Ingalls to Chandler, January 12, 1876, *Microcopy M234*-865, 1310½-76.

26. Smith to Secretary of the Interior, February 6, 1877, *Microcopy M348*-28, 512; Nicholson to Smith, February 17, 21, March 1, 17, May 9, June 1, August 14, September 26, November 28, 1876, in Schurz to Commissioner, April 21, 1877, Thompson to the President, November 13, 1876, and Thompson to Smith, February 28, 1877, *Cherokee Citizenship File,* T112-77.

27. Smith to Thompson, December 8, 1876, *Cherokee–Freedmen (Tahlequah).*

28. Thompson to Smith, February 28, 1877, *Cherokee Citizenship File,* T112-77.

29. Smith to Secretary of the Interior, February 6, 1877, *Microcopy M348*-28, 512.

30. Will P. Ross et al. to Grant, January 9, 1877, Indian Archives Division, Oklahoma Historical Society, *Cherokee–Intruders (Tahlequah);* Schurz to Commissioner, April 21, 1877, and Smith to Marston, May 3, 1877, *Cherokee Citizenship File,* 1348-77; *Cherokee Advocate,* July 7, 1882.

31. Thompson to Marston, August 30, 1877, and Marston to Smith, September 10, 1877, *Cherokee Citizenship File,* U208-77.

32. In October and November the following freedmen from Sequoyah and Cooweescoowee Districts filed affidavits: Bettie Bean, Charles Bollin, John Morgan, Lewis Whitmire, Dennis Whitmire, Anderson Johnson, Mose Smith, Matilda Denningburg, Sandy Vann, Isaac Rogers, and Jonas Ragsville. Affidavits, *Cherokee–Citizenship (Tahlequah).*

33. E. A. Hayt to William P. Ross and H. T. Landrum, November 7, 1877, *Microcopy M21*-138, 152; *Cherokee Advocate,* July 7, 1882.

34. Thompson to the Senate, January 9, 1878, *Cherokee–Citizenship (Tahlequah);* "An Act Providing for the Appointment of a Special Commission to Try and to Settle Claims of Cherokee Citizenship," *Laws and Joint Resolutions of the National Council. Passed and Adopted at the Regular Sessions of the National Council, 1876, 1877 and Extra Session of 1878* (n. p.: Printed by Authority of the National Council, 1878), pt. 2, 13-16.

35. "Act Providing for the Appointment of a Special Commission," December 5, 1877, and 45th Cong., 3d sess., *Senate Report 744,* 594-596.

36. *Cherokee Advocate,* February 9, 1878; petitioners to Rutherford B. Hayes, February 20, 1878, and Daniel C. Finn to Ingalls, July 3, 1878,

Cherokee Citizenship File, Union P131-78, Union I1170-78; William M. Leeds to Marston, March 13, 1878, *Microcopy M21-*138, 546.

37. C. W. Holcomb to Adair and D. H. Ross, February 28, 1878, *Cherokee—Citizenship (Tahlequah);* "Argument of the Cherokee Delegation before the Honorable Commissioner of Indian Affairs," March 16, 1878, *Cherokee Citizenship File,* Union C235-78.

38. W. M. Davis, Jack Davis, Arthur Bean, and W. Tailor to Secretary of the Interior, July 2, 1878, *Cherokee Citizenship File,* Union L475-78; R. N. Sanders et al. to Commissioner of Indian Affairs, July 28, 1878, and notice of Sanders, May 14, 1878, *Cherokee—Citizenship (Tahlequah);* Leeds to Sanders and George Meigs, September 13, 1878, *Microcopy M21-*144, 193.

39. Louis Carter to Commissioner, July 18, 1878, and William Hudson to Commissioner, July 1878, *Cherokee Citizenship File,* Union C455-78, Union H1187-78.

40. Harriet Ward vs. Cherokee Nation, August 20, 1878, Visey Foreman vs. Cherokee Nation, August 20, 1878, Peter Hudson vs. Cherokee Nation, August 20, 1878, Zelfrey Holt vs. Cherokee Nation, August 20, 1878, statement of Jack Nelson, with summons, May 23, 1878, Caesar Smith vs. Cherokee Nation, August 20, 1878, Polly Ann Whitmire vs. Cherokee Nation, August 20, 1878, Johnson Webber vs. Cherokee Nation, August 20, 1878, Peter Meigs vs. Cherokee Nation, August 20, 1878, George Meigs vs. Cherokee Nation, August 20, 1878, Santa Anna Nevins vs. Cherokee Nation, August 20, 1878, list of intruders, Saline District, December 3, 1878, and list of intruders, Cooweescoowee District, December 3, 1878, *Cherokee—Intruders (Tahlequah);* application of Santa An Nevins, October 19, 1875, *Cherokee—Freedmen (Tahlequah).*

41. Leeds to Daniel Landrum and Davis, July 16, 1878, *Cherokee Citizenship File,* Union L475-78.

42. Thompson to Schurz, September 18, 1878, and Thompson to Hayes, December 3, 1878, in Thompson to Hayt, January 16, 1879, *Cherokee Citizenship File,* Union T467-78, Union T42-79; Thompson to E. A. Hayt, October 9, 1878, and Thompson to Attorney General of the United States, October 30, 1878, *Cherokee—Citizenship (Tahlequah).*

43. 45th Cong., 3d sess., *Senate Report 744,* 590-597.

44. Affidavit of Columbus McNair, September 1, 1875, *Cherokee—Freedmen (Tahlequah);* summons of Columbus McNair, August 30, 1878, list of intruders, Cooweescoowee District, December 3, 1878, and Joseph Ross vs. Cherokee Nation, November 6, 1878, *Cherokee—*

Intruders (Tahlequah); Nancy Vann vs. Cherokee Nation, November 6, 1878, and Abraham Ward vs. Cherokee Nation, November 6, 1878, *Cherokee—Citizenship (Tahlequah);* Thompson to Hayes, December 3, 1878, *Cherokee Citizenship File,* Union T42-79. Existing lists of intruders appear to be incomplete. List of intruders, December 3, 1878, *Cherokee—Intruders (Tahlequah).*

45. Thompson to Hayt, January 16, 1879, *Cherokee Citizenship File,* Union T42-79; "Act Amending the act of December 5, 1877," in Dew M. Wisdom to Commissioner, February 17, 1878, *Irregularly Shaped Papers,* shelf 6, 8756-98.

46. *Cherokee Advocate,* October 13, 1880; Thompson to Hayt, January 16, 1879, *Cherokee Citizenship File,* Union T42-79; Thompson et al. to Hayt, February 25, 1879, *Microcopy M234-*872, T145-79.

47. Hayt to Thompson et al., February 25, 1879, *Cherokee—Citizenship (Tahlequah); Cherokee Advocate,* October 13, 1880, July 7, 1882.

48. Thompson et al. to Hayt, February 28, 1879, *Microcopy M234-*872, T152-79.

49. *Cherokee Advocate,* October 13, 1880; W. S. Watkins et al. to Schurz, February 12, 1879, and Leeds to Landrum and Davis, July 16, 1878, in Arthur Williams et al. to Commissioner, February 13, 1879, *Cherokee Citizenship File,* Union W444-79, Union W442-79.

50. Williams et al. to Commissioner, February 13, 1879, *Cherokee Citizenship File,* Union W442-79; *New York Times,* February 26, 1879; E. J. Brooks to Secretary of the Interior, March 7, 1879, *Microcopy M348-*32, 402.

51. I. G. Vore to Hayt, January 28, 1879, and W. P. Boudinot to Secretary of the Interior, January 30, 1879, *Cherokee Citizenship File,* Union V21-79, Union B134-79; statement of Allen Wilson, June 18, 1883, in Henry Ward and Cyrus Beede to H. M. Teller, June 2, 1883, National Archives Record Group 75, *Letters Received,* 12339-83.

52. Boudinot to Secretary of the Interior, January 30, 1879, Vore to Hayt, January 28, 1879, and Thompson to Henry C. Barnes, February 5, 1879, *Cherokee Citizenship File,* Union B134-79, Union V21-79, Union T108-79; Hayt to Barnes, February 5, 1879, *Microcopy M21-*144, 38.

53. Boudinot to Commissioner, February 5, 1879, *Cherokee Citizenship File,* Union B178-79; Thompson et al. to Schurz, March 3, 1879, *Microcopy M234-*872, T167-79; Schurz to Charles Devins, April 21, 1879, *Microcopy M606-*20, 297; *Cherokee Advocate,* October 13, 1880.

54. *Cherokee Advocate,* October 13, 1880.

55. Maryland Beck to Secretary of the Interior, June 9, 1879, Wil-

liams et al. to Secretary of Interior, June 30, 1879, and Isaac Rogers to Schurz, August 9, 1879, *Cherokee Citizenship File,* Union B684-79, Union W1490-79, Union R572-79.

56. Adair et al. to Hayt, July 9, 1879, *Microcopy M234*-871, A485-79; *Cherokee Advocate,* December 4, 1885; "Voters Challenged at the Vinita Precinct by W. H. Drew," August 4, 1879, *Cherokee–Citizenship (Tahlequah).*

57. *Cherokee Advocate,* October 13, 1880.

58. "An Act Providing for the Appointment of a Special Commission to Try and Settle Claims to Cherokee Citizenship," November 26, 1879, *Compiled Laws of the Cherokee Nation* (Tahlequah, Cherokee Nation: National Advocate Print, 1881), 227-236, and *Cherokee–Citizenship (Tahlequah); Cherokee Advocate,* October 17, 1884; D. W. Bushyhead to the Hon. Senate, December 4, 1879, and Roach Young to Bushyhead, February 7, 1880, *Cherokee–Citizenship (Tahlequah);* "An Act Instructing and Empowering the Delegation to Washington, D.C., Appointed under the Act Approved November 25, 1879," *Microcopy M234*-873, C1155-80.

59. Brooks to Phillips, December 24, 1879, *Microcopy M21*-152, 152; *Cherokee Advocate,* August 4, 1882; Devins to Schurz, December 12, 1879, Adair to Bushyhead, December 22, 1879, and Bushyhead to William F. Rasmus, December 27, 1879, *Cherokee–Citizenship (Tahlequah).*

60. *Cherokee Advocate,* July 30, 1879.

IMPASSE AND A
FREEDMAN
chapter **6**   VICTORY

During the 1870s, the Cherokee freedmen had had little to do directly
with the fight for their cause. All they could do was to file protests, appeals, and memorials and to send a delegation to Washington, looking on
while the bureaucratic machinery in Tahlequah and Washington ground
out their cases. Fortunately they had found a champion in the federal
government. During the next few years, events in the Cherokee Nation
would stir the freedmen to more independent action, which gave them
a larger role in determining their future. The freedmen also had a spokesman in Dennis Wolfe Bushyhead, who appealed to the National Council
to adopt them and who later vetoed legislation that denied the freedmen
the right to share in tribal funds. Bushyhead had been elected as a result
of political realignment in the Cherokee Nation. The Downing party was
in a shambles, and the National party, which had replaced the old Ross
party and had elected Bushyhead, was rapidly becoming the party of the
full bloods. The Downing party would be revived as the party of the mixed
bloods, but not before Bushyhead had been reelected to his second term.
During Bushyhead's terms of office, U. S. officials would insist on their
right to oversee Cherokee citizenship. But they would not stop there.
They would begin an attack on Cherokee autonomy on another front
by insisting on the right of the citizen freedmen to share in the national lands and national funds, a right the Cherokees tried to deny
them.

The controversy over citizenship that Bushyhead confronted during
the early months of his administration was complex. Attorney General
Devins had supported Interior Department officials' position on jurisdic-

tion, yet the National Council of 1879 had created another court of commissioners, who went directly to work, holding sessions in January 1880
and disposing of a large number of cases, for the most part decided unfavorably. The court's action complicated a situation that was already confusing to both the Cherokees and freedmen. By the time Chief Charles
Thompson had suspended the sale of intruders' improvements in the spring
of 1879, many had already been sold. In some instances the intruders stubbornly refused to vacate the premises. Purchasers asked district clerks to
issue writs of ejectment against the intruders, but the clerks did not know,
under the circumstances, if the law applied. Also, some Cherokees apparently gave the freedmen the alternative of signing oaths renouncing
their claims to citizenship in exchange for employment opportunities or
of leaving the Nation. The freedmen constantly complained of the lack of
schools, of voting privileges, and of voice in the National Council. Many
still did not know whether the Cherokee court of commissioners had jurisdiction or whether they should respond to it, and some lacked the money
to pay lawyers to appear for them. To earn the money required them to
leave their families and go out of the Nation to find work. Still others
complained that before they were rejected by the commission, they had
sat on juries and had voted but that subsequently they had been denied
these and other privileges, including free schools.[1]

In February 1880 the Cherokees listed seventy-six freedman families as
intruders and requested that they be removed. Commissioner E. A. Hayt,
displeased with the Cherokee method of determining citizenship, refused.
The lists grew. In April the solicitor of Cooweescoowee District reported
the names of eighty-six freedman families in that district alone; most of
them had been rejected by the court in January. The freedmen on the
doubtful lists were always anxious about their improvements. They had
come back to the Nation after the war, they said, and had seen the big
farms of the Cherokees, farms that they, as slaves, had built. But they
had not coveted the farms. They had established small farms that they
were afraid to improve greatly because of the constant threat of ejection.
But now, they charged, the Cherokees had turned a greedy eye toward
these small farms and were confiscating them one by one. A case in
point was William Hudson, who claimed to have returned to the Nation
in compliance with the treaty, made a place on Big Creek, and lived
there undisturbed until the spring of 1880, when Bill Martin, a white
man, came before the clerk of Cooweescoowee District and claimed the

improvement in compliance with the ejectment act. Hudson was ejected and denied a right to come before the clerk because he was on the list of doubtful claimants.[2]

The freedmen were encouraged by the secretary of the interior and the Union Agent John Q. Tufts to meet in convention to air their grievances. In June 1880 they held meetings in each neighborhood and selected delegates to a convention in Fort Gibson to be held on July 5. Six districts were represented; Thomas Mayfield and C. M. Ridge were elected president and secretary. The convention members selected thirty delegates to present their grievances through a petition to Agent Tufts at Muskogee. The delegates claimed to represent more than two thousand persons, but Tufts thought the number too large. However, he did believe that in many cases the Cherokees had failed to carry out the treaty stipulations regarding the freedmen; he therefore asked for formal government investigation.[3]

Meanwhile, getting no cooperation from the Interior Department in removing intruders, Cherokee delegates had taken the matter directly to Congress, hoping to settle the question of citizenship once and for all. They obtained introduction of a bill authorizing negotiations between the government of the United States and the Cherokee Nation for the settlement of the status and rights of the freedmen in the Nation, but it failed to pass before the session of Congress ended. The delegation then asked the commissioner of Indian affairs to send a special commission to the Cherokee Nation during the next session of the National Council to negotiate a final settlement of the freedmen's status.[4]

When the delegation again submitted a list of intruders for removal in July 1880, Indian Office officials instructed Tufts to do nothing that would tend "to recognize the authority of the Cherokee Nation to determine or fix the legal status" of the freedmen and other claimants to citizenship. Tufts was to issue a certificate to those with prima facie claims, enabling them to remain in the Nation until their cases could be determined under rules adopted by the department. But he was also warned to proceed no further than determining prima facie cases and to direct those who could not present such a case to remove immediately from the Cherokee Nation. The freedman cases were held with the hope that they could be decided after negotiations between the government and the Cherokees at the next meeting of the National Council.[5]

The Cherokee census taken in the summer of 1880 showed the magnitude of the citizenship and intruder problem. The census takers enumerated freedmen entitled and not entitled to citizenship. All listed as having doubtful claims were required to appear before the commission on citizenship at Tahlequah in September. There were 1,976 freedmen whom the Cherokees recognized as citizens of the Nation; 531 new claimants to citizenship, of whom 32 were blacks who claimed rights under the Treaty of 1866; and 1,821 "genuine intruders" who had never had claims to citizenship and had no permits from either the Cherokees or the United States to reside in the Nation. Of this last group, 757 were black, and of the latter, 463 had been rejected by the Cherokee courts, 30 had work permits, and 44 had claims not yet decided.[6]

Chief Bushyhead issued a proclamation to those who had been listed as doubtful citizens, published a list of their names, and ordered them to appear before the commission on citizenship in Tahlequah to have their claims adjudicated. Dates were given for the appearance of residents of each district. Under the leadership of Roach Young, the commission took its difficult and tedious work seriously, and despite the obvious need for prompt action, it was not able to get through half of the cases brought before it.[7]

The commission found many names that the census takers had erroneously listed as doubtful. Believing it unfair to declare by default against the 182 cases that had failed to appear before them, the commissioners wanted to meet again in early 1881 to hear them. During September and October 1880 they heard only the cases of those the Cherokees admitted might have a claim to citizenship. There remained, as always, the problem of those who were barred from citizenship by the limitation of the treaty and whom the government had steadily refused to remove. It was apparent to some Cherokees that those cases must be dealt with. One possibility was their adoption, and those who entertained that idea believed that if the Nation did not voluntarily adopt the blacks, the United States would take a part in the matter.[8]

Acting Secretary of the Interior E. N. Marble, responding to earlier requests of the Cherokees, ordered Agent Tufts to attend the National Council and work for legislation to secure rights for the freedmen, whether they had returned within the specified time or not. A bill for their adoption was introduced, but it failed to pass. Its rationale was that this numerous class of residents, because of circumstances beyond their control, had not been able to return in time and had become a grave problem to the Nation. It was to the Nation's benefit to have legal jurisdiction over them. The council instead passed an act providing for the appointment of three commissioners to confer with Tufts and to draft articles of agreement to establish the status of the resident freedmen who were embraced within the Treaty of 1866. The agreement was to be approved by the next annual council and be sent to Congress for ratification. Tufts, of course, was disappointed to find that action would be put off a year. He believed that legislation in favor of the freedmen was unpopular at the time because of recent difficulties between the Cherokees and certain Creek freedmen, during which two freedmen had been hanged and a Cherokee killed. However, Tufts, Bushyhead, and some of the other leaders of the Nation professed hope for favorable legislation at the next annual council and believed that the matter could be settled amicably. Tufts believed as well that the department should demand, for the freedmen's sake, what was provided by the treaty if the council failed to pass proper legislation.[9]

The council's most significant action regarding citizenship was authentication of the census of 1880. A joint committee examined the roll and marked for examination the names of persons they thought were clearly not entitled to rights of citizenship. They also added the names of any bona fide citizens whose names had been omitted. The amended roll, submitted to the chief, was authenticated as a "true and correct list of persons acknowledged and recognized to be citizens of the Cherokee Nation." Citizens whose names were inadvertently omitted could apply through the principal chief, with evidence, for admission by the National Council of 1881. Those whose names were deleted by the joint committee would be summoned by the chief to appear before the commission on citizenship at the September session of 1881. "New claimants" listed in the census were to be heard by the commission at other sessions.[10]

Throughout the first half of 1881, the *Cherokee Advocate* ran notices to citizenship applicants to appear before the commission in Tahlequah in September, warning that failure to do so would result in their names being dropped from the docket. In addition to the cases already docketed were those that arose from the authentication of the census of 1880. In examining the rolls, the council committee had marked as doubtful some persons whom the census takers had listed as citizens. The chief published their names in a proclamation on August 24, 1881, ordering them to appear before the commission during the next month. Failure to do so would result in being declared an intruder. A special plea was made to Cherokee citizens to check the list for persons they knew and to make sure that those persons received notification so that all those summoned might have opportunity to appear.[11]

The commission heard 115 cases already on the docket, admitted most of the claimants, and left pending most of the cases arising out of Bushyhead's proclamation. The *Advocate*'s editor supported the commission, and some of the elected officials became active in pursuing the matter of citizenship. James Keys, solicitor of Cooweescoowee District, had notices put in the newspaper telling the citizens to report all intruders in the district to his office in Chouteau. He planned visits to all communities before his term expired, and anyone having intruders on their places without labor permits would be "dealt with as the law directs without fear or favor." Chief Bushyhead, too, was concerned. It had been two years since the attorney general's pronouncement that the Cherokees had no jurisdiction in the matter of citizenship. Yet no final solution had been found. There had been a continued influx of noncitizens, due, in part, to the commissioner's policy of issuing prima facie certificates, a policy he reaffirmed on November 8, 1881. Because the government had failed to remove those the Cherokees declared intruders, Bushyhead felt that the Nation was endangered. In his annual message to the council of 1881, he applauded the council of 1880 for having recognized the rights of those who appeared undisputed on the census rolls and for ordering a copy kept "for perpetual reference." It was up to the council, he said, "whether one of the main bulwarks of the rights of the Cherokee people shall remain longer inoperative, and the status of a large and increasing class of our residents be left undetermined."[12]

Agent Tufts attended the council of 1881, hoping that the election of a new council would bring a change in attitude toward the freedmen. He met several times with the committee, which had been appointed in 1880 to talk with him, but the members were convinced that it was useless to present any measure granting privileges to the freedmen unless those who already had full rights of citizens should surrender part of their rights. That was impracticable, so no action was taken. Said Tufts, "It is unpopular in the Cherokee Nation to advocate a measure that provides for placing the colored man on an equality with Cherokees, and the politicians are civilized enough to do nothing that might lessen their chances for political success; hence until the sentiment shall undergo a revolution there will be no favorable action." That was unfortunate, Tufts felt, for those who had

been slaves of the Cherokees spoke the language and were accustomed
to their ways. They would starve if they were removed. While he admitted
that only a few of the Indians would ever demand the removal of those
who had been Cherokee slaves, he wanted more definite action. He wanted
their status so fixed that the United States would not have to remove as an
intruder any freedman who had formerly been a slave of the Cherokees,
whether he had returned in time or not. But the Cherokees simply resorted
to their old mode of dealing with the citizenship question: still another
commission was formed in December 1881, with Thomas Tehee as president and Alex Wolf and T. F. Thompson as members. It met in January
1882 and left thirty cases to be heard at its next regular session in September, when several new cases were docketed.[13]

One major result of the January session was a definition and publication of the rules under which the commission operated. All applicants
were required to file their evidence in the same term at which their cases
were docketed, unless specially ordered otherwise by the court. They were
allowed to appear by attorney, who would be heard orally or in writing.
Once an applicant presented his evidence and closed his testimony, he
could give further evidence only if he could show it was not available at
the time he first gave testimony. All claims for citizenship were to be
presented by petition, in writing, and all witnesses had to appear in open
court and make their statements. Affidavits taken out of court were not
accepted. All motions had to be made in writing. Those who wished a
case continued had to show written proof of its justification.[14] These
legal requirements were difficult for the freedmen to meet. Most had no
money for lawyers, witnesses, or travel. They had no education, and
their understanding of legal technicalities was poor.

In January 1882, having twice failed with the National Council, Tufts
asked that the Department of the Interior appoint a commission to come
to the territory to ascertain which of the freedmen claimants qualified
for citizenship under the Treaty of 1866. Later in the spring, he asked
W. A. Phillips, attorney for the Cherokees, to investigate the matter in
Washington and to push for an explicit statement on the matter from
the department in order to avoid further complications.[15]

Meanwhile the freedmen complained that they were being denied
marriage licenses and that their children were not being admitted to the
schools. Some claimed that about five hundred of their numbers were
starving; some of them were doubtful citizens, but others had voted.

They had met in November 1881 to appeal to the Cherokees for relief, but the Indians would allow them no bread money. They had planted crops but could not cultivate them because of their weakened physical condition. They appealed to the commissioner of Indian affairs for relief funds. Commissioner Hiram Price recommended a congressional appropriation of $10,000, but it was not made. On June 1, 1882, a committee of freedman claimants called at Tufts's office in Muskogee to find whether progress had been made in their case. Disappointed, they proposed to petition Congress for an investigation of their condition.[16]

During the summer of 1882, the *Advocate* ran a series of articles on citizenship by "A," who with clear logic, tempered with a faint touch of fatalism, argued for a more realistic attitude on the part of Cherokee officials toward the growing problem of citizenship. His purpose, he said, was to bring the matter before the people, to show them its "dangerous complications," to cause them "to make one grand and determined effort in some way that will be final in its effects, and put an end to this trouble." To "A," the entire matter had not changed since Commissioner Smith's letter to Chief Thompson in December 1876: final authority in matters of Cherokee citizenship rested ultimately in the department. The government had conceded to the Cherokee Nation the right to approve a system of rules and regulations for observance by the courts and for the reinvestigation and approval of all rejected cases. The Cherokee Nation had conceded to the government the power to remove intruders. It was apparent to "A" that more compromise was necessary. To him, the recommendation that those who had returned to the Nation too late be admitted as citizens was an ominous warning of the government's intention in the matter. In effect, a stranglehold had been put on the Cherokees. He saw Commissioner Hayt's suggestion of a joint commission as simply another face of the same ultimatum, which showed a lack of faith in Cherokee competence and good faith in the matter. It was time for the Cherokees to act. As long as alleged intruders could present nothing more than a prima facie case for their rights, the government would not remove them. Therefore "A" called for the establishment of any kind of commission necessary, even if it meant surrendering some of the Nation's right of authority. All attempts to determine citizenship unilaterally had been abortive, and the Nation was no nearer to solving the problem than it had been when the supreme court had been resolved into a commission on citizenship in 1872. The magnitude of the problem now demanded that something be done.[17]

"A" waged a long and informative campaign, but there were few signs of its effects. The citizenship commission met as usual in September, and its record demonstrates some of the futility of which "A" spoke. When the commission adjourned in October, it had brought before it 79 cases involving some 259 applicants. The cases multiplied, and the editor of the *Advocate* urged vigilance against "this drifting tide of immigrants."[18]

While the verbal battle raged concerning the noncitizen freedmen, the National Council created another serious problem in Cherokee-freedman relations. In January 1883 the Cherokees asked for the balance due them of an original $678,655.55 paid for their western lands on which the government had settled Pawnees, Poncas, Osages, Nez Perce, Otoes, and Missouris. On March 3, Congress appropriated $300,000 for Cherokee lands west of the Arkansas River, contingent upon the Cherokee Nation's furnishing deeds of conveyance to the United States in trust for the western tribes. The act provided that the money would be paid into the Cherokee treasury and thence expended as the National Council should decide. In consequence, the council passed an act providing for the money's division among only Cherokees by blood, thus eliminating not only the freedmen but the adopted Shawnees and Delawares as well.[19]

Chief Bushyhead vetoed the bill, objecting to the exclusion from the payment of the adopted whites, freedmen, Shawnees, and Delawares, who the Cherokees claimed had paid nothing for their interest in the lands of the Cherokee Nation. Although Bushyhead held that view, he believed that the Cherokee Nation had the right to share its property with others for as large or small a consideration as it chose. He argued constitutionally that the adopted freedmen and Indian citizens had been vested with the rights of "native-born Cherokees" by treaty and law. Congress's directive to spend the money as the council saw fit did not give that body the right to exclude any class of its citizens entitled to the payment under the law. Despite these arguments, the National Council passed the bill over Bushyhead's veto on May 19, 1883. The act provided for the making of a correct roll of the "citizens of the Cherokee Nation by blood," to whom payments would be made at Tahlequah, Vinita, Fort Gibson, and Webbers Falls.[20]

Meanwhile the doubtful freedmen filed individual appeals for help from the U. S. government. George Vann, the self-styled leader of those who had earlier said that they were starving, claimed to have been the slave of Jim Vann and to have been in the Cherokee Nation at the time of the treaty's ratification. Yet he, his wife, and their eight children had been denied their share of the bread payment of 1880 as well as the benefits of the school fund, but he held that it had never been denied that he had citizenship. The children of Moses Hadrick were excluded from a primary school near Grand River in Delaware District on the ground that he was a doubtful citizen. He had been owned by Lewis Ross, brother of former chief John Ross. Hadrick appealed to Bushyhead through Will P. Ross, the former chief. Bushyhead knew Hadrick's father, Old Cy, or Cyrus. There was no question about Hadrick's origin, but his doubtful status turned on the date of his return to the Cherokee Nation.[21]

In the spring of 1883 Secretary Henry M. Teller, much to Agent Tuft's delight, ordered an investigation of the freedmen's status by Indian Inspector Henry Ward and Special Agent Cyrus Beede. The case that apparently helped prompt the secretary's decision was that of Florence Lane of Cooweescoowee District. She was a former slave of Joseph Vann, but her husband was from the United States. They had made improvements in Cooweescoowee District four years earlier. Action was begun against them in the spring of 1882 when a number of freedmen in the neighborhood signed a petition for their removal because their cattle intruded on the citizen freedmen's range. Then in 1883 a decree of the Cherokee court had ordered the sale of their property, alleging that they were noncitizens. Tufts had been ordered to investigate, and he persuaded Bushyhead to suspend action in the case until the question of their citizenship was determined. Commissioner Hiram Price asked that Mrs. Lane's case be turned over to Beede and Ward and requested the Cherokees to suspend action until after the investigation. The Cherokees agreed.[22]

In their report in June 1883, Ward and Beede presented the department's alternatives regarding the freedmen. It could give the Indian courts exclusive and final jurisdiction over the matter, in which case some injustice and violence would follow, or the government could assume jurisdiction through the U.S. Court for the Western District of Arkansas. The latter course, the investigators believed, would generally satisfy the Indians, who wished a final settlement "of this vexed problem." If the additional cases would overburden the U. S. court, the Interior Department should assume jurisdiction directly and exercise it through a commission of three persons to whom claimants could appeal from the Indian courts. The commission, one member of which should be a Cherokee, should have the power to rehear all cases previously decided adversely by the Indian courts; its action should be final. Many of the freedmen, barred by the letter of the treaty, could obtain special attention to their rights, which Beede and Ward believed they deserved under the spirit and equities of the treaty.[23]

By the fall of 1883, some freedmen were so discouraged that about five hundred made tentative plans to go to the Oklahoma lands west of the Indian Territory and asked for federal help. They were convinced that they could not live among the Cherokees, whom they charged with intimidation during recent elections; if they did not vote as the old Confederate faction wanted them to, they were shot at. They alleged that the Cherokees went around in "squads," got drunk, and committed depredations on the freedmen. Finally the Indians would not allow blacks to teach in the freedman schools, and the Nation provided the freedmen with no insane asylum. Other freedmen petitioned the commissioner of Indian affairs to protect them in their rights. The department was powerless to act on such petitions in the absence of acceptable legislation on the subject by the National Council or by Congress. Therefore the commissioner urged them to present their grievances in the form of petitions to the next National Council and to the next Congress, asking for legislation to secure the rights guaranteed them by the Treaty of 1866. Through their counsel, the freedmen offered suggestions for the creation of a board of arbitration to assume jurisdiction over Cherokee citizenship. Their plan was to give the board full and unlimited authority in all cases of doubtful citizens then pending in the Cherokee Nation. It would also hear cases of those whose property had been sold; if they were found to be citizens, the board would restore their property.[24]

The Cherokees rejected these suggestions as well as those in the Ward-Beede report, steadfastly insisting on their exclusive jurisdiction over citizenship of their own nation. The investigators had reported 752 cases of intruders involving 2,000 to 3,000 persons and concluded that the present remedies to that problem were sufficient if applied faithfully. However, the agent's issuing prima facie permits had led to grave abuses and wrongs to all parties. Bushyhead offered to reopen the rejected cases in order to correct any wrong committed by previous Cherokee citizenship courts in rejecting residents and declaring against them by default. Many had not appeared because their cases were weak, and they would probably refuse to appear again. Therefore he suggested that the agent notify those concerned and, to insure fair play, sit in on the hearings. Commissioner Price, in turn, reaffirmed the Devins report of December

12, 1879, and again suggested that Congress authorize the establishment of a commission, composed of one member chosen by the Nation
and two by the secretary and empowered to investigate and determine
the rights of freedmen growing out of the treaty.[25]

Bushyhead's offer to compromise had been the result of a report
from the Cherokee citizenship commission. When they reported in
September, they had heard 79 cases involving 259 applicants. Of this
number, 17 were freedmen. Aware that any adverse decision was subject to appeal to the Indian Office, the commissioners felt it necessary
to eliminate, if possible, as many of the objections to their procedures
as possible, and they attempted to make their rules for gathering evidence
and testimony conform to those used in the U. S. courts. There were
obvious flaws in their procedure. First, the commission had refused to
take fugitive affidavits in order to protect itself from baseless claims.
People were required to appear in person. Yet some applicants, because
of advanced age, sickness, distance, or hardship could not. Therefore
the commission suggested legislation whereby depositions could be safely
taken. Second, claimants were left to their own resources to get witnesses
to appear in their behalf. People in business were hesitant to give up two
or three days of their time without ample compensation. The commission
suggested that the council establish a fee rate and then empower the commission to compel witnesses to attend. Third, the work of the commission
was hampered because the solicitor was not paid while the commission
was not in session, and as a result, he was not ready to proceed when the
commission met, failing to have prepared his cases ahead of time. The
commission suggested a reasonable salary for the solicitor during vacation
of the commission. Finally, the commission advised the rehearing of a
large number of cases disposed of under the Chambers court. Those cases
had been disposed of by default and had been stricken from the docket.
The Tehee commission felt that many freedmen doubtlessly had been
negligent but that many had been indisposed and had failed to appear
through no fault of their own.[26]

At the National Council of 1883, the citizenship question occupied
much time. The council refused to sanction a proposed committee of
eight to consider and define the rights of each citizen of the Cherokee
Nation under the treaty and the constitution. It did, however, pass an
act prohibiting claimants for citizenship from making improvements, cutting timber, buying property, or commencing merchandising or other

business until their rights had been determined. Violators were subject to fines of from ten to one hundred dollars or ten to ninety days at hard labor, or both. Citizens who were found guilty of aiding noncitizens in such enterprises were subject to the same penalties. Bushyhead submitted the Ward-Beede report to the council and called attention to the citizenship cases that had theretofore been decided adversely by default for failure to appear. At his request the council reopened all such cases that had been decided by the Chambers court. Claimants were given ninety days to present their cases before the citizenship court. Until they were settled, the claimants were forbidden to cut timber, build houses, buy property, or commence merchandising or other business. But before the commission could get underway on the cases, in August 1884 Commissioner Hiram Price asked Bushyhead to request an end to the investigations.[27]

The commission's compliance was due, as well, to other pressures from Washington. In the spring of 1884, a bill was introduced into the House of Representatives authorizing the secretary of the interior to create a commission to dispose of the claims for citizenship not only in the Cherokee Nation but in all nations of the Five Civilized Tribes. However, the bill was reported unfavorably on the grounds that the United States could not, under the 1866 treaty, unilaterally appoint a commission on citizenship. In the Senate, the Committee on Indian Affairs, with Henry L. Dawes as chairman, decided to visit the Indian Territory during the congressional recess to inquire into the rights of freedmen among the Cherokees, as well as among the other tribes. When Commissioner Hiram Price asked the Cherokees to postpone further examination of citizenship cases until after the committee's visit, Bushyhead made it clear that by their compliance the Cherokees in no way acknowledged any authority of the Senate committee to decide who were or were not citizens of the Cherokee Nation, nor would they recognize any inquiry or conclusion of the committee as a valid basis for a complaint. Therefore, Bushyhead doubted the committee's ability to examine both sides of the claims of doubtful residents.[28]

The Senate committee took testimony regarding the freedmen during May 1885 at Muskogee, Fort Gibson, and Tahlequah. It is unlikely that the senators made a fair valuation of the situation because of conflicting testimony. More than a score of freedmen testified, some of them recognized citizens, some of them on the doubtful lists, and some of

them married to freedwomen. Depending upon their status, they were
allowed or refused voting and educational privileges. Some who had
been allowed to vote in some instances had been refused in others. Some
claimed that whites were hired as laborers in preference to blacks, but
others said that they had no difficulty finding work. Some claimed to
have been dispossessed by the Cherokees, but others had had no problems.
Some claimed to have been denied the right to sit on juries; others claimed
that they could not sit on cases involving Cherokees, but Cherokees were
allowed to sit on cases involving blacks. The freedmen, however, were
agreed on certain points: they were denied access to the high schools, the
insane asylum, and the orphan asylum, and they believed that their school-
teachers were of inferior quality, that the courts were partial to Cherokees,
that blacks who had gone north during the war were discriminated against,
and that adopted whites fared better than the freedmen.[29]

The testimony of the freedmen was further confused by the ignorance
of the blacks. Most had been slaves and had therefore had no access to the
educational process. Denial of full access to the courts had resulted in a
general ignorance of the law and legal processes. Some had no sense of
numbers. They had little idea of how many freedmen there were in the
Nation. They had little knowledge of freedman activities outside their
communities or districts. Many had no sense of time. They could only
guess at their ages. One, for instance, who claimed to be thirty-three or
thirty-four, claimed to have come west with the Cherokees in the late
1830s. Another said he had returned to the Cherokee Nation in October
1866; he knew that it was October, because the peaches were ripe (they
ripen in late spring and summer in that climate zone).

The Cherokees, including Bushyhead, refuted many of the freedmen's
charges and remained firm in their position on the citizenship issue. Those
who were not recognized as citizens, Bushyhead maintained, had no rights.
The Cherokees had been generous by not having them removed. He con-
demned the Ward-Beede report for not suggesting a manner of settling
the citizenship question. According to some of the Cherokees, the blacks
were denied access to the high schools and asylums because of racial
prejudice similar to that in the white South. According to one, most Cherokees wanted a strict enforcement of the six-months' rule for economic
reasons. It was "a matter of dollars and cents—you make a man a citizen
and it gives him that much land and money."[30]

During its regular session of 1885, the National Council was once again unsuccessful in dealing with the matter of citizenship. Bushyhead called the council into special session, at which time an act was passed to provide for the appointment of a joint commission to settle citizenship claims. The commission would be comprised of two people appointed by the principal chief and one by the secretary of the interior. The secretary was to prescribe a set of rules, with the chief's approval, for the commission's guidance. If the secretary disliked any provisions of the act, the chief was empowered to negotiate the matter with him and make any arrangement for adjustment of claims upon which the commission disagreed.[31]

This act clearly demonstrated Cherokee willingness to compromise. However, Bushyhead was not satisfied with just the passage of the bill. He asked his executive council to provide him with a formal statement expressing the Nation's position on the question of citizenship and a construction of the treaty and the Cherokee constitution regarding it. The executive council was composed of Rabbit Bunch, Daniel Redbird, Edward Christy, and David Muskrat—all full bloods, who, as a social group, were developing an antipathy for the blacks. When there was any doubt about the citizenship of a freedman, they said, the parties who had conferred citizenship on the freedmen must decide who was included in that class of citizen or devise some plan for enrolling the members of the class. Therefore the parties to the treaty by which the freedmen became citizens—the United States and the Nation—must agree upon some method of finding out who had returned within the six-months' limit. A negative answer to either question settled the matter. Every freedman not enrolled should have his claim considered and decided by a proper commission under rules agreed upon by the Nation and the United States.[32]

Here was further evidence that the Cherokees were willing to allow the United States to participate in the settlement of the citizenship question. Bushyhead made their intentions clear on February 1, 1886: the Cherokees wanted to leave nothing undone, short of sacrificing their "plain and acknowledged rights," to remove all obstacles in the way of enforcement of the treaty regarding the removal of intruders. The stalemate daily added to the difficulties. Intruders were in the Nation by the thousands, and thousands more would arrive if nothing was done. The Cherokees regarded with alarm "the indifference" of the government in removing intruders. Thus Bushyhead asked the department to approve the act and establish a joint commission.[33]

The new Union agent, Robert L. Owen, supported the Cherokees in their appeal. Under the effective policy regarding intruders, a claimant armed with a few bogus affidavits could come into the Cherokee Nation, improve a place, cut timber, graze cattle, plow up the fertile land, and stay there for years, free of rent and taxes and, if removed, be assured of reimbursement for his improvements. Sometimes intruders trespassed on native citizens and even killed them and escaped punishment. The Cherokee courts had no jurisdiction over them because they were not citizens, and when they were taken before the federal district court, that court refused jurisdiction because they presented prima facie cases that they were citizens of the Cherokee Nation. Owen was obligated to issue prima facie certificates to anyone who could present such a case. Many of those cases appeared to have been manufactured in Baxter Springs, Kansas, where Owen charged "a literal citizenship mill" existed. Thus, he established several classes of persons not entitled to have protection papers issued. Among them were freedmen of the United States who had married Cherokee freedwomen, formerly slaves of Cherokees, who had not returned within the six-months' limitation set by the treaty.[34]

Relief in the matter of prima facie protection papers finally came from an unexpected source. On March 1, 1886, the United States Supreme Court handed down a decision in the case of the *Eastern Band of Cherokee Indians* vs. *the United States and the Cherokee Nation*. The decision gave exclusive right in determining citizenship to the Cherokee Nation, but only regarding those who had entered the Nation after August 11, 1886, the date on which the opinion went into effect.[35] The decision meant that the United States still was not willing to recognize the Cherokees' right to decide the status of the freedmen, who must have claimed to have returned within six months after the Treaty of 1866 in order to qualify for citizenship.

The Cherokees asked Secretary L. Q. C. Lamar to stop the issuance of prima facie certificates, to direct the agent to forbid any claimant to citizenship to cut timber until his case was decided, and to remove all who were in the Cherokee Nation in clear violation of the law and the treaty. Finally, they asked the secretary to recognize their right to determine in all cases who were citizens. In response, Commissioner J. D. C.

Atkins instructed Owen not to issue permits to persons hired by prima facie claimants and to refer all such applications to the Cherokee authorities. He then forwarded the Cherokee request to the secretary with the recommendation that the issuance of prima facie certificates cease, that those named intruders be allowed to sell their property in the Cherokee Nation, and that claimants be allowed to remain unmolested until their cases were decided. The Cherokees were willing to allow the intruders to take their movable property out of the Nation, even though they felt the greater part of it had been made in the Nation, and they would allow them to take their crops. However, they insisted that anyone who had been in the Nation for six months or more without making application to the National Council for a permit should be expelled at once. Neither could they agree to allow claimants to reside in the Nation until their cases were settled favorably. Those the agent felt were good cases would be investigated by the Cherokees, and those he thought bad would be removed immediately. Secretary Lamar revoked the orders for issuing prima facie certificates. The concession, however, was a nominal one. When the Cherokees requested a list of those to whom such certificates had been issued, they found that Owen had issued only six of them. They had to wait until a list could be secured from the late agent John Q. Tufts.[36]

The National Council of 1886 created the legislative machinery to deal with the citizenship cases of those who had entered the Nation after August 11, 1886, by establishing a citizenship commission of three. Most of the claimants with whom this commission would deal would be whites and Indians. The council also established a commission to hear the cases of claimants who had entered the Nation before August 11, 1886. The act provided for the appointment of one commissioner by the principal chief and one by the secretary of the interior; the Cherokee authorities were also to appoint a clerk, an interpreter, an attorney, and a sheriff to serve the commission. Sessions were to be held at Tahlequah at times agreed upon by the chief and the secretary after sixty to ninety days' notice in the *Cherokee Advocate*. Claimants failing to present their claims for docketing within six months of the date the commission began its work were forever barred from citizenship. Freedmen were to show proof that they were entitled to citizenship in accordance with the language of article 9 of the Treaty of 1866. The attorney could summon any person believed to be fraudulently upon the adopted Shawnee or Delaware rolls, and the commission was given jurisdiction of all rejected cases from the previous commissions, as well as the right to investigate any fraud formerly used to gain a favorable decree. If the commissioner disagreed, the third person was to be selected as an umpire. The decision of the commission was to be final. Those failing to establish citizenship were to be deemed intruders subject to removal by the principal chief and would be given ninety days to sell their improvements; if they failed to do so, the Cherokee Nation would sell the improvements at auction. Clerks of the several districts of the Nation were prohibited from issuing permits to those rejected. The act was effective, contingent upon the appointment of the U. S. commissioner within six months after January 1, 1887. The Cherokees appointed W. P. Ross commissioner, George O. Sanders clerk, A. N. Chamberlain interpreter, and Wesley Walker attorney.[37]

Commissioner J. D. C. Atkins generally approved of the act but had reservations concerning some of its specific provisions. He suggested that sessions of the commission be held at various locations in the Nation, not just Tahlequah, since many freedmen were too poor to travel, that notice be served on doubtful cases since decisions of the commission were to be final, and that the commission appraise the improvements of rejected cases to be purchased by the Nation at appraised value in order to ensure the freedmen's receipt of a fair price for their property. Finally, he felt that the clause relating to Shawnees and Delawares should be stricken. Atkins asked for the appointment of a U.S. commissioner, but the session of Congress was about to close.[38]

Meanwhile the Cherokee commission set about its work, but it did not confine its ponderings to those claimants who had entered after August 11, 1886. It denied rights of citizenship to many who had entered the Nation before that date and declared them intruders. Many of these had valuable improvements and farms, and the Department of the Interior refused to abide by the decisions of the commission in such cases when the claimants could show prima facie that they were Cherokee citizens. As a result, some confusion concerning jurisdiction resulted. Indian Office officials decided that since the Cherokees had taken the determination of claims into their own hands, there was no need for action on the part of the department except to inform the Cherokees that the department would determine for itself whether any person would be removed as an intruder and that it would not permit any person to be deprived of his improvements without fair compensation. In the summer of 1887, Agent Owen was ordered to make clear to the claimants that the authority of the Cherokee commission extended only to claimants who entered the Nation after August 11, 1886. He was to stress that those entering in good faith before that date were to be protected until their cases could be decided by "competent authority." Owen published a notice to claimants on June 20, saying that no one entering after August 11, 1886, could make improvements on the public domain until admitted to citizenship by the National Council.[39]

In his annual report for 1887, the commissioner of Indian affairs appealed for legislation to establish a method whereby the cases in question could be settled.[40] However, no legislation was forthcoming. In fact, several years were to pass before cases of those declared intruders who had entered the Nation after August 11, 1886, were finally settled. In the meantime, there remained the problem of those who entered before that date, many of whom were black.

Events were soon to take a more favorable turn for both the citizen freedmen and many of those who had been denied citizenship previously. The long tug of war over jurisdiction between the Cherokee Nation and the Department of the Interior was over, for the matter was taken out of their hands as Congress began to assume a larger role in Cherokee affairs. Congressional action was the outcome of the citizen freedmen's reactions to their exclusion from the per-capita payment in the spring of 1883, which created a cause that they could rally behind. It resulted in their first successful suit against the Cherokee Nation and became a means by which the government tried finally to settle the cases of freedmen who were not recognized as citizens.

By the time the bill that had excluded them had passed the National Council, the Cherokee freedmen had organized. On May 19, 1883, the day the act was passed over Bushyhead's veto, Berry Mayes of Fort Gibson, the spokesman for one segment of the freedmen, petitioned Secretary Henry M. Teller on their behalf. Signed by fifty residents of Four Mile Branch community and Tahlequah District in general, the petition protested the act, asked the secretary to delay action on the per-capita money, and called for an investigation. The freedmen also proposed to send a delegation to Washington. They met in convention at Fort Gibson with Frank Vann acting as president and Andy Tiner as secretary. Another group met in Cooweescoowee District on May 29, with Edward Vann as president and Isaac Rogers as secretary. They drafted a protest against the violation of their rights under the Treaty of 1866, charging that their status had never been determined and that the Cherokees recognized them only as they wished, even though the Department of the Interior had denied the Indians' exclusive authority in the matter. This group, who elected Rogers and L. D. Daniels as delegates to present their complaints in Washington, wanted their status fixed and asked the government to police their rights. Still another group from Vinita telegraphed the secretary of the interior, and a group in the northern part of the Nation formally protested against the prejudicial vote of the National Council and pressed their claim to civil, religious, and political rights equal to those of the Cherokees. Their assertion was based on their fifteen years of service to the Nation in voting and serving as guards and jurors. J. B. Butler, president of their group, submitted the names of forty-three bona fide citizen freedmen who subscribed to the protest.[41]

Another meeting was called at Fort Gibson on June 5, 1883. Henry C. Hayden and William Madden of Lightning Creek, Cooweescoowee District, urged the freedmen of Grand River to send a representative from each neighborhood. He also tried to postpone the convention one day in order to give more people time to get there. Both Hayden and Madden were suspicious of Lewis Daniels and Isaac Rogers, who, they claimed, had the sanction of only a few freedmen and had unspecified questionable motives for wanting to represent the freedmen in Washington. They were supported in their suspicion by the freedmen of doubtful status at Vinita, who also had no faith in the freedmen delegates. They charged, through spokesman William Davis, that the delegates could be bought off by the Cherokee delegates. Meanwhile Rogers and Daniels had made their way to Washington. When they reached Secretary Teller, they were armed with a letter of recommendation from O. C. Haskell, a congressman, saying that the freedmen's grievances were valid and needed to be remedied. He promised to use his influence to see that moneys were withheld until the Cherokees were willing to make an equitable distribution of the per capita funds. On June 14, through their counsel J. Amble Smith, Rogers and Daniels filed an appeal for help from the secretary. "Should the full blood Cherokees be allowed to perpetrate this wrong upon us," they said, "who can say when they will stop?"[42]

Word came back to the Cherokee Nation that Secretary Teller had begun to hesitate concerning the per-capita funds. The money would not be available for disbursement until the deeds conveying title to the Cherokees' western lands to the United States were executed, and that could not take place without Teller's approval. The *Washington Dispatch* reported that Teller was "inclined, under the present phase of the question, to withhold his consent to the deeds unless a fairer division of the money is made in regard to the rights of the colored people." This was no doubt journalistic flap, aimed at keeping the issue alive at home, for all of the freedman protests and appeals apparently had little effect. Work on the deeds had steadily progressed. The Cherokee delegates elected to convey the deeds were Chief Bushyhead, R. M. Wolfe, and Robert B. Ross, who by June 9, were ready to sign the documents. In answer to the protests of the freedmen, the delegation stressed that if they had cause for grievance under the Cherokee constitution, the courts of their country were open to them, and the law provided for suit against the Nation as against an individual. But they added bluntly that the latest law on the subject governed the per-capita payment. The deeds were executed and conveyed to the commissioner of Indian affairs, on June 14.[43]

On the home front, the freedmen decided to make themselves felt politically. Even before the act of May 19, there were indications that in the election in August the freedmen would vote as a bloc. In April William Brown, a freedman active in Canadian District politics, promised to deliver fifty to eighty votes from the district for Bushyhead if the chief would promise to work for the rights of freedmen under the Treaty of 1866. The freedmen had planned a meeting for the first week in May on Greenleaf Creek in Illinois District to decide which candidate to support. As Brown put it, they had decided to "go one way" and not scatter their votes, but they wanted to talk to Bushyhead before they made up their minds. The Cherokee act of May 19 apparently convinced them what to do. At a barbecue on Four Mile Branch in mid-July, they agreed to vote as a bloc against the full bloods, the National party, headed by Bushyhead. They were evidently a group to be reckoned with, for from the editorial tone of D. H. Ross, editor of the *Cherokee Advocate,* there was some desire that the freedmen remain disorganized and split in order to blunt their political effectiveness. He argued, rightly enough, that the full bloods had had as much to do with securing the freedmen what rights they enjoyed as had the mixed bloods. He argued also that if injustice had been done the freedmen, it was no more at the hands of the full bloods than at the hands of the mixed bloods. The motive of Ross's argument becomes clear in his final statement: "Their true policy is to exercise moderation; to look to the Courts and to the National Council for the redress

of wrongs; and to vote independently for good, capable men regardless of color or class or party." Ross asked the freedmen to do
something that most of the full bloods or mixed bloods would not do,
for at that time in Cherokee politics, party lines were being clearly drawn
and tensions ran high. An essential issue in the campaign was whether
adopted citizens should share in the $300,000 per-capita payment. The
New York Sun charged that both the newly revived Downing party and
the National party had "carefully cultivated" the adopted citizens for
their votes.[44] But the Downing party had not regained its political
strength, and Bushyhead was reelected.

The freedmen of several districts petitioned the National Council
in the fall of 1883 for repeal of the act of May 19. Freedman representatives of Tahlequah District included Joseph Brown, Berry Mayes, William Humphries, and Jack Pack. Brown had been the first and only freedman to be elected to the Cherokee National Council (he won the office
in 1875), and Mayes had been active in petitioning the government earlier
in the spring. William Thompson, Stephen Smith, and Jake Crapo signed
for Illinois District; Jack Campbell, Zack Foreman, R. Foreman, and
Harrison Foreman for Sequoyah District; and Coffee Sheppard and William Brown for Canadian District.[45] The National Council did not repeal
the act.

The freedmen began to organize. At a meeting at the Lightning Creek
School in Cooweescoowee District on December 6, J. Milton Turner, a
black lawyer from St. Louis who had been active in urging the opening of
the Oklahoma lands, spoke to the freedmen concerning their rights. They
elected Moses Whitmire, Frank Ross, and Henry C. Hayden to represent
them to the United States and empowered them to raise money to pay
for all necessary expenses, to hire attorneys and make contracts with
them to represent the freedmen, and to investigate and settle, if possible,
the question of doubtful citizenship. On December 11 a mass meeting of
freedmen from Illinois, Tahlequah, Canadian, and Sequoyah districts was
held at the AME church in Fort Gibson. The freedmen adopted the resolutions of the Lightning Creek group and elected William Thompson (Illinois), William Brown (Canadian), Berry Mayes (Tahlequah), Jack Campbell (Sequoyah), and Joseph Brown (ex-officio) to join the Lightning
Creek committee. The latter group accepted the Fort Gibson resolutions,
and both groups chose Turner as the attorney for the freedmen. A meeting of freedmen from all five districts met at Fort Gibson on December
21. Moses Whitmire and William Thompson were selected to go to Wash-

ington to press the freedman claims. J. Milton Turner was charged with
presenting to the government the subject of the freedmen's exclusion
from the per capita payment. Evidently in an attempt to ingratiate himself with Bushyhead, Turner wrote the chief a most flattering letter in
late December, informing the chief of his election by the freedmen and
asking for a copy of the Cherokee laws and of Bushyhead's veto message
of May 18.[46]

Under Turner's direction, the freedmen drafted a petition, had it at-
tractively printed, and sent it to Congress, charging that the Cherokees had
violated the ninth article of the Treaty of 1866 by refusing to pay them
their per-capita share of the $300,000. They argued constitutionally for
the money on the ground that it was the purchase price of part of the
public domain of the Nation, which was held in common by all citizens.
To deny their right to a share would set a precedent whereby the Cherokee council could exclude them forever from any future share in the proceeds from the public domain. They argued emotionally that as slaves
they had contributed much materially to the Nation and that since
emancipation, they had "entered upon pastoral life" and had tilled the soil.
The petition read in part: "They have in a humble, but honest way, aided
the Commerce of their Country with crops of Corn, Wheat, and of Cotton. They have without material aid cared for their sick; for their aged
and helpless ones. Also, they are seeking the knowledge contained in the
text books; therefore, to endure this wrong so unexpectedly wrought
would indeed prove a dire and discouraging circumstance." They asked
Congress to withhold from any moneys then due the Cherokees the
amount owed the freedmen and to reverse the act of the Cherokees to
prevent the freedmen from being defrauded of their rights in the future.
G. W. Ingalls, the U. S. agent at the Union Agency, also received a copy
of the petition with a request that he investigate the matter. The Cherokee authorities received their copy in March 1884. Upon review of the
situation, the commissioner became convinced that there was "no question
that the Cherokees have failed to fulfill their obligations to these people."[47]

No significant action regarding the matter occurred for nearly two
years. In November 1885 J. Milton Turner filed a brief asking Congress
to compel the Cherokees to observe the stipulations of the treaty and
to withhold the freedmen's pro-rata share from any fund then due or
to become due the Cherokees from the United States. If Congress did
not, Turner argued, then the Cherokee council had set a precedent by
which the freedmen could be forever "excluded, ejected, and driven

out from their rightful pro rata in the public domain of the Cherokee Nation, as contemplated in the treaty of 1866, and from any and
all proceeds or share *whatsoever* arising out from the sale thereof."
In early 1886 the issue was finally taken up in Washington. With the
aid of Senator Henry L. Dawes, Turner brought the petition of his
constituents before the President, asking for an executive order re-
storing the funds. Instead the President asked the secretary of the interior to prepare legislation to effect the restitution of the funds to
the freedmen.[48]

Commissioner J. D. C. Atkins believed that the Cherokee act of
May 19, 1883, was a violation of the freedmen's rights under the ninth
article of the Treaty of 1866, which entitled them to their pro-rata
share as if they were native Cherokees, and a violation of the act entered into between the Cherokees and the Shawnees and Delawares, of
their right to due process, of their right to the uniform application of
the law, and of the spirit and intent of the law of Congress. The act
gave the council "the power to say how, or rather for *what object*,"
the money was to be extended to the whole Cherokee people (this had
been Turner's argument). It did not give them the right to say who was
to receive the money. Finally he believed that the act was a violation
of "every principle of equity and justice." Atkins also pointed out that
the President was empowered by article 4 of the treaty to ensure that
justice was obtained for the freedmen. He recommended that Congress
appropriate a sum to make a per-capita payment to the freedmen,
Shawnees, and Delawares equal to that received by the Cherokees by
blood and make the sum a lien on the unassigned lands of the Cherokees west of the ninety-sixth meridian to be deducted from any future
payments on the lands. The Cherokee census of 1880 listed 15,307 Cherokees by blood. Therefore Atkins estimated that the Cherokee payment
was slightly less than $20 per capita. The same census listed 1,976 freed-
men, 672 Delawares, and 503 Shawnees, for a total of 3,151. Therefore
a little over $63,000 was necessary to equalize the payment. However,
Atkins asked for an appropriation of $75,000 or as much of that as nec-
essary to take care of any increase in the number of the three classes of
citizens. Any excess would return to the Treasury. Atkins's draft of a
bill was presented to Congress in early March 1886.[49]

By late March it appeared to Cherokee observers in Washington that
J. Milton Turner would be able to secure passage of the appropriations

bill. He appeared before the Senate committee in behalf of it, and Chief
Bushyhead spoke against it. Bushyhead found himself in a rather awk-
ward position regarding the law, which he had previously declared un-
just to the freedmen. He was forced to defend the general opinion of
the Cherokee people himself since he and the Cherokee senate had failed
to name a delegation to Washington on behalf of the Nation. The editor
of the Vinita *Indian Chieftain* believed that Bushyhead had handled the
entire matter poorly. He wrote in an editorial: "Three years will soon
have passed since a fraud was perpetrated upon the people, out of which
have grown the complaint of our adopted citizens, the criminal charge
against [W. A.] Phillips, the creation of caste lines, revival of old prejudices, and many other troubles that surely would have been avoided,
had a different course, wholly consistent with the facts of the case, been
pursued in reference to the $300,000. . . . What he maintained was right,
he now has to oppose as the wrong, because law is considered to be the
expression of justice."[50]

The Cherokee council made the matter even more complex through
legislation passed at a special session held in April 1886. The session was
called to enact legislation providing for the per-capita distribution of
$300,000 in rents paid to the Cherokees by the Cherokee Strip Live-
stock Association for grazing rights in the Cherokee Strip. But before the
legislators got down to the business at hand, they drafted and approved
a "Construction of the Rights of Cherokee Citizenship as Designed to be
Conferred upon Freedmen and Friendly Indians in the 9th and 15th
Articles of the Treaty of 1866." The articles were defined in the following manner: Cherokees by blood originally owned all Cherokee lands
and owned them at the time of the treaty; before the Civil War, whites
were admitted with all the rights of native Cherokee under the Cherokee
government, but such citizenship did not carry with it title to the lands
or to the proceeds from them at their sale; the Cherokees understood the
term *rights of native Cherokees* not to extend to title of national lands
and money unless those lands had been paid for or right had been ex-
pressly granted.[51]

The council construction meant that the adopted Shawnees and
Delawares were entitled to lands and invested funds that they had paid
for along with their equal rights under the laws of the Cherokee Nation.
On the other hand, the adopted whites and freedmen had all the rights
of native Cherokees as subjects of the government but none to the land

or proceeds from its sale because they had paid nothing for that right.
The Cherokees considered the right of these citizens to benefit from
the investments for governmental and school purposes as "a gift attached
to the grant of citizenship." According to the *Indian Chieftain*, this construction said that the only difference between the native and adopted
citizen was that the latter could cultivate the soil and use it as his home
without paying rent.[52]

Once more, the National Council omitted the freedmen and other
adopted citizens, directing the money to be paid to Cherokees by blood
as had been done in 1883. In the senate, the argument against including
the freedmen followed the logic of the construction. It was argued also
that if the freedmen were included, then more privileges would be granted
them than to the native Cherokees, for the former would be getting something from the Cherokees while the Cherokees would be getting nothing
from the freedmen. The other side quoted the treaty and urged a construction to allow the freedmen to participate in the property and funds.
President of the senate L. B. Bell presented the latter side while George
Sanders, a full blood, presented the former. The senate passed the measure
by a vote of eleven to six, and the act was approved on April 28, 1886.[53]

Meanwhile in the U. S. Congress the proposed appropriation of $75,000
for the freedmen's share of the first $300,000 was still alive. Bushyhead
and the Cherokee delegates argued against the bill, and J. Milton Turner
continued to argue for it in committees. He was supported by petitions for
justice from blacks in Missouri, Illinois, New York, Mississippi, and Indian Territory, and Turner maintained that the bill was in accordance with
the recommendations of President Grover Cleveland. But the Cherokees
were indignant, for to them its implications were clear and prophetic of
future events:

> The transaction, even to the extent it has gone, is rather humiliat-
> ing, as it suggests the idea that the independent sovereignty as
> claimed by some of our nation, is only a myth, and can be blown
> into invisible vapor, as a bubble in the air, by the breath of a few
> hundred law-makers. How often such a thing may be repeated is
> only limited by the pleasure of congress and intestine complaint
> to interfere with our affairs. There is no such a thing as complete
> sovereignty belonging to the nation, nor has there been since the first

treaty with the United States. This the government knows, and
hence the settlement of troubles on account of per capita payments. The suit of the North Carolina Cherokees against the
nation before a foreign court is convincing proof of this. The
arrest and conviction of our citizens before an alien court for
offenses committed within our limits settles the question.[54]

J. Milton Turner took the matter to the Cherokee people. In a
letter to the editor of the *Indian Chieftain,* he insisted that in his prosecution of the freedmen's case over the previous three years, he had
avoided any "tendency toward disrupting the harmony and friendliness
so necessary to the peace and welfare of all the several classes interested
in this matter." If the problem was not settled, however, the Cherokee
government would remain dissatisfied, and serious dissensions might
result. Turner argued that the act of March 3, 1883, did not give the
Cherokee Nation the right to abrogate treaty guarantees to the freedmen,
Shawnees, and Delawares and ended his letter with an emotional appeal
by forecasting the possible destruction of the Cherokee Nation, as well
as the nations of the other Civilized Tribes. He said that "powerful cap-
italists and corporations" desired possession of the Indian Territory,
and the survival of the Five Civilized Tribes depended upon "the degree
of internal harmony and comity, which those people and civilized tribes
are able to maintain among themselves." Turner concluded, "United we
stand, and divided we fall."[55]

While the appropriation bill was being debated, Turner began proceedings concerning the second per-capita payment of $300,000, par-
ticipation in which the freedmen had been denied by the council on
April 28. On June 14 he asked the President to intercede on behalf of
the freedmen, but remedy lay with Congress. The freedmen and Cherokees could do nothing but wait for the legislative process to take its course.
In the meantime the pending legislation became a political issue. In the
election of 1887 in the Cherokee Nation, the freedmen figured prominent-
ly once more. Early that year, a freedman spokesman under the pseudo-
nym "A. Freedman" urged a bloc vote by freedmen, for the per-capita
question was a vital one. He supported Downing party candidate Joel B.
Mayes, a mixed blood who, he believed, would be just to the freedmen;
the National party candidate, Rabbit Bunch, was a full blood who advo-

cated making the per-capita payment to Cherokees by blood only. At this time there were about twenty-four hundred adopted freedmen in the Nation, of whom about a thousand were voters. Both parties courted these voters and made the per-capita payment an issue. The Downing party, comprised mainly of mixed bloods, offered to give the freedmen all rights guaranteed by treaty. The National party, comprised mainly of full bloods and some half bloods, agreed to let the matter go to the U. S. court of claims for adjudication and to abide by its ruling.[56]

As the political campaign heated up, some Cherokee citizens charged political interference from outside the Nation, particularly by J. Milton Turner. Agent Robert L. Owen took affidavits from both Cherokees and freedmen who said that Turner had allegedly boasted of receiving pay to campaign for the National party. Owen asked for protection against "political tramps" and for Turner's removal from the Nation until after the election: "Political excitement runs high enough without having Demagogues from the states coming in here and making bad blood between neighbors." Owen's petition contained fifty-three names. The *Indian Chieftain* published what purported to be a statement of the bylaws of the United Keetoowah organization of full bloods, in which they vowed, among other things, to trample under foot the Downing party, adopted whites, former Confederate sympathizers, the blacks, and the Delawares and Shawnees. The statement was allegedly approved by Rabbit Bunch. There was evidence that some National party sympathizers were defecting because of the association with it of people like J. Milton Turner, W. A. Phillips, and others. Some Nationals had become disenchanted during Bushyhead's second term because he had allegedly fallen under the influence of these people.[57]

When the ballots were counted, Downing candidate Joel B. Mayes was elected principal chief, but a majority of National candidates were elected to the senate and council of the National Council.[58] Bushyhead was the last National party candidate to serve as chief. Until the Nation was dissolved, the Downing party had political dominance. The Nationals became bitter, and politics became divisive. The old resolve had gone out of the new leaders, who offered little resistance to the desires of the United States.

In the Fiftieth Congress, a bill to make the $75,000 appropriation finally passed and became law on October 19, 1888. It charged the amount against the Cherokee Nation and placed a lien on Cherokee lands west of the Arkansas River. The money was to be distributed to those Cherokee freedmen and their descendants described in the Treaty of 1866, as well as to the Delawares and Shawnees. Each person was to receive a payment equal to the amount paid to Cherokees by blood in accordance with the act of the Cherokee National Council on May 19, 1883. The news of the act was not well received in the Cherokee Nation. Cherokee newspapers continued to insist on the Cherokee position in the matter: that the land sold was held by Cherokees by blood only at the time of the 1866 treaty and that adopted citizens had only those rights transferred to them by the Cherokees by blood. The latter, the newspapers insisted, had not transferred title to the land to adopted citizens in the Treaty of 1866. Finally, they insisted that it should be the Cherokees, and no one else, who decided who should share in the proceeds from the sale of tribal lands.[59]

According to the appropriations act, the secretary of the interior was to distribute the money per capita. The amount paid each person presented no problem, for it was well known how much each Cherokee by blood had received. Neither did the method of payment present a problem. But determining which freedmen and others were entitled to share in the distribution of funds was another matter, and the department immediately set about finding a way to do so. The new commissioner, John W. Oberly, asked Agent Owen to study the act and make suggestions. Owen believed that the United States had equal voice in saying who were freedman citizens of the Cherokee Nation and proposed the establishment of a joint commission of three—one chosen by the United States, one by the Cherokees, and one by both. He thought it important that the department say immediately on what terms it would be willing to settle the question of who was entitled to citizenship. It should be firm but as liberal as consistent with justice. Secretary William Vilas, unlike his predecessors, believed that there were limits to the department's jurisdiction over Cherokee citizenship. There was no law by which the United States could establish such a commission as Owen had suggested. Neither had the department the authority to confer Cherokee citizenship on any person or to appoint a commission. But Vilas found no objection to the Office of Indian Affairs' handling of the matter. Therefore he authorized the appointment of a special agent, with one appointed by the Cherokees, to hear the cases. All those accepted by the Cherokees would be placed on a roll of admitted claimants. The cases of contested claimants would be referred to Congress with a recommendation for legislation that would allow the department to act in conjunction with the Cherokee Nation in determining the rights of contested claimants.[60]

At Owen's suggestion, Chief Joel Bryan Mayes had taken the matter directly to the National Council, reminding the Cherokees that they had twice before made provision for the establishment of a joint commission to settle the matter of freedman citizenship. And when news came that the commissioner had appointed Special Agent Henry Heth, Mayes asked the council to cooperate with him as he worked with someone appointed by the Nation. Heth was to consult with Owen and the Cherokees, decide how to proceed, and then enroll the freedmen, Shawnees, and Delawares. Commissioner John Oberly's only instructions were to consider all evidence and testimony submitted. However, Acting Commissioner J. George Wright shortly thereafter concluded that congressional legislation was necessary to secure the proper handling of the enrollment and relieved Heth.[61]

On March 2, 1889, Congress appropriated five thousand dollars for the enrollment and for making the per-capita payment, and on July 6, John W. Wallace was appointed enrollment commissioner. Commissioner of Indian affairs T. J. Morgan instructed Wallace to receive and consider all testimony submitted to him regardless of race and to allow the claimants to appear with counsel if they desired. Although the department had no authority to confer citizenship on any person, Morgan saw no objection to having Wallace, as a special agent, investigate the matter and act in conjunction with a person appointed by the Cherokees to prepare a roll of the people whose claims to share in the appropriation were not contested. Thus Wallace was instructed to make a roll of admitted and doubtful citizens of all three groups. Evidence relating to doubtful claimants was to be forwarded to the Indian Office. Wallace was to confer with the new Union agent, Leo E. Bennett, and adopt some plan by which to make the enrollment. He was to give the enrollment the essential publicity and the claimants ample time to make their applications. However, Morgan warned Wallace that his job would not be an easy one because of the ignorance of the freedmen and the lack of data bearing on their claims.[62]

Commissioner Morgan could not have made a more accurate prediction. Wallace quickly ran into difficulties in making the roll, but they arose from a source that apparently neither he nor Morgan had anticipated—

the Cherokees. The Indian officials placed obstacles in his way in an effort to thwart his attempt to enroll the freedmen, and they charged Wallace with fraud in making the roll. When Wallace finally succeeded in enrolling the freedmen, the Cherokees refused to accept the validity of his work. They had no way of knowing that their refusal to help Wallace make an accurate roll of the freedmen would later prove to be a costly mistake for their nation. All they knew was that Congress had struck a heavy blow to their autonomy by usurping their right to determine who were citizens of the Cherokee Nation.

NOTES

1. C. O. Frye to D. W. Bushyhead, December 31, 1879, Indian Archives Division, Oklahoma Historical Society, *Cherokee–Intruders (Tahlequah)*; John Q. Tufts to E. J. Brooks, February 17, 1880, George W. Lynch to Secretary of the Interior, January 22, 1880, Lynch to President Hayes, February 29, 1880, Nathaniel Duffie to Secretary of the Interior, April 24, 1880, M. A. Daniel to Secretary of the Interior, April 8, 1880, William Hudson et al. to Secretary of the Interior, March 31, 1880, and Sam Barnes to Carl Schurz, May 22, 1880, National Archives Record Group 75 (Records of the Bureau of Indian Affairs), *Letters Received Relating to Cherokee Citizenship, 1875-89* (hereafter cited as *Cherokee Citizenship File*), Union T259-80, L120-80, L464-80, D337-80, S1341-80, C602-80, B404-80.

2. W. P. Adair et al. to Hayes, April 17, 1880, *Cherokee Citizenship File;* "Cases submitted to the 'Commission on Citizenship' at the January Term of Said Commission in 1880," "List of Intruders Now Residing in the Cherokee Nation, Sequoyah District," February 6, 1880, James Keys to Bushyhead, April 6, 10, 1880, and A. H. Norwood to Bushyhead, August 25, 1880, Indian Archives Division, Oklahoma Historical Society, *Cherokee-Citizenship (Tahlequah);* Jesse Ridge et al. to President, April 10, 1880, National Archives Microfilm Publications, *Microcopy M234* (Records of the Office of Indian Affairs, Letters Received)-875, R4301-80.

3. Tufts to R. E. Trowbridge, July 17, 1880, *Cherokee Citizenship File,* Union T866-80. Delegates from Cooweescoowee District were H. C. Hayden, Moses Whitmire, Joseph Boggs, Riley McNair, J. J. Rose, Sandy Thompson, Nelson Merrel, Eman Vann, Nathan Duffie, Sam Vann, Reuben Sanders, and Peter Meigs; from Saline, Thomas Mayfield and Arthur Bean; from Delaware, Jack David, Jack Bean, and Berry Mayes; from Tahlequah,

Joseph Rowe, Charles Nave, and Joseph Ross; from Sequoyah, Jesse Mc-
Clure and Coley Albert; and from Illinois, Richard Fields, Lewis Caton,
William Thorne, Jake Brown, Daniel Roach, Russel Mackey, and Jake
Crapo.

4. Adair to Trowbridge, June 28, 1880, *Microcopy M234*-873, C1115-
80; W. A. Phillips to Schurz, September 29, 1880, *Cherokee Citizenship
File,* Union P1188-80.

5. Brooks to Tufts, July 20, 1880, *Cherokee–Intruders (Tahlequah);*
Bushyhead and Phillips to L. Q. C. Lamar, April 1886, *Cherokee Citizenship File,* 7846-87; *Cherokee Advocate,* December 4, 1885.

6. "Act Providing for Taking the Census of the Cherokee Nation in
the Year 1880," in H. Price to Secretary of the Interior, November 17,
1883, *Cherokee Citizenship File,* P21353-83; "Summary of Colored
Citizens and Colored Intruders Resident in the Several Districts . . . 1880,"
Indian Archives Division, Oklahoma Historical Society, *Cherokee–Freedmen (Tahlequah).* Of the citizens, there were 484 males over eighteen. Of
those listed as intruders, 163 were over eighteen; of the rejected claimants,
125 were over eighteen, and of those who still had claims, 7 were over
eighteen. The citizen freedmen, listed by district, were as follows: Cooweescoowee, 546; Delaware, 101; Saline, 122; Going Snake, 5; Flint, 12;
Tahlequah, 456; Illinois, 539; Sequoyah, 125; Canadian, 70. Noncitizen
freedmen families claiming citizenship were distributed as follows: Cooweescoowee, 30; Delaware, 62; Saline, 25; Going Snake, 7; Flint, 7; Tahlequah, 32; Illinois, 29; Sequoyah, 50; Canadian, 7. Intruder freedmen
were distributed as follows: Cooweescoowee, 564; Delaware, 13; Saline, 5;
Going Snake, 2; Flint, 1; Tahlequah, 15; Illinois, 97; Sequoyah, 35; Canadian, 35.

7. Roach Young to Bushyhead, October 4, 1880, *Cherokee–Citizenship (Tahlequah); Cherokee Advocate,* September 15, 1880; proclamation of Bushyhead, July 27, 1880, in Price to Secretary of the Interior,
November 17, 1883, *Cherokee Citizenship File,* 21353-83.

8. Young to Bushyhead, October 4, 1880, *Cherokee–Citizenship
(Tahlequah); Cherokee Advocate,* November 17, 1880.

9. E. N. Marble to Tufts, October 16, 1880, and Tufts to Marble,
January 8, 1881, National Archives Record Group 75, *Letters Received,*
8548-1927 Cherokee Nation 175.2, pt. 1, 662-81; Marble to Tufts,
October 16, 1880, National Archives Microfilm Publications, *Microcopy
M21* (Records of the Office of Indian Affairs, Letters Sent)-158, 370;
bill introduced in Senate by Hon. S. H. Benge, November 30, 1880,
*Cherokee–Freedmen (Tahlequah); Compiled Laws of the Cherokee Na-
tion* (Tahlequah, Cherokee Nation: National Advocate Print, 1881), 325;
Cherokee Advocate, August 4, 1880.

10. *Compiled Laws, 1881,* 318-322.

11. *Cherokee Advocate,* February 16, March 9, July 20, August 24, 1881; proclamation of Bushyhead, August 24, 1881, in Price to Secretary of the Interior, November 17, 1883, *Cherokee Citizenship File,* 21353-83.

12. Young to Bushyhead, October 4, 1881, *Cherokee–Citizenship (Tahlequah); Cherokee Advocate,* October 5, 1881.

13. *Cherokee Advocate,* November 2, 9, 25, 1881; Bushyhead and Phillips to Lamar, April 3, 1886, in H. L. Muldrow to Commissioner of Indian Affairs, March 25, 1887, *Cherokee Citizenship File,* 7846-87.

14. Tufts to Price, January 26, 1882, National Archives Record Group 48 (Records of the Department of the Interior, Office of the Secretary), Indian Territory Division, *Chickasaw Freedmen,* box 392 (60a), 2098-82; *Cherokee Advocate,* December 23, 1881, September 1, 8, 1882. The Chickasaw freedmen file, hereafter cited as *Freedmen File,* was apparently mislabeled, for most of the documents contained in it relate to the Cherokees.

15. *Cherokee Advocate,* February 10, 1882.

16. Tufts to Price, January 26, 1882, *Freedmen File,* box 393 (60b), 2097-82 (documents subsequently referred to are in box 393 unless otherwise indicated); Bushyhead to Phillips, April 28, 1882, and Cherokee Delegation to Secretary of the Interior, May 12, 1882, *Cherokee–Citizenship (Tahlequah).*

17. Alonzo Manly to Bushyhead, April, 1882, *Cherokee–Citizenship (Tahlequah);* Hewston West to Price, May 2, 1882, *Letters Received,* 8540-82; Price to Secretary of the Interior, April 11, 1882, National Archives Record Group 75, *Report Books,* 41: 689; Tufts to Price, June 1, 1882, *Freedmen File,* 10166-82; *Cherokee Advocate,* June 30, August 4, 1882.

18. *Cherokee Advocate,* June 16, 23, 30, July 7, 21, 28, August 4, 1882.

19. Ibid., October 6, 1882.

20. R. W. Wolfe and Robert B. Ross to H. M. Teller, January 5, 1883, National Archives Record Group 75, *Letters Received* (case 48), 28213-85; 49th Cong., 1st sess., *Senate Executive Document 82,* 2; *Cherokee Advocate,* June 8, 1883.

21. 49th Cong., 1st sess., *Senate Report 1278,* pt. 2, "Documents," 20-21, 19-20.

22. George W. Vann to Price, February 27, 1883, and Tufts to Price, April 14, 1883, *Letters Received,* 3982-83, 7058-83 (E. C. Boudinot and J. Milton Turner attested to the truth of Vann's statements); Will P. Ross to Bushyhead, May 9, 1883, *Cherokee–Freedmen (Tahlequah);* Wolfe et al. to Teller, March 24, 1883, *Cherokee Citizenship File,* 5885-83.

23. Florence Lane to Secretary of the Interior, April 4, 1883, *Chero-kee Citizenship File,* 6601-83; petition, May 28, 1882, and S. H. Mayes to Bushyhead, May 21, 1883, *Cherokee–Intruders (Tahlequah)*; Tufts to Bushyhead, April 14, 1883, Price to Tufts, May 5, 1883, and Tufts to Bushyhead, May 9, 1883, *Cherokee–Citizenship (Tahlequah).*

24. Henry Ward and Cyrus Beede to Teller, June 2, 1883, in Price to Secretary of the Interior, November 17, 1883, *Cherokee Citizenship File,* 21353-83; Vann to President of the United States, September 1883, and Vann to Secretary of the Interior, October 3, 1883, *Letters Received,* 18730-83, 18645-83.

25. Price to Arthur Bean, Jack Davis, and Leander Bean, September 17, 1883, National Archives Record Group 75, *Letters Sent,* Land Letter Book 116: 439; "Suggestions Relative to Board of Arbitration," October 30, 1883, and Phillips to Teller, November 5, 1883, in Price to Secretary of the Interior, November 17, 1883, *Cherokee Citizenship File,* 19958-83, 21353-83.

26. Price to Secretary of the Interior, November 17, 1883, *Cherokee Citizenship File,* 21353-83.

27. Admitted freedmen were Joseph Watie, Coose Baldridge, Pose Gibson, Amiretta Gibson, Mary Stover, Eliza Stover, Jane Stover, Bessy Stover, Lydia Stover, Angelina Stover, and Mary Stover (second by this name). Left pending was the case of Isaac Rogers. Thomas Tehee et al. to Bushyhead, September 10, 1883, and September 30, 1883, and Tehee to Bushyhead, October 3, 1883, *Cherokee–Citizenship (Tahlequah).*

Cherokee Advocate, November 16, 1883, September 19, October 17, 1884; Bushyhead to the Hon. Senate and Council, November 6, 1883, *Cherokee–Freedmen (Tahlequah); Constitution and Laws of the Chero-kee Nation, Published by an Act of the National Council, 1892* (Parsons, Kan.: Foley R'y Printing Co., 1893), 384-385; Joint Resolution of the National Council, November 26, 1883, *Cherokee–Citizenship (Tahlequah);* Bushyhead to the National Council, December 3, 10, 1883, *Cherokee–Intruders (Tahlequah);* George O. Butler to Secretary of the Interior, January 22, 1884, *Cherokee Citizenship File,* 1826-84.

28. Abstract, April 15, 1884, 48th Cong., 1st sess., *Report 1037,* and Price to Bushyhead, June 30, 1884, *Cherokee–Citizenship (Tahlequah)*; H. L. Dawes to Teller, June 24, 1884, and Bushyhead to Price, August 11, 1884, *Freedmen File,* 12002-84, 15651-84.

29. Those testifying included several who had aired grievances against the Cherokees during the preceding years. Their testimony is reproduced in 49th Cong., 1st sess., *Senate Report 1278,* pt. 2, 3-43, 81-95.

30. Ibid., 44-81, 90-94, 99-138.

31. Bushyhead to the Senate, December 8, 1885, Indian Archives Divi-

sion, Oklahoma Historical Society, *Cherokee—Ejectment (Tahlequah); Cherokee Advocate,* December 4, 1885; Senate Bill 4, December 8, 1885, *Cherokee—Freedmen (Tahlequah);* Muldrow to Commissioner, March 25, 1887, *Cherokee Citizenship File,* 7846-87.

32. Executive Council to Bushyhead, December 15, 1885, *Cherokee—Citizenship (Tahlequah);* Muldrow to Commissioner, March 25, 1887, *Cherokee Citizenship File,* 7846-87.

33. Bushyhead to Lamar, February 1, 1886, *Cherokee—Citizenship (Tahlequah);* Muldrow to Commissioner, March 25, 1887, *Cherokee Citizenship File,* 7846-87.

34. Robert L. Owen to J. D. C. Atkins, February 27, 1886, in Muldrow to Commissioner, March 25, 1887, *Cherokee Citizenship File,* 7846-87.

35. *Annual Report of the Commissioner of Indian Affairs to the Secretary of the Interior for the Year 1887* (Washington, D. C.: Government Printing Office, 1887), lviii-lix.

36. Bushyhead and Phillips to Lamar, April 3, 1886, and Bushyhead and John Chambers to Lamar, July 13, 1886, in Muldrow to the Commissioner, March 25, 1887, Lamar to the Commissioner, August 5, 1886, and Bushyhead to Atkins, August 31, 1886, *Cherokee Citizenship File,* 7846-87, 20920-86, 23633-86; Owen to Rabbit Bunch, June 1, 1886, and Owen to Bushyhead, October 16, 1886, *Cherokee—Citizenship (Tahlequah).*

37. "An Act Providing for the Appointment of a Commission to Try and Determine Applications for Cherokee Citizenship," and L. B. Bell to Bushyhead, December 18, 1886, *Cherokee—Citizenship (Tahlequah); Cherokee Advocate,* February 23, March 9, April 20, 1887; C. J. Harris and W. T. Landrum to Lamar, January 19, 1887, *Freedmen File,* 2095-87; "An Act Providing for the Expenses of Collecting Testimony before the Commission on Citizenship," "An Act Providing for the Appointment of a Joint Commission," Bushyhead to the Senate, December 17, 1886, and Bell to Bushyhead, December 18, 1886, *Cherokee—Citizenship (Tahlequah).*

38. Muldrow to Commissioner, February 21, 1887, *Freedmen File,* 5159-87; Atkins to Secretary, February 7, 1887, National Archives Record Group 75, *Letters Sent,* Land Letter Book 156: 59.

39. *Cherokee Advocate,* March 9, 1887, and July 6, 1887; *Annual Report, 1887,* lix; Upshaw to Owen, April 14, 1887, *Letters Sent,* Land Letter Book 158: 434; Commissioner to Owen, June 16, 1887, *Cherokee—Intruders (Tahlequah);* open letter of Owen, June 30, 1887, *Cherokee—Citizenship (Tahlequah).*

40. *Annual Report, 1887,* lix.

41. Berry Mayes et al. to Secretary of the Interior, May 19, 1883, Frank

Vann and Andy Tiner to Secretary of the Interior, May 21, 1883, credentials of Isaac Rogers and L. D. Daniels, n.d., J. M. Fields, J. Glass, and S. Webber to Teller, May 30, 1883, and J. B. Butler et al. to Hiram Price, June 1, 1883, *Letters Received* (case 48), 984-83, 9837-83, 2425-83, in 10861-83; Muskogee *Indian Journal*, May 31, 1883. Many records relating to the per-capita payment of 1883 were consolidated under the *Letters Received* number 10861-83 and labeled *Case 48*, by which further references to this file will be indicated.

42. Hayden and William Madden to the People of Grand River, June 4, 1883, William Davis to Secretary of the Interior, June 6, 1883, credentials of Rogers and Daniels, n.d., Rogers et al. to Teller, n.d., and Rogers and Daniels to Commissioner of Indian Affairs, June 9, 1883, *Case 48*, 10463-83, 2425-83, 10490-83, and 10861-83.

43. *Cherokee Advocate*, June 8, 1883; "Act Appointing D. W. Bushyhead, R. M. Wolfe, and R. B. Ross Delegates to Convey Lands to U. S.," May 17, 1883, Cherokee Delegation to Teller, June 9, 1883, Bushyhead et al., to Teller, June 13, 1883, and Teller to Commissioner, June 14, 1883, *Case 48*, 2278-83, 2513-83, 2547-83, 10861-83.

44. William Brown to Bushyhead, April 27, 1883, *Cherokee–Freedmen (Tahlequah); Cherokee Advocate*, July 27, November 16, 1883.

45. "Petition of Colored Citizens of the Cherokee Nation," November 14, 1883, *Cherokee–Freedmen (Tahlequah)*.

46. "Cherokee Freedmen–Petitions for Redress, etc., Received February 12, 1884," *Freedmen File*, box 392 (60a), 2873-84; J. Milton Turner to Bushyhead, December 24, 1883, *Cherokee–Freedmen (Tahlequah)*.

47. Petition to the Honorable, the Senate and House of Representatives of the United States in Congress Assembled, *Cherokee–Freedmen (Tahlequah);* John J. Ingalls to Secretary of the Interior, January 30, 1884, *Letters Received*, 2268-84; Price to the Secretary of the Interior, February 12, 1884, *Letters Sent*, Report Book 47: 307.

48. Turner to Bushyhead, November 20, 1885, *Cherokee–Freedmen (Tahlequah);* 49th Cong., 1st sess., *Senate Report 1278*, pt. 2, "Documents," 22-23; Turner to President, February 8, 1886, *Freedmen File*, 4194-84; Lamar to President, February 27, 1886, National Archives Microfilm Publications, *Microcopy M606* (Letters Sent by the Secretary of the Interior)-44, 159; 49th Cong., 1st sess., *Senate Executive Document 82*, 6; *New York Times*, February 10, 1886, *Indian Chieftain*, February 11, March 4, 1866; *Indian Journal*, March 4, 1886.

49. 49th Cong., 1st sess., *Senate Executive Document 82*, 3-4, 11; Bill S. 1800, *Cherokee–Freedmen (Tahlequah)*.

50. *Cherokee Advocate,* March 26, 1886; *Indian Chieftain,* April 1, 1886.

51. *Cherokee Advocate,* May 7, 1886. An act of May 19, 1883, provided that the treasurer of the Nation hold such pyaments until the amount reached $300,000, at which time it was to be paid per capita under the direction of the National Council. "Construction of the Rights of Cherokee Citizenship as Designed to be Conferred upon Freedmen and Friendly Indians in the 9th and 15th Articles of the Treaty of 1866," April 27, 1886, *Cherokee–Citizenship (Tahlequah).*

52. *Cherokee Advocate,* May 7, 1886; *Indian Chieftain,* May 20, 1886.

53. *Cherokee Advocate,* April 30, 1886.

54. *Indian Chieftain,* May 28, June 24, 1886.

55. Ibid., July 22, 1886.

56. Atkins to Secretary of the Interior, June 25, 1886, *Letters Sent,* Land Letter Book 149: 377; *Indian Chieftain,* January 20, 1887; *Annual Report, 1887,* 113.

57. Owen to Atkins, June 7, 1887, *Letters Received,* 14871-87; *Indian Chieftain,* July 27, 1887.

58. *Annual Report, 1887,* 113; Gaston L. Litton, "The Principal Chiefs of the Cherokee Nation," *The Chronicles of Oklahoma* 15 (September 1937): 267.

59. HR 5066, 50th Cong., 1st sess., National Archives Record Group 75, *Printed Matter Concerning Attorneys' Claims against the Old Settler Cherokees, 1888-95; Cherokee Advocate,* April 4, December 5, 1888; *Indian Chieftain,* October 11, November 15, 1888, March 21, 1889.

60. John W. Oberly to Owen, November 2, 1888, and Oberly to Secretary of the Interior, November 10, 1888, *Letters Sent,* Vol. 18 (Letter Book 177-178): 258, 255; William Vilas to Commissioner, November 15, 1888, *Letters Received,* 28325-88.

61. Owen to J. B. Mayes, November 5, 1888, and Mayes to National Council, November 16, 1888, *Cherokee–Freedmen (Tahlequah);* Mayes to Council, November 20, 1888, Henry Heth to Mayes, November 28, 1888, and "An Act to Create a Joint Commission," n.d., *Cherokee–Citizenship (Tahlequah);* Oberly to Heth, November 21, 1888, *Letters Sent,* vol. 90 (Letter Book, 179-180): 426.

62. John W. Wallace's oath of office, July 6, 1889, *Letters Received,* 20921-89; T. J. Morgan to Secretary of the Interior, July 11, 1889, *Letters Sent,* Finance Letter Book 163: 27; Morgan to Wallace, July 11, 1889, *Letters Sent,* Land Letter Book 187: 93; *Indian Chieftain,* August 29, 1889; 50th Cong., 1st sess., *Senate Executive Document 83,* 5-6.

THE WALLACE ROLL AND

THE FREEDMAN'S

chapter 7 COMPROMISE

It quickly became obvious to John W. Wallace that the Cherokees would not cooperate with him in making a roll of the freedmen since they did not recognize the government's right to authorize him to do so. When he arrived in Tahlequah in late August 1889, he found a letter of protest from Chief Joel Mayes, precipitated by a recent article in the *Cherokee Advocate* opposing his mission. In order to mend his political fences, Wallace asked Mayes to appoint someone to help him revise the rolls of the admitted citizens. Mayes complied but quickly changed his mind, claiming that he lacked authority to do so. Thus Wallace obtained a copy of the authenticated rolls of 1880 and went alone to Vinita where he started working on them. He neither requested nor expected further help from the Cherokees and accused Mayes of being obstinate.[1] Government officials should have anticipated Mayes's resistance. Not just the per-capita payment was at stake; Cherokee autonomy was being trampled on.

By the end of October, Wallace had received nearly thirty-eight hundred applications from freedmen, Shawnees, and Delawares in Cooweescoowee, Saline, and Delaware districts, a much larger number than had originally been expected. He corrected the rolls for these districts, eliminating deaths and adding births and current places of residence. Each claimant's statement was accompanied by the affidavits of witnesses who were citizens by blood or who were on the authenticated rolls. Wallace found the witnesses necessary because of the ignorance of most of the claimants and the "unreliability of much of the evidence which they would submit if permitted to do so." Many of the freedmen did not know how old they were, and some could not count. Some went by more than one name.

Thus getting vital statistics was difficult. Wallace asked them, among other things, if they had been slaves at the outbreak of the war, who their masters were, where they were at the close of the war, how they obtained their freedom, where they had been since the war, where they then resided, and if they were recognized as a voter by the Cherokees.[2]

Applicants came in such numbers that great crowds collected near Wallace's office. Poverty stricken, the people had no means of getting food or shelter. To disperse the crowds as quickly as possible, Wallace took the sworn statements with corroborative evidence, wrapped each case separately, and listed it alphabetically for future reference when he had time to make final lists of admitted and doubtful claimants. In November he moved his office to Tahlequah and there found the same conditions with the same rush of freedmen he had met at Vinita. In order to cope with the crowds, Wallace employed a rather large staff. He had four clerks: W. H. Rowe, C. S. Shelton, S. S. Clover, and W. W. Breedlove. All except Rowe were Indians. He had an interpreter, for many of the freedmen and witnesses spoke no English. Freedman Luster Foreman was his messenger and go-between with the freedmen. Porters and messengers publicized the enrollment locations to those in out-of-the-way places and performed labor around the office—bringing water, chopping wood, making fires, and cleaning up after the crowds. It took several people to handle the crowds, and a marshal or sheriff was necessary to maintain order, for wherever Wallace went, "an unruly crowd of obstructionists unfavorable to the enrollment of the freedmen gathered about the office every day."[3]

Wallace's work was also hampered by rumors and intrigue. Secretary of the Interior John Noble had, on the basis of a report from "good authority," already asked Union Agent Leo Bennett to investigate rumors that Wallace was an intemperate man. And there was a rumor among the Cherokees that Wallace had been promised a certain amount of money for each freedman he admitted to the roll. Wallace complained, "The country is full of schemes, and plans of every description have been insinuated to me. All for one purpose. To secure the lion's share of the money to be disbursed." He incurred the wrath of the salesmen, merchants, and creditors when he refused to furnish them any information, to issue any certificate, or to accept any orders by which they might place a hold, for the collection of debts, on future payments to the freedmen.[4]

At this time, most of those who presented themselves to Wallace were

authenticated citizens whose names appeared on the roll of 1880. However, he was informed that large numbers of freedmen were en route from
Texas, New Mexico, and Arkansas to present claims. Wallace found it
convenient to work in Tahlequah during the meeting of the National
Council. Its members and other Cherokees from all parts of the Nation
visited Wallace, testified for applicants (he received from 50 to 125 each
day), and praised Wallace's thoroughness, maintaining, however, that
they doubted the validity of his mission. The Cherokee executive office
furnished him official statements that corrected clerical errors and omissions in the authenticated rolls. Finally, his being at the capital prevented,
to some degree, unscrupulous persons who, for a fee per capita, sent applicants from neighboring states to Wallace with false statements. It was
difficult for Wallace to estimate the number who would ultimately be
entitled to citizenship, for those arriving each day told of large numbers
in their neighborhoods yet to come.[5]

Toward the end of 1889, Wallace became apprehensive about the safety
of the great mass of evidence he had collected and kept at his residence.
On December 18 he went to Fort Gibson and took his records by train
to Fort Smith, Arkansas, where he secured storage in a government vault
under the control of the custodian of records. In January 1890 he moved
his residence to Fort Smith from which point he could visit all remaining
neighborhoods. By that time he had received over six thousand applications with an estimated twenty-five hundred to three thousand to go.
There were several settlements with two hundred to four hundred persons each, and the mail indicated that many would come from Louisiana,
Texas, Arkansas, and the Choctaw Nation. Wallace hoped to have the rolls
completed and ready for the distribution of funds by April.[6]

For the next month, Wallace took testimony in Sequoyah District. The
work was difficult. Because of its easy access from Arkansas, many blacks
from that state had entered the district and had been allowed to remain.
Wallace found the inalterable ignorance of most of them "beyond com-
prehension." By the middle of February, he had nearly eight thousand
names, many of whom were contested cases. However, Wallace could see
the end of his work. He was nearly finished in Sequoyah District; then he
had a few Shawnee and Delaware cases to investigate and a few days to
spend at Vinita regarding freedman cases.[7]

In March he finished taking testimony and began making his decisions
and completing the rolls. The task was monumental. He had seen nearly

every black resident of the Cherokee Nation and great numbers from adjoining states. He had had to see all of the Shawnees and make a new roll
and had spent more time among the Delawares than he had expected. As
the work went on, Wallace came under fire again. Cherokee Elias C. Boudinot pointed out to Secretary Noble the difficulties that lay in store for
the department after the enrollment. The government had had only an ex
parte estimate by the Cherokees of the number of freedmen when Congress had appropriated the $75,000. Boudinot estimated that the final
count would reach seven thousand, which would require another appropriation. He praised Wallace for his "industry, skill and faithfulness" in the
work. Noble was surprised at the number of freedmen applicants, although
he should not have been since Wallace had pointed out the great number
who had come before him. Noble began to distrust Wallace. He ordered
Commissioner Thomas J. Morgan to look carefully at Wallace's report
and, if necessary, verify it by means other than Wallace's accounting.
He mentioned, "merely as a warning," that there had been at one time
adverse reports about Wallace's character.[8]

Noble's suspicions were further aroused when J. Milton Turner gave
him a letter from Cherokee Ridge Paschal to Turner, alleging that Wallace and "a powerful combination at Fort Smith" had conspired to take
money from the freedman payment. Luster Foreman, the freedman who
had assisted Wallace in taking testimony, was supposed to have called a
meeting of the freedmen at Vinita for March 4. Described as "Wallace's
man," Foreman was allegedly going to tell the freedmen that if they
would sign papers agreeing to take $7.00 or $7.50 per capita, they would
get their money immediately. The remainder of the money due each
would supposedly go to Wallace and his friends. Foreman allegedly
boasted that his pay went on even while he was not assisting Wallace. Paschal also charged that Wallace and his other assistants, J. L. Adair, Jr.,
and C. S. Shelton, were "extremely rebel democratic." He therefore
recommended that Noble send someone to the territory under secret
orders to probe the situation. On the letter, Noble wrote confidentially
to Morgan: "There are a good many such statements about Wallace's
habits. Be careful."[9]

On March 7 a group of freedmen met at Fort Gibson. They selected
an executive committee composed of a freedman from each of the nine
districts. The committee drafted a resolution to be presented to the chief,
the President, the secretary of the interior, and both houses of Congress.

They expressed their thanks to Congress for appropriating the $75,000, praised Wallace for his work, asked that Congress provide an additional appropriation, if necessary, to make the payment, asserted their right to a share of the second $300,000, which had been paid in 1886 to Cherokees by blood, expressed their favor of the proposed sale of the Cherokee Strip, and praised Boudinot as a "bold, unselfish and true friend of the freedmen, as well as of all the Cherokee Nation." Finally, they rejected both the National and Downing parties, which had in the last election incorporated into their platforms support for "equal and exact justice to the freedmen." Yet the council had met for nearly sixty days, and not a word had been uttered in the freedmen's behalf. They pledged to vote in the future for their friends, regardless of party. After drafting the resolution and making plans to convene again on March 20, the freedmen adjourned.[10]

Complaints about Wallace's activities came from Chief Mayes and former chief D. W. Bushyhead, and Secretary Noble decided not to send Wallace any money to distribute until he learned if the enrollment was well done. Noble did not wish any injustice done the freedmen, yet he himself did not want to do any to Wallace. He wanted to know if Wallace was an improper person to do the enrolling, and he encouraged Fred W. Strout, a resident of Vinita, to inform him of anything "beyond a mere suspicion" that might incriminate Wallace. Perhaps it was Noble's anxiety that caused Commissioner Morgan to suggest that Wallace go to Washington to complete the work of revising the rolls and arranging the papers related to them. Wallace refused, saying that he could do his work more rapidly at his own residence in Fort Smith with the help of his two able assistants: a Cherokee freedman of "unusual intelligence" who had worked with him from the start and knew the status of almost every black in the Nation and a clerk who was familiar with the incidents connected with the hearing of each case.[11] The freedman was Luster Foreman who had, without Wallace's knowledge, apparently involved Wallace in schemes to defraud the freedmen and by boasting, evidently falsely, about his salary. The clerk was Shelton, who later turned on Wallace.

Wallace's work had not grown any more palatable to the Cherokees as it approached completion. J. A. Scales, a prominent leader of the Downing party, said in a letter published in the *Indian Chieftain* on March 20: "I do not believe the Negro entitled to a cent of our money, or to a foot of land." One had only to look at the Creek Treaty of 1866 to see

the intention of the government at the time. The Creeks by that document were required to take in their freedmen with"all the rights and
privileges of native citizens, including an equal interest in the soil and
national funds," while the Cherokees were required to give theirs "all
the rights of native Cherokees." Said Scales, "If the 9th article of the
Cherokee treaty conveys any rights of property to the Negro, it is the
first recorded instance of the kind where property was conveyed without
naming it since the 'earth was divided' in the days of Peleg."[12]

With his job nearly finished, Wallace found himself increasingly more
under fire from the Cherokees. They again charged him with enrolling
great numbers of interloping freedmen at so much per capita; Wallace
countered that the Cherokees themselves had encouraged the applications
of many who had no claim just to slow down his progress and that they
were now trying to make it appear that he had encouraged the applications for profit. There was so much excitement about his work among
the Cherokees that it was unsafe for him to travel in the Nation. Agent
Leo Bennett offered the assistance of a squad of Indian police whenever
Wallace needed to go into the Indian country. Cherokee concern about
the enrollment was manifested by their passage, in April, of an act creating a joint United States and Cherokee court of eight members to redo
Wallace's work.

To counter the charges, Wallace filed statements made by W. Y. H.
Foreman, Luster Foreman, Claude S. Shelton, and W. W. Breedlove, all
of whom worked or had worked for him. W. Y. H. Foreman said that
Wallace had worked hard against great odds. All had been treated equally,
and all business had been conducted with open doors. He had heard of
neither irregularities nor sales of certificates of citizenship. The others
supported that testimony, stressing that the evidence was objectively
taken, carefully marked, and safely stored and that Wallace was evaluating the evidence and making the final rolls. Wallace also came under fire
from the secretary of the interior. Always suspicious of him, Noble wrote
him early in April that his funds were nearly spent and that he was liable
for not conforming to his instructions. But Wallace protested that his only
instructions had been to keep accurate accounts of his expenditures and
to enclose them with his final report.[13]

Later that month, Wallace informed Morgan that he had the Cherokee
freedman and Shawnee rolls and evidence ready to mail but that he had
several Delaware families requiring inquiry. On April 30, before he could

mail the rolls to Washington, they and all of the original papers relating
to the Cherokee freedman enrollment were stolen from Wallace's home in
Fort Smith. Mrs. Wallace was at home when Claude Shelton, the clerk who
no longer worked for Wallace, and another man, whom she did not recognize, broke in. She resisted, but they forcibly removed the papers. Agent
Leo Bennett saw the importance of recovering the papers and consulted
the U. S. attorney at Fort Smith, who advised the department to seek the
aid of the Department of Justice in the search. Bennett hired a detective,
with whose aid he found the papers in the government vault, where they
had been put with the consent of Judge Isaac Parker, who had assured
Shelton that the papers would remain there until Wallace settled accounts
with his clerks. There remained for Bennett, then, the problem of getting
the papers back without having to go through the local courts and thereby saving expense and, more important, time. Bennett then entered negotiations with Shelton's attorney and, by the aid of a telegram from Noble,
succeeded on May 6 in getting back the papers, which he immediately sent
to Washington. Wallace followed the papers two days later.[14]

Wallace had completed his reports by the first week in June. Noble
directed Commissioner Morgan to have someone go over the reports with
Wallace to see that they were correctly made. The commissioner chose
R. F. Thompson, a clerk in the Office of Indian Affairs, who thought that
Wallace had done a good job in light of adverse conditions. Cherokees who
wanted to undermine his work had sent claimants to him, knowing well
that they had no rights, hoping to build a case for invalidating his work.
The Cherokee Nation had refused to appoint a commissioner to help him.
The freedmen's ignorance made the work more difficult. There was often
a confusion of names and ages. Wallace had found 1,998 living freedmen
whose names appeared on the Cherokee authenticated roll of 1880 or
who descended from those on the roll. He added to it 1,243 names of
freedmen he felt entitled to share in the payment. When Thompson eliminated duplications and rejected several, his total came to 3,351, while
Wallace's came to 3,369.[15]

Settling Wallace's accounts and obtaining additional funds to pay for
the disbursement of the per-capita funds was a drawn-out affair, but by
the time Noble presented the request to the secretary of the treasury, he
was convinced that Wallace had done his best. He justified the request on
the ground that Wallace had been antagonized by the Cherokees and had
had to examine large numbers of people and their witnesses. The work

had required much more time and money than had been expected. Noble also defended Wallace before the Senate Appropriations Committee against charges that he had put immense numbers of freedmen on the roll, saying, "Mr. Wallace has my confidence."[16]

Although Wallace had evidently been honest in hearing and evaluating evidence, his activities might be somewhat questionable. He made only verbal contracts with his clerks, he fell behind in the payment of their salaries, and he refused to give them statements of what was due them before he left Fort Smith. As a result there was a discrepancy between his account of what was owed them and theirs. Some aspects of his relationship with Luster Foreman might also be questionable, but not so much because of a lack of ethics as of poor judgment in choosing his partners. Wallace knew that the act of October 19, 1888, and the subsequent enrollment of the freedmen would result in future litigation. Therefore he sought to take J. Milton Turner's place as attorney for the freedmen in future suits. The March meeting in Fort Gibson had obviously been held by the freedmen, in part, for his support. It had been to rally his support that Foreman had called the meetings in Vinita in the early weeks of the year and had created suspicion of fraud. Wallace unfortunately left it to Foreman to organize the freedmen for him. Foreman became president of those he could organize in the northern part of the Nation. Wallace's man in the southern part of the Nation was William Brown, who was to see Joe Brown, Frank Vann, and Richard Foreman, particularly. The object was to have Wallace named attorney by an executive committee of the freedmen at a fee of 15 percent of all money recovered by the freedmen and 10 percent of the value of their proportion of lands obtained in future suits. Wallace was determined to unseat Turner, who, Wallace said, had "got the best of everyone that filed claims before him." Those who rallied around him, including E. C. Boudinot, had been Turner's opponents for some time. But it had been Turner who had got the legislative results in the freedmen's behalf, and Wallace failed to get his contract.[17]

Wallace's service as special agent ended on October 14, 1890. He left in his wake a controversy concerning his freedman roll that would last for years. In the fall the work of examining and revising the rolls continued. Wallace had taken evidence for nearly 7,000 applications about which decisions had to be made, and those which had no base had to be eliminated. When the rolls were finally completed, there were 3,216 on the authenticated roll and 130 on the doubtful roll. These figures explain, in part, the Cherokee opposition to Wallace's work, for their census of 1890 showed only 2,052 admitted freedmen.[18]

Meanwhile the freedmen clamored to be paid. One group assembled at Fort Gibson on October 17 to consider what steps to take. Another met at Goose Neck Bend, Cooweescoowee District, in early December. Most of the freedmen were farmers, and because of drought, their crops had failed that year. Winter was now upon them, and they faced hardship. The convention, chaired by R. M. Sanders of Hudson, elected a committee—David Vann, David French, G. W. Lane, Louis Nave, and David D. Mayes—to petition the secretary to proceed with the disbursement to those who were on the authenticated list.[19]

It was decided that Agent Leo Bennett would make the payment to save the cost of a special commissioner. He was to pay the freedmen first to stop the clamor. The freedmen made so many inquiries of Bennett that they became an annoyance to him. He finally asked the commissioner to tell him when and where the money would be paid and give him authority to make the fact public so as to relieve their anxiety. Near the end of December, the commissioner sent the rolls, evidence, and payment books to Bennett, who planned to pay those on the authenticated roll and investigate the cases of those on the doubtful list and those who had died since the roll had been made. From his reports the department would prepare supplemental lists. Morgan warned Bennett against publishing a copy of the approved list to avoid a rush of appeals by rejected claimants.[20]

On January 15, 1891, Bennett published a notice in several papers in the Cherokee and Creek Nations that he would pay $15.50 per capita to the 3,216 who had been duly enrolled. Satisfied that more of them were within reach of Braggs than any other railroad station or easily accessible point, he would begin there on January 27 and pay for six to ten days. Heads of families could draw for themselves and their families. Guardians and administrators of estates were required to furnish duly processed documents to establish their right to draw. From Braggs, Bennett planned to go to as many other points in the Nation that he could reach with the funds he had. Many of the people were without the means to appear unless the payment was made in their immediate area. However, he believed that payment would be protracted because the supplemental roll of the cases yet to be decided would have to be made.[21]

There was trouble from the start. When he arrived at Braggs, he found that there had been an effort to concentrate the entire payment there. Reports had circulated that, despite his notices, Bennett would pay only at Braggs. The freedmen descended upon him like "a herd of cattle on a stampede." Some were afraid that the money would run out, and they wanted to get theirs before it was gone. Bennett ordered the Indian police at Muldrow to notify the freedmen at Vinita, Nowata, and elsewhere in Cooweescoowee District to wait two weeks for a payment there. For a few days, these notices seemed to check the influx of people.[22]

J. Milton Turner was responsible for the great rush of freedmen to Braggs. On January 21 he had endorsed a letter signed by H. C. Townsend, general passenger and ticket agent for the Missouri Pacific Railway Company, promising a round trip ticket at reduced rates to Braggs from points on the Kansas and Arkansas Valley Line. Tickets could be bought at Lenapah, Nowata, Talala, Segeeyah, Claremore, Wagoner, Fort Gibson, Illinois, Vian, Sallisaw, and Muldrow. Turner came to Braggs, saying that he had not been paid for this services as attorney for the freedmen. Stories circulated that he was collecting money from some. Bennett thought that he should be removed but, since he was their attorney, awaited instructions. Bennett later found that the freedmen were contributing from twenty-five to forty cents each for a contingent fund for the prosecution of the case they had taken to the U. S. court of claims concerning the second $300,000.[23]

Meanwhile some of those who had been paid returned home. Those who had not been paid became anxious, and then Bennett faced another onslaught, with people coming from as far away as Nowata, Lenapah, and Claremore. Then news came that the freedmen from Vinita were preparing to come. Again Bennett stayed them with a telegram. He closed his books at Braggs on February 4, having paid 1,491 freedmen.[24]

During this first payment, Bennett found that the names of many freedmen who were recognized as citizens by the Cherokees did not appear on the roll. Commissioner Morgan instructed him to make a separate roll of those people, but Bennett thought it impractical to delay the payment of those who were present and had come long distances. Also, the number of recognized freedmen omitted was greater than Bennett had at first thought. They had evidently relied on their recognition by the Cherokee authorities and had failed to appear before Wallace for enrollment; many of them lacked evidence at hand to establish their identities. Finally, much time would be needed to investigate cases not entitled to a rehearing, for many came to draw who were not recognized citizens; they had been presented to Wallace but had been rejected by the department. Thus Bennett told those recognized citizens that an early opportunity would be offered to them to present their claims. In some cases children were left off while the parents' names appeared. In others brothers and sisters were listed but other children of the same parents were not. Bennett directed all such claimants to present the legal evidence of their claims, supported by other testimony as they saw fit to furnish, and to forward it to the department.[25]

Bennett began the payment for Cooweescoowee District at Vinita on February 10, 1891, for Tahlequah District on February 16, and for Saline District on February 23. During March he made payments at five different places on the Missouri, Kansas, and Texas and on the Kansas and Arkansas Valley railways as well as at the Union Agency. By the end of that month, Bennett had only 393 shares to go. Of those, he had refused payment to twelve who were born after March 3, 1883, to four who were unknown to the heads of the families with whom they were listed, to seven not satisfactorily identified, to four who were Creek freedmen and did not wish to draw with the Cherokees, to seven who were classified as Cherokees by blood and had drawn in 1883, to twelve who were duplications, and to eighteen who did not correspond with their description on the roll. The remaining 327 had failed to appear.[26]

Bennett was also prepared to make a supplemental roll of those listed as doubtful claimants on the Wallace roll but who were entitled to payment. He had notified each person from one to three times that he would be required to supply the lacking evidence specified in each case. Of the number, eighty-nine were admitted, eighteen were not, seven were duplications, and thirteen had failed to appear. Bennett said "These people move very slowly, and it may be they will yet file proof." These claims were paid when the Shawnees were paid the following December.[27]

There still remained to be dealt with those freedmen who were recognized Cherokee citizens but whose names did not appear on the rolls. Secretary John W. Noble listened to complaints that five hundred to six hundred freedmen had been left off the Wallace roll but were recognized as citizens. Noble informed the freedmen that if they could get statements to that effect from the Cherokees, their names would be added to the supplemental rolls. It would take at least sixty days to take the evidence, and in order for Bennett to keep up the agency business, he had the investigations at his office, giving the claimants a specified time to file their proof and complete the enrollment. Bennett received applications until early 1892, when the rolls were closed on January 28. J. Milton Turner applied to the commissioner for an extension of the deadline, estimating that six hundred to twelve hundred additional freedmen could prove their rights. Morgan refused, defending Wallace's work. However, the enrollment was suspended only temporarily so Bennett could complete the payment of the newly admitted before the close of the fiscal year. By then the enrolled freedmen numbered 3,278, subject to adjustment in case of duplications, fact of birth after March 3, 1883, or death before that date. Of these, 2,957 had been paid, and Bennett believed that the remaining shares would never be called for. He had paid at the principal towns and at the agency, advertised in the papers and through the mails. He had received 134 applications, none of which had been presented to the secretary but which had prima facie evidence of right to citizenship, and Bennett recommended their enrollment.[28]

In the fall of 1892, the secretary approved a supplemental roll, and Bennett began payment in October. He paid eight days at Braggs, twelve at Vinita, three at Alluwe, and one each at Lenapah, Claremore, Fort Gibson, Muldrow, and Chouteau. He then kept the rolls open for payment at the agency offices for five weeks. He announced payments at Alluwe in January 1893, at Vinita in February, and at the agency office every Saturday during January, February, and March. By the end of this period, 3,429 freedmen had been enrolled; of those, Bennett could neither identify nor locate nearly 200.[29]

Inquiries and applications had continued to flow into Bennett's office. Marcus D. Shelby was sent as a special agent to replace Bennett until a new agent was named. On July 14, 1893, he forwarded 261 applications to the department. The secretary approved 99 names for enrollment, and a supplemental schedule was forwarded to the new agent, Dew M. Wisdom, for payment. This number brought the total on the Wallace roll to 3,524.[30] Thus four years after Wallace had begun his work, the rolls were closed.

Compiling the roll had demonstrated quite dramatically the complexities of the matter of Cherokee citizenship. Most marked was the conflict between the laws of the state and the laws of humanity regarding the freedmen. Many were denied enrollment because they could not prove that they had returned to the Nation within six months of the ratifica-

tion of the treaty. Yet the Cherokees often could not prove that they
had not. Many who had occupied the same farms for over twenty years
were thus declared intruders.

The matter was rendered more complex by the application of those
who obviously had been born in the Cherokee Nation but no longer resided there. There was the case of Jack Thompson, who with his mother
was taken to the Chickasaw country during the war and left there. At the
end of the war, they went to Texas where Thompson was educated. He
returned to the Nation in 1885 to join his father, Barney Brady, a recognized citizen freedman. Another case concerned a group of blacks from
Mapleton, Kansas, who appeared before Wallace. Although they were
clearly residents of Kansas and alleged to have been since 1863, some
succeeded in getting on the roll and receiving per-capita payments. Others
from Chetopa and Fort Scott, Kansas, also made applications. At Fort
Scott about a hundred formed a committee to represent them in their
attempt to get a per-capita payment. Other applications came from Cherokee freedmen and their descendants who resided in the Creek Nation
and the newly formed Oklahoma Territory. Finally, there was the case
of Richard Vann of Colorado City, Colorado, who had been born in the
Nation but had been out of the territory for over twenty years. He had
nevertheless appeared before Wallace in 1889 and processed an application.[31]

Many such applications were the result of ignorance on the part of
the freedmen concerning the operation of the law. If many who had
lived in the Nation since the 1860s could not prove their right to citizenship, those such as Vann certainly could not. There is evidence, however,
that many applications were prompted by lawyers who received a fee
from the blacks whether or not they were enrolled. One woman from
Chetopa, Kansas, wrote to Noble, "I have spent near all I have riding on
the Railroad to get my rights and it seems like we will get beat out of it
in spite of what Uncle Sam does." She said that the lawyers had told the
freedmen that they could get their rights "fixed up," and she added that
"the Lord and Satan only knows who to trust in there." Another freedwoman claimed that a lawyer at Coffeyville, Kansas, had told her that
he worked for the agent and would see that she got on the roll, but she
had been rejected after all. Others applied directly to the secretary for
assistance, saying that although the lawyers had promised that they could
get the cases "straightened out," the freedmen would rather pay Noble, fo

they knew that his fee would not be as much as that the lawyers charged.[32]

The Cherokees had opposed the Wallace roll from the start; now they distrusted it even more. They charged that at least a thousand "too late" freedmen had been placed on the roll by false evidence or intrigue. They referred to their census of 1880 as the authentic roll and pointed out that the Wallace roll was unfair since the Cherokees had not had a judge present during the taking of evidence.[33] (But it must be remembered that the Cherokees had refused to cooperate in that respect.)

Although the Cherokees did not recognize the Wallace roll as authoritative, they did use it as a means of declaring as intruders those freedmen whose names did not appear on it. Shortly after the initial payment in early 1891, a number in Cooweescoowee District had their places advertised and sold by the sheriff. Even some whose names had appeared on the roll were harassed by Cherokee officials, who claimed they had obtained citizenship through fraud by paying witnesses.[34]

Some freedmen whose friends and relatives had been excluded joined the Cherokees in charging Wallace with carelessness. But the department defended Wallace's work, placing the blame for difficulties on the Cherokees and the freedmen. Commissioner Morgan wrote, "In my opinion, Wallace gave ample time to every freedman in the Cherokee Nation to present in person or by attorney, his claim to enrollment." Gross ignorance and lack of knowledge of business methods caused many claimants not to complete or perfect their evidence. Wallace's method was such that it guaranteed justice to the freedmen. And his work, added Morgan, "while not professing to be perfect, is to be commended for its many good qualities."[35] Despite its "good qualities," however, the Cherokees in the years to come steadfastly refused to accept the roll.

The congressional act of October 19, 1888, had been clearly a victory for the citizen freedmen. For the first time their right to share in the lands and moneys of the Cherokee Nation was firmly established. The per-capita payment for many was a pyrrhic victory, for it ultimately cost them as much to establish their right to it as it was worth. But they had established their stake in the future affairs of the Nation. The situation was not the same for those who had not been recognized as citizens before the Wallace roll. What may have appeared as victory for them was fleeting, for officials of the Cherokee Nation refused to accept the validity of the roll as long as the Nation existed. In fact, during the next few years, they were so intent on invalidating Wallace's work that they made some errors in judgment that were more costly than acceptance of the Wallace roll would have been. One of those errors resulted in what became known as the freedman's compromise, which gave strength to the trend toward congressional control over Cherokee destiny, created dissension among the Cherokees, and delivered a severe blow to Cherokee resistance to federal policies, resistance that had already begun to weaken.

By the time the Wallace roll was officially closed in 1893, forces were already set in motion to bring about the freedman's compromise. As soon as congressional legislation had secured the freedmen their right to share in the $300,000 per-capita payment of 1883, the freedmen's representative committee had set about settling accounts with J. Milton Turner, their attorney. However, from the start there was controversy, which indicated dissension in the freedmen's ranks. Although there would be several years of factionalism, it would be overcome, and the freedmen would score a second victory in their struggle for rights.

The first controversy was begun by William Brown, a member of the freedman committee. The freedmen had agreed under contract to pay Turner a fee of 25 percent of whatever amount was appropriated by Congress to pay them per capita. Brown maintained that the committee had gone to considerable expense and had raised money to defray Turner's expenses in Washington and to pay telegram and mail expenses. Brown claimed to have advanced most of the money himself and wanted repayment from Turner's fees. Speaking for the committee, he said that they were willing to settle fairly with Turner but asked the commissioner of Indian affairs to refuse him payment until the committee's claim had been settled. Turner denied having received anything from Brown. He had spent five years, he said, in securing the congressional appropriation. The freedmen had subscribed a little money for him, and he had credited them with it in the account he filed with the commissioner. Brown was simply a member of the committee empowered to hire counsel for the freedmen and could therefore have no claim on the freedmen for attorney's fees.[36]

G. H. Ten Broek, an attorney at St. Louis, claimed over $5,000 of the attorney's fee because of money he had loaned to Turner, who, he claimed, had sought funds from him in early 1888 because the freedmen could advance him no more. Ten Broek said that he had advanced some cash and had made six trips to Washington to confer with and assist Turner in pushing the freedmen's cause. E. C. Boudinot, the Cherokee, claimed half of

Turner's fee for having assisted Turner in handling the claim. Boudinot
held that it was his suggestion that the freedmen hire Turner, that they
had a verbal agreement to divide the attorney's fee equally, that Turner
was to have been concerned with only the freedmen and not the Shawnees and Delawares, who shared the appropriation, and finally that
Boudinot was to have assisted in getting the freedmen to pay Turner's
expenses. Boudinot claimed to have advised the Shawnees and Delawares
and to have presented a memorial to Congress on behalf of the freedmen. Because his agreement with Turner was verbal, Boudinot asked
the secretary of the interior for sixty days to prove his case. In July
1889, the entire amount of the fee was granted to Turner so the
others could settle their claims in court, but $5,000 was withheld
until after the per-capita payment was made to the freedmen. Congress had required the Cherokees to pay $15,000 as attorney's fees, and
on July 27, 1889, the Department of the Interior paid Turner one-half
of it and held the other half for thirty days to allow for the filing of
counterclaims.[37]

That summer Turner was accused of meddling in Cherokee political
affairs as he had in 1887. In a letter to the editor of the *Indian Chieftain*,
"Junebug" accused Rabbit Bunch and his National party backers of trying "to bring state influence to bear upon Cherokee national affairs."
"Junebug" felt that the Cherokee citizens, especially the freedmen, should
be cautious since the party in power had been antagonistic to the interests
of the blacks for years.[38] How much of this attack on Turner was in-
spired by Boudinot's claim is uncertain.

In the fall Boudinot and Turner took their claims directly to the freedmen. Turner published an open letter in the *Indian Chieftain*, explaining
how he had exhausted his personal funds and those advanced by the freedmen. His total bill was $28,000. He had expended $15,000, the amount
that had been appropriated, and he requested the additional $13,000 as a
fee for his services. Turner asked the freedmen to pay him that amount in
accordance with their agreement and to reject Boudinot's claim. G. H.
Ten Broek supported Turner, saying that Turner was often without funds,
that his family was in actual want, and that he had turned down other
offers of employment while working on the freedman case. He pleaded
with the freedmen to reject Boudinot's claim and to pay the additional
$13,000. Boudinot published a similar letter, and William Brown, who
still claimed a share of the fee, hired an attorney to collect what he said

was due. In the spring of 1890, Turner received the balance of the $15,000, and during the per-capita payment to the freedmen allegedly tried to collect more money from individual freedmen after they had been paid.[39] Thus ended the first squabble among attorneys and others over fees for their work in behalf of the Cherokee freedmen. Most were no doubt simply opportunists who sought to prey upon the vulnerable freedmen. There would be other such squabbles before Cherokee affairs were brought to a final close.

At about the time this matter was settled, the citizen freedmen began to plan their strategy for recovering other of their rights, specifically their share of the second $300,000, which had been distributed to the Cherokees by blood in 1886. They had met in March 1890, praised Wallace's work, and announced their intentions in the form of a resolution. On June 1 at Fort Gibson, their platform committee—Joe Brown, Simon Lynch, Doug Webber, Charles Mayfield, and Richard Foreman—presented a simple platform for the freedmen of the Nation to consider. They agreed to send a delegation to Washington and to make a contract with a lawyer who would work for their rights as citizens of the Nation. The freedmen selected delegates from their respective districts: Henry Still, Dunk Vann, and David Nave (Cooweescoowee); Simon Lynch, Thomas Mayfield, and Charles Mayfield (Saline); Richard Foreman and Lewis J. Johnson (Sequoyah); Joe Brown, Bass Harlan, and Davy Webber (Tahlequah); Lewis Rowe, Blue Thompson, Luster Foreman, and Thomas H. Moore (Delaware) and Crow Vann, Bill Brown, and Frank Vann (Illinois). These men met in convention at Fort Gibson on June 19, with Luster Foreman as president and Thomas H. Moore as secretary. An executive committee was selected and empowered to attend to all business that might arise concerning the freedmen, to inform the leaders of each district when an election was to be held, and to call a meeting whenever the president of the committee thought it necessary. The executive committee was comprised of J. A. Brown (president), John Burgess, and Bass Harlan of Fort Gibson; Luster Foreman, Thomas H. Moore, and Simon Lynch of Vinita; Moses Whitmire of Alluwe; Richard Foreman of Redland; and Washington Nave from near Coffeyville, Kansas.[40]

A congressional act of October 1, 1890, conferred upon the U. S. court of claims the jurisdiction, subject to appeal to the Supreme Court, to determine the rights of the freedmen, Delawares, and Shawnees and to decide if they were entitled to recover a share of the money derived from the grazing lands of the Cherokee Nation west of the Arkansas River. It also authorized the attorney general to appoint from the Department of Justice a person competent to defend the Cherokee Nation.[41]

Joseph Brown, chairman of the freedmen's executive committee, and Luster Foreman, president of the Cherokee Freedmen's Brotherhood, called the freedmen delegates to meet at Fort Gibson from October 27 through October 29, 1890. Five of the seven districts with sizable freedman population were represented. On the third day of the meeting, they elected a trustee in whose name the suit would be brought for them in the court of claims. Sixty-two-year-old Moses Whitmire of Alluwe was elected by a vote of six to one over Joseph Brown, and the election results were forwarded to Secretary John Noble for approval. Joseph Brown and William Brown immediately protested Whitmire's election, calling Whitmire the choice of J. Milton Turner and charging Turner with trying to "run the country." Whitmire was illiterate, and Turner had "improperly influenced" the delegates to that Whitmire would select Turner to act as attorney for the freedmen. The Browns challenged the election on the grounds that some districts had not been represented. Chief Joel B. Mayes, however, endorsed Whitmire's election, calling him "a man of integrity and every way trustworthy to occupy the position confided in him."[42]

Secretary Noble, however, thought the Browns' protest "of such serious import" to justify withholding approval until the charges were answered. Agent Leo Bennett was instructed to find whether the selection was regularly and lawfully made at a convention that had met after due notice and that had had fair representation. Battle lines were drawn, and the Browns gave fuller voice to their charges. William Brown claimed that the convention had been "informally constituted," with only five of the nine districts represented by delegates, that noncitizens had been a leading element in the deliberations, that Whitmire was unfit because of his age and his illiteracy, and that Whitmire would engage Turner, who Brown believed was unfit to represent the freedmen as their attorney. It appears that Brown opposed Turner more than he objected to Whitmire. He still smarted from his failure to collect the fees he claimed Turner owed him and alleged that Turner had called him aside at the convention and told him that if he would not oppose Whitmire, then Turner would get the fees he claimed the freedmen still owed him and would pay Brown. Joseph Brown made similar charges: neither the president nor the secretary of the Freedmen's Brotherhood had been present, and the meeting had not been representative. He had called the meeting "for general consultation," he claimed, since the freedmen could not take binding action. Turner and Henry Hayden, both noncitizens, had taken over the meeting, Brown alleged. Turner had told those assembled that their purpose was to elect a trustee and that the convention had the authority to do so. He had lobbied among those present and had brought in several freedmen "picked up in the streets of Fort Gibson." On the third day, Turner had succeeded in getting a vote. Brown also suggested that bribes had been offered and taken.[43]

Published reports that Turner had received a contract to prosecute the freedmen's claims drew a protest from Luster Foreman, president of the Freedmen's Brotherhood. The freedmen needed no attorney, he said, and no contract had been made. If there was one, it was bogus. He asked Secretary Noble not to approve any contract with Turner, for the freedmen had not selected Whitmire as trustee. A story in the *Muskogee Phoenix* said that the freedmen were being swindled out of more fees by Turner.[44]

Supporters of Whitmire countered with their claims, and their evidence was overwhelming. Henry Hayden answered the Browns' charges by saying that William Brown was a resident of the Creek Nation and was not identified with the Cherokee freedmen. He denied that Joseph Brown had put any reservations on the right of the convention to do business, and he said that there was evidence that Brown was a "paid conspirator." Turner was recognized as a friend by the freedmen and as "one of the highest of our black race in scale of intellect and civilization." William Brown opposed Turner because on October 27, in an address at Fort Gibson, Turner had charged that Brown was the only one of the freedmen's committee who had betrayed his people regarding the $75,000. As far as Brown's claim against Turner for fees, Hayden said that he had been secretary of the executive committee since 1883 and knew that the claim was not valid.[45]

Turner produced a statement by one James Piper of St. Louis, who had been in Fort Gibson during the convention and who testified that Turner was highly popular among the freedmen and that the only ones who seemed to be against him at the time were William and Joseph Brown, the latter a candidate for the trusteeship. That candidacy, it was rumored, was backed by "several lawyers residing at Muscogee" who were to receive appointment as attorneys for the freedmen. Piper also observed that the freedmen seemed to respect Whitmire, whose election was finally made unanimous.[46]

Numerous private citizens came to Whitmire's support. A physician named Frazer from Vinita said that Whitmire had been elected "by the very best and most upright element of the freedmen" and called him "one of the most intelligent, industrious and honorable men of the race." Whitmire was "father and grandfather of a large, industrious and sober family, in fact one of the few families who reflect credit on their race, in this nation." Whitmire was not for purchase; opposition to him had its origin in Washington, Frazer said, because he was too honest to be bought by those who would enrich themselves at the expense of the Cherokee Nation. Turner, he said, was the choice for attorney of every honest freedman in the Nation. W. J. Strange of Chelsea endorsed Whitmire and reported that the opposition had tried to call conventions through the Cherokee papers but had failed. Several petitions supporting Whitmire, signed by large numbers of freedmen, were sent to the Department of the Interior. A group of "bona fide Cherokee Freedmen" met at the Goose Neck Bend schoolhouse on Decmeber 4, endorsed Whitmire's election, and sent their sentiments to Noble. Finally Whitmire himself denied that he was an instrument in Turner's hands but insisted, instead, that "the whole body" of the freedmen wanted Turner to represent them and regarded him as "a superior man of their race."[47]

Turner offered an explanation of the Browns' enmity toward him. He alleged that they appeared at the convention with attorney Dew M. Wisdom of Muskogee, who told Turner that he had been a Confederate captain in General Forrest's command and had commanded a company at the Fort Pillow massacre. Wisdom allegedly told James Piper that he represented a syndicate of six or seven lawyers who wanted Joe Brown elected trustee to ensure that one of them would get the freedman case. He also was alleged to have said that "all rights of native Cherokees, was too damn much money and lands, for the damn niggers to have."[48]

Meanwhile Agent Leo Bennett had held his investigation as ordered. In his opinion the selection of Whitmire had been lawfully made, and he felt that the choice was a good one because Whitmire was honest and had "business ability." Thus Whitmire was confirmed by the secretary as trustee on January 7, 1891.[49]

Reports immediately circulated that Turner had been confirmed attorney. The Browns again protested, and Commissioner Thomas J. Morgan informed them that Turner had been "screened" at the time Whitmire was being considered and that the matter would not be reopened. However Turner was not selected as the attorney to represent Whitmire. That position fell to Robert H. Kern of St. Louis, who engaged Henry D. Laughlin and Turner to assist him. They were to receive 10 percent of whatever was recovered through the court of claims. The arrangement between Kern and Turner was probably made to appease the factions among the freedmen, for Turner's role in succeeding events was subdued.[50]

The act of October 1, 1890, had given the plaintiffs a year to institute their suit. The brief Kern filed was lengthy; it asked for a judgment concerning the freedmen's right and title to the lands of the Cherokee Nation, including the Cherokee Outlet; to the trust, stocks, and funds of the Nation; to rents already paid and to be collected for grazing lands; to money paid for land on which the friendly tribes were settled; and to money received for the sale of the Neutral Lands in Kansas.[51]

Before the case was heard, however, there were several complications. On November 25, 1890, shortly after Whitmire's election as trustee, the Cherokees had distributed still another (a third) $300,000 per capita to Cherokees by blood for rent on grazing lands west of the ninety-sixth meridian. They had also agreed to sell the Cherokee Strip to the United States. By an act of March 3, 1893, Congress appropriated $8,595,736 for the tract, paying the Cherokees $295,736 out of the Treasury of the United States and holding the balance, at 4 percent interest, for payment in five installments beginning March 4, 1895. A sufficient amount was to be held in the Treasury to pay the Shawnees, Delawares, and freedmen if their pending cases were determined favorably for them. The Cherokees, however, were given the right to borrow against their deferred payments. Taking advantage of this option, they borrowed $6,640,000 from the Union Trust Company of New York and paid that amount, per capita, to Cherokees by blood.[52]

In June 1893 the court of claims rendered a decision regarding Shawnee claims, using a census taken by the Cherokees in 1893 in determining the number of Shawnees. That census also listed 2,052 freedmen. The Shawnee case was appealed to the Supreme Court. It was significant for the freedmen, for if the Court upheld the court of claims and established the Cherokee census as authoritative of citizenship, then only those freedmen enrolled in it would be entitled to rights in the Cherokee Nation.

Kern claimed that his clients numbered about 4,000, and he asked that those not listed in the census be protected from removal until the present case was heard. In view of the Shawnee decision, Commissioner D. M. Browning refused to consider individual cases until the freedmen's case was heard, and Secretary Hoke Smith used it as an excuse to close the Wallace roll by ceasing payment of outstanding claims.[53]

Kern had thought the freedmen's case would be heard by the court of claims during the October 1893 session, but a decree was not handed down until March 4, 1895. The Cherokee Nation argued, first, that the ninth article of the Treaty of 1866 was intended to confer upon the blacks in the Cherokee Nation such rights only as were conferred on blacks in the United States. Any other construction of the article would place penalty on the people of the Cherokee Nation not put on the people of the United States. If any penalty were to be imposed for holding slaves, it should be on only those who had held them, not all Cherokees. Second, the Cherokees claimed the exclusive right to manage their internal affairs, a right that the United States had once recognized; therefore no act of the U. S. government or Congress could take away the right. The Cherokees had an "absolute unrestricted right of self-government" regarding its internal affairs. Third, the United States was simply a trustee of the Cherokee funds now in its Treasury and had no control over funds that might come into possession of the Cherokee Nation. Finally, the Cherokees asked why the freedmen of the Cherokee Nation should have acquired a right to the land with their freedom. The freedmen of Georgia received no such right. The Cherokees had been good to their freedmen, who had been allowed to till as much land as they could improve and had never been denied the right to vote, to sit on juries, to sue and be sued, and to receive benefit of the public schools.[54]

In its decision, the court ruled that there had been two inconsistent principles operating in the Cherokee Nation since the constitution of 1839. The "common mind" clung to the idea of communal lands to which the Cherokees had only the right of occupation. Yet by the constitution, the title of the lands passed from the communal owners and became vested in the newly founded government. The communal owners became "citizens," whose rights were defined and limited by the constitution and laws. The idea of common property under the constitution meant only that it was never to become individual property. The Treaty of 1866 became part of Cherokee law. That the Cherokees at the time

did not envision the sale of their property was true. However, while the
freedmen made their foothold through the interposition of the United
States, it was the Cherokees who fixed their status by giving them all
the rights of native-born Cherokees in the constitution of 1866. The
National Council's legislative authority was not absolute. It was limited
by the constitution, and it had no power to control or abrogate the
treaty obligations. Any funds or annuities that were originally treated
as communal and not national by distribution remained as such, and the
freedmen had no share in them. The court declined decision on what
their share in other funds was because the number of freedmen had not
been presented in the arguments. It suspended decision to entertain suggestions from counsel.[55]

The freedmen did not accept the Cherokee census that listed 2,052
freedmen. Counsel for both sides agreed that taking a new census would
involve a great deal of expense and delay and would lead to more bad feelings in the Cherokee Nation. The Wallace roll was then brought before the
court and explanation was made concerning how it had been compiled and
how the Cherokees had been invited to participate in its making but had
refused.[56]

The court of claims then handed down another decision on March 18,
1895. In the name of expediency and in order to avoid any difficulties in
the Cherokee Nation, it affirmed the Wallace roll as correct, denying that
the roll was ex parte since the Cherokees had had opportunity to participate in its making. Thus 3,524 freedmen, less those who had died since
March 3, 1883, plus those born between that date and May 3, 1894, were
entitled to participate in $903,365. The secretary of the interior was di-
rected to appoint a commission to correct the roll. Kern was allowed
$18,067.30 in fees and compensation, as well as 4 percent of the amount
recovered, or $36,134. Whitmire, as trustee, was awarded $5,000 for
compensation and expenses. At the same time, the court decreed that the
Cherokee acts of April 28, 1886, November 25, 1890, and May 3, 1894,
as far as they related to the freedmen, were null and void. The freedmen
and their descendants were thereafter entitled to participate in the common property of the Cherokee Nation. The court reaffirmed this decision
on May 8, 1895.[57]

The Cherokees did not like this decision. Chief C. J. Harris believed that
the only way to escape the hated Wallace roll was to appeal to the Supreme
Court. He made plans to call the Naitonal Council into extra session to
take up the matters of the freedmen and intruders and ask the members to

decide if the Nation should appeal. The common opposition to the Wallace roll manifested itself in Cherokee politics in the summer of 1895. Robert B. Ross and S. H. Mayes, nominees for principal chief on the National and Downing party tickets, respectively, issued a joint statement of their opposition to the roll and their support for an appeal to the Supreme Court. Since the interests of the United States were in no way involved in the case, the commissioner did not recommend an appeal on the part of the United States. Any action toward an appeal, then, was left to the Cherokee Nation. Harris claimed that there were nine hundred names illegally on the Wallace roll; thus the Cherokees appealed to the Supreme Court not on the grounds of the justice of the decree but on the legality of the Wallace roll.[58] The freedmen had wanted the Wallace Roll, plus an added percentage of it to represent the natural increase of freedmen, accepted as the aggregate of freedmen. The court had rejected that plea, so the freedmen, too, filed an appeal to the Supreme Court.

In order to strengthen their arguments, the Cherokee National Council passed a bill on September 25, 1895, authorizing the chief to appoint three persons to take evidence of the mistakes in the Wallace Roll and to invalidate it "as a true, correct and reliable showing of the number of freedmen who were entitled to and were exercising the rights to Cherokee citizenship under the 9th article of the treaty of 1866." The commissioners were given only two weeks to report. The Vinita *Indian Chieftain* was a hard critic of the Cherokee government. It charged that many on the Wallace roll were only married to Cherokee freedpersons and were therefore not entitled to citizenship; it called the roll "notoriously corrupt" and attacked Wallace's method of taking testimony as "an outrage on the Cherokee government." But the *Chieftain* laid the blame on the Cherokee government itself, which at the time "made no effort to get a fair deal and really let their day of grace pass."[59]

The commission consisted of R. F. Wyly, C. S. Shelton, and Isaac Rogers. Shelton had worked for Wallace, and Rogers was a freedman. They visited Nowata, Lenapah, Goose Neck, Ruby on Salt Creek, and Vinita before their two weeks expired. They took some affidavits, but for the most part their efforts failed because the freedmen were suspicious of them and doubted their motives. Many thought it was a trick to delay, or prevent altogether, their receiving the money awarded them by the court of claims. That, and a lack of time, resulted in a practical failure of their mission.[60]

In view of the Cherokees' "wide-spread, if not controlling prejudice" against the Wallace roll, the freedmen offered a compromise. An earlier offer had been turned down, but now they felt that the Cherokees would be more receptive. The freedmen wanted to equalize their payment with that already made to the Cherokees, and they sought Cherokee legislation to carry it out. The freedmen proposed, first, that both sides withdraw their appeals to the Supreme Court; second, that the decree in the case be modified so that the aggregate allowed would be $1.3 million so that each freedman would receive $295.65, the amount the Cherokees had received per capita, instead of $256.34; third, that in lieu of the Wallace roll, the Cherokee authenticated roll of 1880 be considered final as far as the persons on it and their descendants were concerned; fourth, that three commissioners—one selected by the Cherokees, one by Whitmire, and one by the judge of the U. S. Court for the Third District of Arkansas— be approved by the court of claims; fifth, that these commissioners enroll the freedmen and free blacks to participate in the payment, the names enrolled being approved by the secretary; sixth, that the Cherokees be allowed to appear by counsel before the commission; seventh, that the final roll be treated as authentic; and finally, that provisions be made for the payment of lawyers' fees. If the compromise was made, the Cherokee Nation was to ratify it through proper legislation and appoint commissioners to act for it.[61]

Chief S. II. Mayes approved the compromise, and on December 7, the National Council passed an act to carry it out, appointing E. C. Boudinot, Jr., to represent the Nation. Kern and Boudinot submitted the proposition to the court of claims. However, much to the disappointment of all, on January 27, 1896, the court of claims refused to reopen the decree, to appoint commissioners to take a new census, and to render a judgment of $1.3 million. The increase of $400,000 was properly the duty of the National Council, it said. Kern, Turner, and Whitmire held an immediate conference with Chief Mayes, Boudinot, and the Cherokee delegation in Washington in an attempt to reach a settlement. On January 28 they agreed that the Wallace roll should be stricken from the decree, that the Cherokee roll of 1880 should be accepted as authentic and brought up to date, and that a commission of three should be appointed by the secretary to hear such evidence as might be offered by any other freedmen claiming a right to citizenship. One was to be selected by the Cherokees and one by the freedmen. The Cherokees agreed to call the National Council to meet at an early date in order to appropriate the money necessary to bring the award total to $1.3 million.[62]

The Cherokees were anxious to cooperate because they hated the Wallace roll. If the compromise did not work, the Wallace roll would still be binding. Again Kern and Boudinot petitioned the court of claims, and on February 3, it modified the decree and validated the compromise, limiting the payment to each freedman to $256.34. All parties agreed not to appeal the case; thus the decree was final. The Cherokees kept their bargain. They passed a bill appropriating $400,000 to equalize the payments of the Cherokees and freedmen whose names would appear on the roll approved by the secretary as provided in the decree of February 3. Mayes approved the bill on March 27, 1896. On June 25, D. W. Lipe, the Cherokee treasurer, asked Secretary Smith to deduct from the first installment of the Cherokee Outlet proceeds the money due the freedmen under the act of council.[63]

The Cherokees looked on the freedman compromise as a victory, for it had eliminated the Wallace roll. But it had cost them. If the Wallace roll had been retained, it would have required only $1,040,813.40 to pay the freedmen.[64] However, their victory was to be short-lived, for the succeeding roll was to be even more controversial than the Wallace roll, and in succeeding elections, the National party members made an issue of the compromise, calling it "the million dollar nigger steal." There was no doubt that the compromise was a victory for the freedmen. For the second time within a decade, they had had their rights upheld by the legislative and judicial systems of the United States. Those victories formed the groundwork for their participation in the division of the national assets when the Nation was dissolved during the next decade.

NOTES

1. John W. Wallace to T. J. Morgan, September 7, 1889, National Archives Record Group 75 (Records of the Bureau of Indian Affairs), *Letters Received,* 25517-89; *Indian Chieftain,* September 5, 1889; Wallace to Joel B. Mayes, September 9, 1889, Indian Archives Division, Oklahoma Historical Society, *Cherokee—Freedmen (Tahlequah); Annual Report of the Commissioner of Indian Affairs to the Secretary of the Interior for the Year 1889* (Washington, D.C.: Government Printing Office, 1889), 211.

2. Wallace to Morgan, October 12, 26, 1889, *Letters Received,* 29502-89, 31054-89; *Indian Chieftain,* September 19, 1889.

3. Wallace to Morgan, November 6, 1889, June 30, 1890, *Letters Re-*

ceived, 32220-89, 19840-90; 51st Cong., 1st sess., *House Executive Document 456,* 4.

4. Secretary of the Interior to Commissioner of Indian Affairs, September 11, 1889, and Wallace to Morgan, November 6, 1889, *Letters Received ,* 25932-89, 32220-89; Morgan to Wallace, November 15, 1889, National Archives Record Group 75, *Letters Sent,* Land Letter Book 191: 318.

5. Wallace to Morgan, November 6, December 9, 1889, *Letters Received,* 32220-89, 35701-89. One inquiry from a lawyer at Silver City, New Mexico, for instance, said that "several parties" residing there claimed to be entitled to rights as Cherokee freedmen. Arthur H. Harllee to Secretary of the Interior, September 3, 1889, *Letters Received,* 25530-89.

6. Wallace to Morgan, December 26, 1889, January 2, 17, 1890, *Letters Received,* 37429-89, 335-90, 2214-90.

7. Wallace to Morgan, February 15, 1890, *Letters Received,* 5295-90.

8. Wallace to Morgan, March 11, 1890, Elias C. Boudinot to John W. Noble, February 10, 1890, and Noble to Commissioner, February 15, 1890, *Letters Received,* 8131-90, and 4945-90.

9. Ridge Paschal to J. Milton Turner, February 27, 1890, *Letters Received,* 6812-90; "Rouge et Noir" (clipping), March 8, 1890, Oklahoma Historical Society Library, Fred S. Barde Collection.

10. "Rouge et Noir."

11. Noble to Commissioner, March 17, 1890, and Wallace to Morgan, March 18, 1890, *Letters Received,* 8533-90, 8494-90; Noble to Fred W. Strout, March 18, 1890, National Archives Microfilm Publications, *Microcopy M606* (Letters Sent by the Secretary of the Interior)-64, 164.

12. Quoted from Carolyn Thomas Foreman, "Joseph Absalom Scales," *The Chronicles of Oklahoma* 28 (Winter 1950-51): 418-432.

13. Wallace to Noble, April 9, 1890, and Wallace to Morgan, April 25, 1890, *Letters Received,* 11547-90, 13112-90; statement of W. Y. H. Foreman, April 10, 1890, statement of Claude S. Shelton, April 11, 1890, statement of Luster Foreman, April 11, 1890, and statement of W. W. Breedlove, April 12, 1890, National Archives Record Group 75, *Affidavits, 1891-92.*

14. Wallace to Morgan, April 25, 1890, Leo E. Bennett to Commissioner, May 4, 14, 1890, and Breedlove to R. L. Owen, August 29, 1890, *Letters Received,* 13112-90, 13683-90, 15338-90, 28916-90.

15. Noble to Commissioner, June 9, 23, July 21, 1890, Wallace to Noble, June 11, 1890, and Wallace to Morgan, July 2, 1890, *Letters Received,* 17763-90, 19029-90, 18065-90, 20018-90, 22414-90; R. F. Thompson to Secretary of the Interior, July 12, 1890, *Affidavits, 1891-92;* R. V. Belt to Thompson, June 12, 1890, *Letters Sent,* vol. 100 (Letter

Book 199-200), 156; Morgan to Secretary of the Interior, July 19, 1890, *Letters Sent,* Finance Letter Book 154: 141B; 51st Cong., 1st sess., *House Executive Document 456,* 3, 2.

16. Noble to W. B. Allison, August 21, 1890, *Microcopy M606*-66, 412.

17. Maxwell and Chase to Belt, September 19, 1890, William Warner to Noble, October 2, 1891, Strout to Noble, November 20, 1890, Wallace to William Brown, June 14, 1890, and Wallace to Luster Foreman, June 14, 1890, *Letters Received,* 28916-90, 30613-91, 36562-90, 19483-90, 892-91; 51st Cong., 1st sess., *House Executive Document 456,* 4; "Rouge et Noir."

18. Noble to Wallace, December 6, 1890, and Bennett to Commissioner, December 25, 1890, *Letters Received,* 7909-91, 40299-90; Belt to Brown, October 22, 1890, *Letters Sent,* vol. 103 (Letter Book 205-206), 39; *Cherokee Advocate,* August 8, 1893.

19. Brown to Secretary of the Interior, September 16, 1890, and David French et al. to Noble, December 4, 1890, *Letters Received,* 30858-90, 38303-90; Belt to Brown, October 22, 1890, *Letters Sent,* vol. 103 (Letter Book 205-206), 39; Belt to Secretary of the Interior, October 8, 1890, and Belt to Brown, October 9, 1890, *Letters Sent,* Finance Letter Book 115: 196, 268; Noble to Commissioner, November 21, *Microcopy M606*-68, 186.

20. Belt to Secretary of the Interior, October 8, 1890, *Letters Sent,* Finance Letter Book 115: 196; Bennett to Commissioner, December 19, 25, 1890, *Letters Received,* 39477-90, 40299-90; Morgan to Bennett, January 19, 1891, *Letters Sent,* Land Letter Book 105: 113.

21. *Indian Chieftain,* January 15, 1891; Bennett to Commissioner, January 16, 24, 1891, *Letters Received,* 2094-91, 3240-91.

22. Bennett to Secretary of the Interior, February 5, 1891, *Letters Received,* 4970-91; Belt to Strout, February 5, 1891, *Letters Sent,* Land Letter Book 211: 42.

23. H. C. Townsend to the Cherokee Freedmen, January 21, 1891, *Letters Received,* 10705-91.

24. Bennett to Secretary of the Interior, February 5, 1891, *Letters Received,* 4970-91.

25. Bennett to Commissioner, February 7, 1891, *Letters Received,* 5312-91; *Indian Chieftain,* February 3, 1891; Morgan to Secretary of the Interior, February 16, 1891, *Letters Sent,* Land Letter Book 211: 303.

26. *Indian Chieftain,* February 3, 12, 1891, Bennett to Commissioner, February 10, March 31, 1891; *Letters Received,* 7031-90, 14291-91.

27. Bennett to Commissioner, April 13, 16, 1891, *Letters Received,* 14291-91, 14704-91; *Indian Chieftain,* December 10, 1891. Typical cases in question appear in Bennett to Commissioner, June 20, August 14, 1891, *Letters Received,* 22310-91, 30014-91.

28. Bennett to Commissioner, April 16, 1891, February 2, June 6,

1892, Thomas H. Moore to Noble, April 16, 1891, and Turner to Morgan, January 13, 29, 1892, *Letters Received,* 14704-91, 4351-92, 21074-92, 14728-91; Morgan to Moore, April 28, 1891, *Letters Sent,* Land Letter Book 215: 395; Morgan to Maxwell and Chase, March 19, 1892, *Letters Sent,* Land Letter Book 233: 273; report of Bennett, February 6, 1892, National Archives Record Group 75, *Supplementary Census Rolls, 1891-92.* Typical cases are presented in Jim Rogers to Noble, March 14, 1891, W. N. Buffington to Secretary of the Interior, March 21, 1891, Bennett to Commissioner, May 7, 28, November 3, 1891, April 28, June 6, 1892, *Letters Received,* 10279-91, 11169-91, 17132-91, 19625-91, 39714-91, 16132-92, 21074-92; Morgan to John Landrum, November 18, 1891, and Morgan to Moses Hardwick, December 8, 1891, *Letters Sent,* Land Letter Book 226: 148, 472; Morgan to Isaac Rogers, March 30, 1892, *Letters Sent,* Land Letter Book 234: 187.

29. *Indian Chieftain,* October 6, December 15, 1892; Bennett to Commissioner, November 29, December 12, 1892, *Letters Received,* 42931-92, 44548-92; Belt to Secretary of the Interior, March 23, 1893, *Letters Sent,* Land Letter Book 254: 490.

30. Marcus D. Shelby to Commissioner, July 14, 1893, *Letters Received,* 26695-93; D. M. Browning to D. M. Wisdom, August 14, 1893, *Letters Sent,* Land Letter Book 263: 206.

31. Jack Thompson to Noble, January 30, 1891, John H. Graham to Secretary of the Interior, March 7, 1891, Washington Jones to Noble, March 21, 1891, B. J. Waters to Secretary of the Interior, September 8, 1891, Humphrey and Hudson to Commissioner, March 27, 1892, Susan Vann to Morgan, January 24, 1893, William Bradley to Secretary of the Interior, April 24, 1893, and L. S. Hess to Morgan, April 4, 1892, *Letters Received,* 4409-91, 9362-91, 11151-91, 33087-91, 11811-92, 3373-93, 16066-93, 12822-92; Morgan to Graham, March 19, 1891, *Letters Sent,* Land Letter Book 213: 118; Morgan to Richard Vann, January 13, 1893, *Letters Sent,* Land Letter Book 250: 337.

32. M. H. Porter to Noble, February 18, 1891, Betsy Reed to Noble, December 26, 1892, and Washington Jones to Noble, March 21, 1891, *Letters Received,* 7598-91, 351-93, 11151-91.

33. Strout to Belt, March 18, 1891, *Letters Received,* 10705-91.

34. Moses Whitmire to Noble, April 20, 1891, and Bennett to Commissioner, May 7, 1891, *Letters Received,* 15147-91, 17131-91; Belt to David Wistoneking, May 4, 1891, *Letters Sent,* Land Letter Book 216: 115.

35. Morgan to Isaac Rogers, June 30, 1891, *Letters Sent,* Land Letter Book 218: 468; Morgan to Turner, January 21, 1892, *Letters Sent,* Land Letter Book 229: 169.

36. William Brown to Commissioner of Indian Affairs, March 28, 1889, and Turner to John H. Oberly, April 6, 1889, *Letters Received,* 8443-89, 8889-89.

37. G. H. Ten Broek to Noble, May 27, 1889, and George H. Shields to Secretary of the Interior, July 15, 1889, National Archives Record Group 48 (Records of the Department of the Interior, Office of the Secretary), Indian Territory Division, *Chickasaw Freedmen,* box 393 (60b), 3043-89, 3044-89, 6036-89; Morgan to Boudinot, July 27, 1889, *Letters Sent,* Finance Volume 146: 397A; Van Manning to Secretary of the Interior, September 20, 1889, *Letters Received,* 2679-89; *Muskogee Phoenix,* July 11, 1889. The Chickasaw freedmen file, hereafter cited as *Freedmen File,* was apparently mislabeled; most of the documents in it relate to the Cherokee freedmen.

38. *Indian Chieftain,* June 8, 1889.

39. Ibid., September 13, October 24, 1889; John V. Wright to Commissioner, October 27, 1889, *Letters Received,* 30585-89; Morgan to Wright, October 30, 1889, *Letters Sent,* finance volume 148: 102A; Noble to H. E. Cuney, April 5, 1890, *Microcopy M606*-64, 357; Noble to Bennett, January 30, 1891, *Microcopy M606*-69, 452; *Muskogee Phoenix,* April 3, 1890.

40. Statement of Luster Foreman, April 11, 1890, *Affidavits, 1891-92;* Convention at Fort Gibson," June 1, 1890, list of Cherokee freedmen delegates, June 19, 1890, and resolution of the freedmen of the Cherokee Nation, June 19, 1890, in *Letters Received,* 892-91; J. A. Brown to Noble, June 21, 1890, *Letters Received,* 20631-90.

41. *Statutes of the United States of America* (Washington, D. C.: Government Printing Office, 1890), 26: 636; Belt to Secretary of the Interior, March 23, 1893, *Letters Sent,* Land Letter Book 254: 490; act of October 1, 1890, *Cherokee–Freedmen (Tahlequah); Indian Chieftain,* October 16, 1890.

42. Henry C. Hayden to Noble, October 29, 1890, and Willian and Joe Brown to Noble, November 2, 1890, in *Letters Received,* 892-91; Morgan to Secretary of the Interior, December 11, 1890, *Letters Sent,* Land Letter Book 208: 263; Mayes to Secretary of the Interior, November 5, 1890, *Letters Received,* 34870-90.

43. Noble to Hayden, November 8, 1890, Noble to Whitmire, November 8, 1890, George Chandler to Commissioner, November 10, 1890, *Microcopy M606*-68, 69-70; Belt to Bennett, November 11, 1890, *Letters Sent,* Land Letter Book 207: 7; William Brown to Secretary of the Interior, November 11, 1890, affidavit of William Brown, November 26, 1890, affidavit of Joseph Brown, November 26, 1890, in *Letters Received,* 892-91.

44. *Indian Chieftain,* November 6, 13, 1890; Luster Foreman to Noble, November 19, 1890, in *Letters Received,* 892-91; *Muskogee Phoenix,* November 20, 1890.

45. Hayden to Noble, November 12, 1890, and affidavit of Hayden, November 21, 1890, in *Letters Received,* 892-91.

46. Turner to Noble, November 15, 1890, in *Letters Received,* 892-91.

47. M. Frazer to Noble, November 20, 1890, *Letters Received,* 37006-90; W. J. Strange to Noble, November 25, 1890, various petitions, n.d., J. H. McGowan to Noble, November 28, 1890, J. E. Campbell to Noble, November 29, 1890, R. M. Sanders to Noble, December 4, 1890, and Whitmire to Noble, November 21, 1890, in *Letters Received,* 892-91.

48. Turner to Noble, December 11, 1890, in *Letters Received,* 892-91. All correspondence of William Brown to the department was attested to by Wisdom and was written in Wisdom's handwriting, on Wisdom's stationery.

49. Bennett to Commissioner, December 3, 1890, and Noble to Commissioner, January 7, 1891, in *Letters Received,* 892-91; Morgan to Secretary of the Interior, December 11, 1890, *Letters Sent,* Land Letter Book 208: 263.

50. *Indian Chieftain,* January 22, 1891, February 27, 1896; Joseph Brown to Secretary of the Interior, March 17, 1891, *Letters Received,* 10923-91; Belt to Joseph Brown, March 25, 1891, *Letters Sent,* Land Letter Book 213: 326; Belt to Secretary of the Interior, May 5, 1892, *Letters Sent,* Land Letter Book 236: 471; *Muskogee Indian Journal,* January 25, 1895.

51. Brief of Moses Whitmire by Kern, n.d., in *Cherokee—Freedmen (Tahlequah).*

52. *Statutes of the United States of America* (Washington, D.C.: Government Printing Office, 1893), 27: 640-641; Moses Whitmire v. the Cherokee Nation and the United States, *Cherokee—Freedmen (Tahlequah);* Belt to Secretary of the Interior, March 23, 1893, *Letters Sent,* Land Letter Book 254: 490.

53. *Annual Report of the Secretary of the Interior for the Fiscal Year Ended June 30, 1896* (Washington, D.C.: Government Printing Office, 1897), 70; Frank C. Armstrong to Frank Pack, November 28, 1893, *Letters Sent,* Land Letter Book 269: 192; Kern to Hoke Smith, June 14, 1893, *Letters Received,* 22720-93; Browning to Huston West, October 16, 1893, and Browning to Lee J. Norwood, June 19, 1894, *Letters Sent,* Land Letter Book 267: 36 and Land Letter Book 282: 397; Smith to Commissioner, January 9, 1895, *Microcopy M606-84,* 29.

54. Kern to Principal Chief, September 6, 1893, *Cherokee—Freedmen (Tahlequah);* 30 *Court of Claims,* 144.

55. 30 *Court of Claims,* 144.

56. Ibid.; Browning to Gore, Brickhalter, and Nevile, March 13, 1895, *Letters Sent,* Land Letter Book 300: 288.

57. 30 *Court of Claims,* 144; *Annual Report, 1896,* 71.

58. C. J. Harris to J. F. Thompson, May 21, 1895, *Cherokee–Freedmen (Tahlequah); Indian Chieftain,* July 4, 25, 1895; Smith to Attorney General, July 9, 1895, *Microcopy M606*-86, 47.

59. *Indian Chieftain,* October 10, 17, 1895; R. F. Wyly, C. S. Shelton, and Isaac Rogers to Harris, November 2, 1895, *Cherokee–Freedmen (Tahlequah).*

60. Wyly et al. to Harris, November 2, 1895, and S. H. Mayes to the Honorable National Council, November 21, 1895, *Cherokee–Freedmen (Tahlequah).*

61. Kern to Mayes, November 25, 1895, *Cherokee–Freedmen (Tahlequah); Cherokee Advocate,* January 8, 1898.

62. Mayes to the Honorable National Council, December 3, 1895, and Mayes to the National Council, December 6, 1895, *Cherokee–Freedmen (Tahlequah); Annual Report, 1896,* 472-473; *Langston City Herald,* December 7, 1895, 31 *Court of Claims,* 147; *Indian Chieftain,* January 30, February 27, 1896; "An Act Relating to the Settlement by Compromise of the Case Now Pending in the Courts of the United States," December 7, 1895, *Letters Received,* 8548-1927 Cherokee Nation 175.2, pt. 2, exhibit D.

63. *Annual Report, 1896,* 72, 472; Smith to Attorney General, February 8, 1896, *Microcopy M606*-87, 430; D. W. Lipe to Smith, June 25, 1896, Indian Archives Division, Oklahoma Historical Society, *Cherokee-Treasurer,* 1462.

64. Thomas P. Smith to George C. Pendleton, May 18, 1896, *Letters Sent,* Land Letter Book 333: 86.

THE KERN-

chapter 8 CLIFTON ROLL

Once the task of reaching a final settlement of the freedman's compromise was over, there remained the still more tedious and difficult task of making a new roll according to the decree of February 3, 1896. The resulting one, however, would be no more to the Cherokees' liking than the Wallace roll had been.

A few days following the court decree, Secretary Hoke Smith directed Commissioner Daniel M. Browning to draft a set of instructions to guide the commissioners who would make the roll. The court of claims amplified its decree by applying it to the free blacks and freedmen, and their descendants, who had been residents in the Cherokee Nation at the time of the Treaty of 1866 or who had returned within six months. All others were excluded. The court also ruled that the six-months' period extended from the date of the promulgation of the treaty—August 11, 1866—and thus did not expire until February 11, 1867.[1]

The commission Smith appointed consisted of Robert H. Kern, William Clifton of Georgia (who was chairman), and William P. Thompson of the Cherokee Nation. J. M. Keys and W. W. Hastings were confirmed as attorneys for the Cherokee Nation. The commissioners were directed to accept the authenticated Cherokee roll of 1880; their only inquiries concerning it were to ascertain which persons on the roll and their descendants were alive on May 3, 1894 (the date of the law providing for payment of Outlet funds to the Cherokees). No evidence was to be taken that tended to disprove the citizenship of any person on the roll. They were, otherwise, to limit their inquiries to those and their descendants who qualified under article 9 of the treaty, were alive on May 3, 1894, and were at that time residents of the Cherokee Nation.[2]

Browning suggested a list of questions to which the applicants must supply answers. When and where were they born? Who were their parents? Were they slaves in February 1863? If so, who were their masters? If not, but if they were the descendants of slaves, who were their parents' owners? Were they residents of the Nation when the treaty was concluded? If not, where did they reside, and when did they return? Had they since lived continuously in the Nation? If not, when did they leave the Nation, how long did they stay away, and what reason did they have for staying away? If they were married women, what were their maiden names and the names of their former husbands if previously married? What were their post office addresses? How long had they lived there consecutively? A majority vote of the commissioners on the evidence entitled the applicant to be enrolled.[3]

The commissioners were to advertise for two weeks in the two most popular newspapers, and post, by handbills or circulars, the times and places where they would hear evidence. They were given four months to complete their work, at the end of which they were to submit a schedule of those entitled to payment, to report the daily proceedings and the evidence taken regarding those not admitted, and to file stenographic notes of all testimony taken.[4]

They began their work on April 23, and their first session was held at Hayden in Cooweescoowee District on May 4. Throughout the succeeding months, they held a second session at Hayden, two at Claremore, three each at Fort Gibson and Vinita, and one each at Tahlequah, Sallisaw, and a point about four miles north of Chelsea. They took 651 applications involving 3,277 persons. Cross-examination took up a good deal of time. The Cherokees, interested in eliminating as many from the rolls as possible, took every opportunity to question the correctness of evidence. Browning suggested that the commissioners limit examination and cross-examination to the issues involved but still give a full and free hearing to all.[5]

Problems quickly emerged. Some freedmen who were on the 1880 roll had children who were eighteen to twenty years old, but the children's names did not appear on the roll. These latter were enrolled. Other problems resulted from the Cherokees' procedure. The commissioners worked from eight A.M. until six P.M. each day and employed a stenographer to take the testimony. The Cherokees did not hire a stenographer, so the commission had to wait for them to make notes of the testimony. Clifton and Kern also felt that the Cherokees were taking a much wider latitude than necessary in cross-examination, requiring the freedmen to state the exact points in the Nation where they had lived, who had seen them there, and so forth. Cross-examination sometimes took thirty minutes, so that in the first three weeks the commission had heard only 195 applicants.[6]

To show the complexity of some cases, Kern and Clifton related the example of Blue Thompson. Thompson testified that at the beginning of the war, he was a slave of James Allen Thompson near Fort Wayne in Delaware District. His master took him to the Chickasaw Nation during the war, but in the fall of 1865, Blue came back to the Nation, settling in Sequoyah District. He was recognized as a Cherokee citizen and appeared on the roll of 1867 and on the Wallace roll. He spent about a third of the time outside the Nation working on the railroad. Because he was on one of his working trips when the census of 1880 was taken, he did not appear on the authenticated roll. The problems of legality and justice presented by this case and others made Clifton and Kern submit, for the secretary's approval, a list of twelve questions to be allowed the Cherokee attorney on cross-examination. The secretary rejected the request because the instructions initially issued to the commission were sufficient. It was far better, he said, to permit the examination to continue as it was than to eliminate any cross-examination, leaving the evidence or method open to attack on the grounds of partiality or injustice. Nevertheless, the commissioners decided to curtail considerably the cross-examination. Otherwise, Kern estimated, it would take up to $5,000 to pay for the transcript of evidence. Kern also wanted to use as evidence the affidavits Wallace had taken, but the Wallace roll had been set aside in the court's decree. Besides, the Cherokees had objected to the roll because the Nation allegedly had not had the opportunity for proper examination of witnesses. If the Clifton commission used the evidence, their roll would be open to the same charges. Convinced, however, that a useless waste of much time occurred in cross-examination, especially concerning those who had been out of the territory, Kern requested a ruling whether such cases were governed by *Elk* v. *Wilkins* (112 U. S. 94), which dealt with the expatriation of American citizens. If the freedmen had been out of the Cherokee Nation long enough, perhaps they could be considered citizens of the United States. But the assistant attorney general held that the case did not apply and ruled that the Cherokee freedmen could become citizens of the United States only by naturalization or by putting themselves within the provisions of the Dawes, or General Allotment, Act of February 8, 1887.[7]

Kern was concerned about writing a final report. The commissioners had been instructed that when they disagreed, the testimony of the case should be written up and forwarded to the department. Those cases would be many. Clifton and Kern thought that "undue latitude" had been allowed the Cherokees in cross-examination. Thus, the examination had gone on to the extent that Kern felt that it would be impossible to write up the voluminous testimony before August 10, 1896, the date the report was due. He asked for permission to write up the substance of what was said in the testimony rather than a verbatim transcript, arguing that the idea of the compromise was to settle the matter of citizenship without referring it to the secretary for revision. Secretary Hoke Smith rejected the request and directed the commission to work within the established budget and to submit a full, not an abbreviated, report.[8]

The commission did not complete taking testimony until August 8. Part of the delay no doubt resulted from the Cherokees' method of investigating cases. Although generally they gave hearty approval of the instructions to the commission, they at times entered vigorous written protests to the commission's interpretation of those instructions. Keeping their own records of proceedings took time. There was an average of five witnesses for each application. Those introduced on the part of the Cherokee Nation had to be subpoenaed and consulted before they took the stand. As a result the chief had to appoint two assistants to Keys and Hastings. Much time was consumed in the process, yet the attorneys for the Nation felt that they were unable to protect the Nation successfully for a lack of time. It was apparent that the commissioners could not submit the roll on time, and they received a thirty-day extension. The stenographer had fallen ill and had gone home to St. Louis, and Kern was nominated for Congress. Thus politics occupied his mind as well as that of Clifton, who was a member of the Georgia state senate. Clifton went home and left Kern with the business of getting the testimony written.[9]

As the September 10 deadline drew near, the stenographer was still unable to work, and another thirty days' extension was granted. Kern thought the testimony would number four thousand pages and renewed his request to be allowed to write only its substance. Kern blamed the delay on Clifton, who, during the taking of testimony, had not wanted to sift through "irrelevant, foolish stuff" and thus had included all testimony, which now had to be typed. In October a third extension was granted, and Kern again asked to abbreviate the testimony regarding the freedmen who had left the Cherokee Nation from time to time. There was not "one scintilla of proof" that any of them had been naturalized anywhere. To omit them would save several hundred pages. The stenographer could note all omitted testimony so that it could be referred to if necessary. Again, however, the secretary refused to modify Kern's instructions. In late October, another extension was granted with a warning that it was the last. Kern grew impatient. He wanted Clifton to convene the commission to begin reviewing the evidence and making decisions regarding the admission of the applicants, but Clifton did not call a meeting until November 25. Angered, Kern charged that they had been "playing" for three months while the interests of the freedmen were ignored. They worked through the four thousand pages of evidence between November 25 and December 9, and the report was completed on December 13.[10]

The final report of the Kern-Clifton Commission reflected the difficulties they had faced. They could not include ages because the blacks had no idea how old they were. Women who were grandmothers claimed to be twenty-five. Many did not know what district they lived in. Even the names were not to be trusted: "In that country we often meet a girl by the name of 'John' and a boy by the name of 'Susan,' hence the name does not indicate the sex." The Kern-Clifton roll contained 2,569 authenticated names and 1,902 unauthenticated names. Some freedmen, however, had not been able to see the commissioners because of illness. Others failed to receive notice of the commissioners' hearings. Commissioner D. M. Browning sympathized with these freedmen as he did with others who had been sold into slavery in Mexico at the end of the war and did not get back to the Indian Territory until years later. Thus when departmental officials reviewed the roll, they eliminated duplications, took some names from the unauthenticated roll, evaluated the special cases, and came up with a supplemental authenticated roll of 144. Those names, added to the adjusted authenticated roll of 2,530 and the adjusted unauthenticated roll of 1,878, made a total of 4,552 freedmen who claimed citizenship in the Cherokee Nation.[11]

Then came the matter of making the per-capita payments to the freedmen. No sooner had the Clifton commission begun its work than inquiries began to arrive at the Indian Office, asking when the money would be paid.

People began as well to vie for the job of paymaster. Robert L. Owen, former agent at the Union Agency and now president of the First National
Bank in Muskogee, asked Hoke Smith to appoint his brother, William
Owen. Owen used political arguments to urge his point. He had twice
been elected to the Democratic National Committee and had recently been
elected a delegate to the National Convention in Chicago. The Indian
Territory would soon become a state, he prophesied, and the freedman
vote would be important. If "a prominent Democrat resident" of the territory made the payment, the freedmen would "strongly remember the
benefits delivered to them." A large number of the freedmen supposedly
wanted Owen to make the payment. In opposition to Owen, Kern wrote,
"I see nothing in all this maneuvering but the expectation of practicing
an infernal lot of rascality. I have made this long fight for the freedmen
without the assistance of a solitary soul in the Indian Territory. A more
rotten and corrupt set of men never walked God's earth than hold the
reins of that country." Kern suggested that an appointment not be made
without consulting the Clifton commission; his hope, he said, was to
avoid the disgraceful proceedings that took place in the Nation every time
a payment was made. William Owen claimed that he had the endorsement
of the community, but evidence indicates that the support was not among
the freedmen of the Cherokee Nation. Kern insisted that there could "be
no reason on earth why the will of a few scheming shylocks from the
Nation should be consulted in preference to the wishes of the freedmen
about paying the money." When the appointment was finally made in
early 1897, it went to James G. Dickson, whom Kern claimed the freedmen preferred because he came from outside the Indian Territory.[12]

Next arose a conflict over the place where the disbursement would
take place. Petitions containing hundreds of signatures came from Fort
Gibson, arguing that three-fourths of the freedmen lived in Illinois
District, most of them within a few miles of Fort Gibson. Nevertheless,
the department chose Hayden as the place where the payment would
begin on February 15, 1897, and asked that a troop of cavalry be sent
to protect Dickson and to preserve order. The payment was expected
to last thirty days. No sooner had Hayden been selected than petitions
began to come in from Vinita, asking that the payment be made there.
The Business Men's League of Vinita pointed out that Hayden was
twenty miles from the railroad and, until recently, consisted only of a
blacksmith shop and a small store that was owned by the black post-

master. However, in recent weeks, Kansas merchants had assisted the postmaster in erecting a pay house and a rude hotel and had promised to build a branch bank there. Vinita, the group argued, was a commercial center with a large freedman population, who kept hotels, blacksmith shops, and restaurants. There was also a local police force.[13]

Dickson was instructed to make no changes in the roll. He was to pay the head of each household unless he could not appear or unless he was "notoriously unfit" to handle money. If parents were separated, Dickson was to pay the one caring for the children. A freedman with more than one wife was to be paid for the wife and minor children who lived with him. If they all lived together, he was to receive the pay for his first wife only, and the other wife or wives were to be paid for themselves and their children. Dickson was to check carefully guardianship papers of orphaned children or incompetents; the payment of those without guardians was to be deposited with the United States until a guardian could be appointed. All payments were to be made by check, directly to the freedmen. Creditors were to be denied access to the immediate vicinity of the payment while it was in progress. Notices were sent out, and the freedmen congregated at Hayden, ready for the payment on February 15, 1897. After a delay of two days and under specific instructions not to accept powers of attorney, to make arrangements in favor of any trader, or to allow any creditor of the freedmen in the vicinity of the pay house, Dickson began the payment. Conditions on the grounds were intolerable. The weather was cold, and rain fell, turning the ground into black, waxy mud. Camped in tents, many of the blacks became sick, some were forced to go home, and at least one—Arthur Williams—died. Dickson paid the sick ones first so that they could return home.[14] This faltering start was a forecast of the difficulties that continued to plague the payment.

After the first installment had been paid out about mid-March, Dickson moved to Fort Gibson because he was afraid of trouble from collectors to whom the freedmen owed money. Prominent among them was F. B. Severs, a merchant from Muskogee, who claimed about $50,000 was owed him; he was collection agent for about $120,000 in debts to others. Difficulties soon arose when the payment began again. On March 26 Judge W. M. Springer of the court for the Northern District of the Indian Territory at Vinita served Dickson with a writ of mandamus, directing him to accept the power of attorney from certain Cherokee freed-

men to their creditors. Dickson wrote for instructions. Should he obey the
writ and have his funds cut off or refuse and face a contempt of court
citation? Indian Inspector J. George Wright informed the secretary that
the writ involved a power of attorney in favor of F. B. Severs for money
due about 950 creditors, an aggregate of $170,000. The commissioner
held that if the federal courts of the Indian Territory compelled Dickson
to pay on powers of attorney, they would lay his accounts liable to dis-
allowance by the Treasury Department on the ground that such payment
would violate section 3477 of the Revised Statutes. He asked that the
U. S. attorney for the Northern District of the Indian Territory be instructed to appear in Dickson's behalf and have the writs revoked. Meanwhile similar writs, issued by Judge Springer and covering claims of other
creditors, were being served on Dickson.[15]

There is some evidence that Dickson had known about the proceedings
against him for several days but had failed to inform the department. Inspector James McLaughlin and Captain J. C. Galbreath of the First Cavalry
became convinced that Dickson was in collusion with some of the creditors
and that he had lost the confidence of the freedmen. He was accused of
having told the freedmen that only those who would agree to pay Severs
would be paid and of having admitted Severs to the room where payment
was made. On May 4 Secretary C. N. Bliss relieved Dickson, sent an army
officer to take charge of the funds, and ordered the freedmen, who were
neglecting their farming, to return home and await notice of the resump-
tion of the payment. He notified Dickson and his clerk to report to the
Indian Office and there to help give the rolls a thorough examination and
to close out his accounts.[16]

Bliss's insistence on a thorough examination of the rolls was the result
of complaints about their gross inaccuracies. While he was at Hayden,
Dickson had called the rolls "unfit for the purpose of payment." They
were carelessly constructed. All members of one family were seldom
found enrolled together, and ages, sexes, names, and family relations were
frequently wrong. Commissioner Browning had asked Judge Springer to
look into the matter as well as into the difficulties surrounding the payment. Springer empaneled a grand jury, which adjourned without returning any indictments but which found that many of the Cherokee freedmen on the authenticated roll of 1880 had been left off the Clifton roll
and that many who had no right to citizenship had been included. Springer
recommended that the rolls be purged by the Dawes Commission, which

had been created by Congress in 1893 and which had been in the Indian
Territory since then, attempting to negotiate agreements by which the
Five Civilized Tribes would dissolve their nations and allot their lands in
severalty. The commission had also been directed to make a roll of the
citizens of the nations and had been much interested in the work of the
Clifton commission. Secretary Bliss asked Frank C. Armstrong of the
Dawes Commission to investigate the Dickson payment and to report.
Armstrong learned that from the start the proceedings had been unsatis-
factory and that the rolls were incorrect and should be corrected before
payment was resumed. However, Bliss refused to suspend the payment.
He did not see how the department, under the decision of the court,
could undertake action for the relief of any person who claimed a share,
nor could he see how the Dawes Commission could add to or take from
the roll. Once the payment had been made, the department could determine what course to pursue, if any, to relieve those omitted.[17]

Bliss appointed Agent Dew M. Wisdom of the Union Agency to complete the payment at Fort Gibson. Those who lived a great distance away
were sent notices to apply directly to the office of the secretary of the interior. When Wisdom began payment in June, trouble persisted. A thousand
or fifteen hundred freedmen camped in the vicinity. Bill collectors hugged
the boundaries of the pay ground, waiting to pounce on freedmen when
they received their money. Severs was there with his attorneys. He told the
freedmen that he had another writ from the federal court and threatened
to stop the payment again if those who owed him did not settle their
debts. Some were intimidated. Traders set up temporary stores in tents
near the pay ground, their wares displayed to tempt the freedmen who
had cash. Violence broke out on June 24 when U. S. deputy marshals
tried to help creditors collect some debts. Two shots were fired, evidently
aimed at the marshals. No one was hit, but a marshal struck a freedman
with his rifle.[18]

When Wisdom completed the payment of the funds granted by the
court of claims, the rolls were turned over to D. W. Lipe, treasurer of
the Cherokee Nation, to disburse what remained, after the attorneys' fees
had been deducted, of the extra $400,000 appropriated by the Cherokees.
Some freedmen charged that Lipe had schemed with Charles M. Ross,
Joel Baugh, P. N. Blackstone, Henry Eiffert, and Dick Dannenberg of the
Cherokee Nation to defraud some of the freedmen of their money. Petitions were circulated to prevent his making the payment. They claimed
that Ross and the others were telling the freedmen that the Cherokee

Nation was going to institute a suit to have certain freedmen stricken from the rolls. By those means, they allegedly got some of the freedmen to sell them their claims to their per-capita share for ten or fifteen dollars, while the shares were worth about fifty-two dollars. The petitioners asked that the money be taken from the Cherokees and paid out by Wisdom. Nevertheless Lipe began the payment at Tahlequah on July 15, 1897, and continued the disbursements there and at Chelsea and Fort Gibson until August 31.[19]

With Lipe's payment ended another significant event in Cherokee affairs. Because of their obsessive determination to do away with the Wallace roll, the Cherokees had agreed to a costly compromise. Accusations of fraud during the making of the Kern-Clifton roll and the subsequent payments proved divisive in later years, and as time passed, the Cherokees grew to hate that roll as much as they hated Wallace's, for the charges and countercharges gave support to congressmen who argued that the Indian nations should be dissolved because Indian leaders were corrupt. There was some evidence that corruption did exist. The charges and countercharges about the various payments from the Kern-Clifton roll reflected the climate that had surrounded freedman affairs for several months. From the beginning, there had been rumors of fraud regarding the freedman compromise and the subsequent enrollment of the freedmen by the Clifton commission.

One concerned the contract Moses Whitmire had made with Kern and J. Milton Turner on January 28, 1896, for their services in obtaining the per-capita funds for the freedmen. On August 15, 1896, D. W. Lipe paid Kern and Turner $126,666 of the additional $400,000 the Cherokees had appropriated as their part of the compromise. Whitmire swore under oath that he had not agreed to pay Kern one-third of the $400,000. His concept of the agreement as it was read to him and signed was as follows. He had originally hired Kern at 10 percent of the money awarded the freedmen by the court of claims, but in rendering the decree, the court allowed him only 6 percent, or $54,201.30. Therefore Whitmire entered an agreement with Kern to pay him the 10 percent, or $36,134 out of the $400,000 appropriation. With this money, Kern was supposed to fulfill his obligation to Turner, his associate. It was after the appropriation that Whitmire allegedly learned that he had agreed to pay Kern one-third. Whitmire, who was illiterate, did not know what was in the contract he had signed.[20]

Whether Kern and Turner took advantage of the illiteracy and infirmity of Whitmire, who was now approaching seventy, is uncertain, but that was the opinion of Allen Lynch, one of the committee of the freedmen who had advised Whitmire in all freedman matters. Whitmire had reported to Lynch, upon his return from Washington, that he had agreed to pay Kern and Turner the remaining 4 percent of the original contract. Lynch thought fraud might be involved. There is no evidence to indicate that Whitmire was anything but an honest man. However, Lipe had refused to pay the money due under the contract as it was originally witnessed, so on August 13, 1896, Whitmire had marked another copy, properly witnessed. It was on this copy that Lipe paid. According to Indian inspector W. J. McConnell, the witnesses were employed by "one of the principal advocates of the appropriation."[21] However, if Whitmire was duped, it occurred twice.

After the payment was made, the Cherokees realized how costly the compromise had been. Rumors were rife that fraud and bribery had been used in obtaining passage of the $400,000 appropriation. In the summer of 1897, Chief S. H. Mayes and others were accused of having taken a bribe to ensure passage of the compromise bill. Mayes first answered the charges through the newspapers. Foremost among those making charges was Frank J. Boudinot, brother of E. C. Boudinot, who had been elected counsel for the Nation at a special session of the National Council in October 1895. According to Frank, his brother had been called to Kansas City to a secret meeting, involving some high-level officials of the Nation. E. C. Boudinot confided in Frank that a scheme was afoot to compromise the matter of the freedmen, Delawares, and Shawnees. The Boudinots agreed that if contracts were to be made, they would attempt to get a share in Frank's name. E. C. and his wife went to Kansas City, and when they returned, he reported to Frank that a verbal agreement of compromise had been reached. All money was to pass through Kern's hands. Out of the fees he would receive as attorney, Kern was to kick back $50,000 to be divided among E. C. Boudinot, Jake Guthrie, J. E. Campbell, W. W. Hastings, ex-Chief C. J. Harris, and Chief S. H. Mayes. Boudinot had some doubts about the plan but decided that he had done all he could for the Nation during an earlier trip to Washington, and that if a deal was made, the Boudinots might as well share in it.[22]

When E. C. Boudinot died on February 10, 1896, Frank told the other members of the party that he knew of the secret contracts and expected his brother's share. The group allegedly met in Tahlequah to draft a council bill to ratify the freedman compromise, which had been agreed to on January 28. Frank Boudinot, Campbell, Kern, Guthrie, and Hastings were there. Later they went to Boudinot's law office to put the final touches on the bill. Hastings allegedly told Kern to go back to his hotel because he should not be seen there at that time, presumably because the ratification was a Cherokee affair. After the appropriation bill passed, the group went to St. Louis to divide the funds. J. E. Campbell returned from St. Louis, saying that Hastings would pay Frank $1,600, which he supposedly did in four checks from the Bank of Tahlequah.[23]

Mrs. Addie Boudinot, widow of E. C., substantiated Frank Boudinot's allegations. However, she said that when she went with her husband to Kansas City, she saw Kern and Campbell but not Hastings, Mayes, Guthrie, or Harris, nor did she hear them spoken of. Just before he died, E. C. told her that he had $7,200 due him from Kern through Campbell and James S. Stapler, a banker at Tahlequah, $1,250 from the Delawares, through Hastings, and $2,200 from the Shawnees, through Harris and Guthrie. Mrs. Boudinot claimed that Hastings had paid her $2,400.[24]

The scandal touched other members of the Cherokee delegation who had served with C. J. Harris in Washington in 1895 and 1897: Joseph Smallwood, Roach Young, and George W. Benge. Benge admitted that the delegation had been called to the rooms of Chief S. H. Mayes in Washington, where Hastings was present, to meet with Kern and E. C. Boudinot. At another meeting in the rooms of C. J. Harris, Kern and Boudinot presented a written agreement between Mayes and Kern whereby Mayes agreed to call an extra session of the National Council and advocate the passage of the $400,000 appropriation. The delegates sanctioned the agreement, but they did so, according to Benge, only because of what the Cherokees were to gain: a purging of the Wallace roll. Benge denied any fraud in the matter, but he admitted that the compromise was a mistake. It had not only failed to get rid of the fraudulent freedmen names but ultimately had added hundreds more.[25]

In the face of allegations and rumors, the National Council passed a resolution on November 25, 1897, charging that the compromise had resulted from a conspiracy between attorneys for the freedmen and representatives of the Cherokee Nation to rob the treasury of $400,000 and to put upon the Cherokee people more than one thousand "useless

and degraded Negroes." Because the officials of the Nation had shared
in the spoils and had brought shame to the name of the National Council,
the council created a committee of seven to investigate the charges. They
were given the authority to subpoena witnesses, administer oaths, and
punish for contempt, but they had only a week to work before they had
to report on December 4.[26]

They did little more than record charges and countercharges. First,
there were the charges. Benge, who had been accused of receiving some
money from the compromise, denied the charge, but he claimed to have
seen papers showing that Mayes, Hastings, E. C. Boudinot, Jake Guthrie,
and Ed Campbell had received $13,000 each. R. L. Fite testified that
he had spoken with Richard M. Wolf at the freedman payment at Hayden. Wolf supposedly named Sam Smith, Roach Young, Benge, Hastings,
and others who had shared in the division of the $126,000. Wolf had al-
legedly said that he had received about $1,500 and that others were get-
ting more than $2,000. Albert Taylor, the auditor of accounts of the
Cherokee Nation, testified that in December 1895 he was approached by
E. C. Boudinot, who told him that if things went right, he would build
a big house in the spring and would allow Taylor to use part of it as a
poolroom. Taylor assumed that Boudinot had meant that if a compromise
was made, he would profit by it. Later Frank J. Boudinot hired Taylor
to use his influence with the full-blood members of the council in getting the compromise bill passed. Taylor was to receive about $2,000 from
the $126,000, but he claimed that he had received nothing. Boudinot
later told him, he said, that Kern and Hastings had beat E. C. Boudinot
out of his share. Taylor did not know if any money was ever paid. On
the other side of the question, James S. Stapler denied that any kickback
money had been deposited in his bank at Tahlequah, and he knew of
no collusion. His statements were supported by the testimony of De-
Witt Wilson. D. W. Lipe claimed to know nothing about collusion; he
had simply paid the $126,000 as fulfillment of a contract.[27]

Because the committee had not finished its work on December 4,
the day the session of the National Council ended, the investigators
reached no conclusions, but they had succeeded in raising a number of
interesting questions. Therefore they turned the problem over to the
National Council, which passed a joint resolution, asking Mayes to call
the council into extra session so the investigation might continue. Mayes

delayed his answer until December 28, 1897, at which time he said that he favored the investigation but thought that it would be less expensive if it was done while the council was in recess.[28] But the council was over, and no law existed for the continuation of the investigation. Therefore all official acts in the matter on the part of the Cherokees ended.

When news of the allegations appeared in the St. Louis papers, Kern came to the defense of Chief Mayes and the others, denying Boudinot's charges of collusion regarding the compromise. Kern also told local reporters that "the compromise between the freedmen and the Cherokees was virtually a bet as to how many negroes there were in the Cherokee Nation." In an effort to invalidate the Wallace roll, the Cherokees had found themselves faced with a still larger Kern-Clifton roll. "It was a plain compromise," said Kern, "in which we, looking out for the interest of our clients, got more money for them than was called for in the judgment." Kern accused the Cherokees of setting up a "howl about bribery and treachery" to detract from the fact that they had made a mistake.[29]

That such remarks were salt in political wounds cannot be doubted. But it is uncertain how much the allegations resulted from the Cherokee national political scene and how much was simply sour grapes. More uncertain is the extent to which the charges were based in truth. If they were not true, it is interesting that E. C. Boudinot's brother and widow would implicate Boudinot in a kickback scheme. One thing was certain: the Cherokees were chagrined at their mistake. They not only attacked the compromise, but they appealed to racist feelings in attacking the mode of making the roll, charging that blacks' testimony was taken at face value while Cherokees' testimony was put to rigorous test, thus allowing many blacks from the United States to get on the roll. The Cherokees were now determined to get rid of the Kern-Clifton roll as they had done the Wallace roll.[30]

By the time Mayes replied to the council regarding the investigation, Indian inspector W. J. McConnell had been assigned to look into allegations of fraud regarding the compromise and the freedman payment. Assisted by George C. Ross, McConnell took up where the Cherokee committee had left off. John P. Welch, interpreter for the National Council, testified that when the compromise appropriation bill came before the council, it was referred to a special senate committee made up of Levi Cookson, Simon Walkingstick, Daniel Gritts, Henry Lowry,

and David Faulkner. The bill was read, and all of the committee seemed
opposed to it. Then Hastings, Benge, and Sam Smith (president of the
senate) appeared before the committee and urged its favorable report.
After that, Welch claimed, the members of the committee lobbied for
the passage of the bill. Ed Campbell and Hastings lobbied for it, and
Walkingstick allegedly told Welch that he had been promised a bonus
if he worked for and voted for the bill. Sam Smith had allegedly told
him that "an old darkey" gave him $25 as a present after he had voted
for the bill. Welch received $150 from Stapler and $25 from Guthrie.
Daniel Gritts testified that he did not know when he voted for the bill
that Kern was to get one-third of the appropriation. Otherwise he would
not have voted for it. Mayes made the same claim and denied, under
oath, that he had received money to be bribed or influenced. And in
like fashion, former chief C. J. Harris denied any complicity.[31]

McConnell, like the Cherokee investigating committee, succeeded in
taking a mass of contradictory evidence. However, in his report to the
secretary of the interior, he stated that Mayes's refusal to continue the
investigation by Cherokee authorities had not been satisfactorily explained,
and there was no doubt in McConnell's mind "that the passage of the
bill was secured by a liberal distribution of money." He said, "Men high
in the Councils of the Cherokee Nation, as well as others trusted by the
Cherokee Freedmen and Free colored persons, have grossly and out-
rageously betrayed the confidence of their too confiding people."[32]

McConnell had heard the story only as it was told by various factions
in the Cherokee Nation. There remained Kern's side of it. When the Cherokees appointed E. C. Boudinot as attorney to appeal the decision of
the court of claims to the Supreme Court, Kern discussed a compromise,
he said, to avoid years of litigation, but he had got nowhere because the
freedmen were not willing to have the Wallace roll set aside and a new
census taken unless they could get additional money. In October Chief
C. J. Harris passed through St. Louis and told Kern that it was in the
best interest of the Cherokees for the litigation to end if the number of
freedmen could be ascertained in some way. In November Ed Campbell
had called at Kern's office and suggested a compromise. Kern talked it
over with his associates—Judge Henry O. Laughlin, Wells H. Blodgett,
Fred Lehmann, and J. Milton Turner—and submitted a proposition to
Campbell, who accepted it. It was the compromise that the Cherokee
council sanctioned on December 7, 1895. It was agreed, Kern said, that

Campbell should have the larger percentage of whatever fee might be recovered in the settlement of the case in excess of the $56,000 allowed Kern and his associates by the court. Campbell agreed to work to procure the passage of the law by which the freedmen could enjoy their full share of the Cherokee common property. The attorneys felt that the number of freedmen had so increased that it would take $1.3 million to pay them.[33]

According to Kern, Boudinot invited him to Kansas City to discuss the compromise. He wanted the amount reduced to $1 million or $1.1 million. Kern denied Frank Boudinot's allegation that Mayes or Guthrie was there and denied that either he or his associates had gone to the Cherokee Nation when the compromise bill passed the National Council in December 1895. After the bill passed, Kern, Laughlin, Whitmire, and Turner went to the court of claims. When the court denied the compromise in late January, each side was determined to go to the Supreme Court. On second thought, Kern and his group decided to try once more to reach a compromise. With Whitmire and Turner, Kern drafted a proposition, went to the rooms of Chief Mayes and the Cherokee delegation in Washington, and told them that if the Cherokees would agree to appropriate the extra money, the compromise could be effected. The Cherokees agreed. The parties went to the court and stated what they wanted, and the court modified the decree. To this point, Kern protested, nothing had been said about compensation. When the National Council met in March 1896, Kern went to Tahlequah and stayed two or three days. He had no sooner reached town when an attack was made on the compromise. He answered the charges through a letter to the *Indian Sentinel* on March 21, in which he fully explained the terms of the compromise and denied being there to influence members of the council corruptly. He left Tahlequah before the bill passed.[34]

Kern did not explain why he dealt with Ed Campbell in St. Louis when E. C. Boudinot was the Cherokee Nation's attorney. Neither did he or any of the others explain why the meeting to discuss the compromise was held in Kansas City. Kern was under fire on other matters as well. McConnell was instructed to investigate not only the circumstances surrounding the compromise but also the possible fraudulent practices of Kern and others during the enrollment of the freedmen before the Clifton commission.

The latter investigation grew out of various charges, the first of which

had come on July 4, 1896, from S. H. Mayes. In a letter to President
Grover Cleveland, Mayes charged that Kern was corrupting the duties of
his position as enrollment commissioner by employing R. P. deGraffenreid to assist J. Milton Turner, attorney for certain freedmen appearing
before the commission and partner of Kern, by helping Turner prepare
freedman cases for presentation before the commission, by receiving part
of the fees collected from the freedmen, and by intimidating witnesses
for the Cherokee Nation by threatening them with prosecution and im-
prisonment for perjury. Mayes submitted affidavits making complaints
against Kern. Those and the rumors of wrong and arbitrary practices by
Kern had been the impetus for his complaint, he said. Secretary Hoke
Smith referred the matter to William Clifton for investigation and report.[35]

Before Clifton could report, however, Kern himself addressed the
secretary on the subject, asking for the papers presented against him.
A freedman at Fort Gibson had handed him a petition that had come
through the mail with a request that the freedman circulate it for signatures. Addressed to the President, the petition charged that Kern,
while sitting as a commissioner, was also acting as attorney in partner-
ship with J. Milton Turner and was receiving pay from persons appearing before him. It also charged that Kern had hired deGraffenreid of
Muskogee to assist him and Turner in prosecuting the cases before him
and that he had succeeded in putting a large number of unauthorized
persons on the roll. Kern denied everything in the petition. Before he
had gone to the Indian Territory, he had suggested to the secretary's
office that the freedmen hire an attorney, but he had been overruled
on the ground that he was on the commission to look after their rights.
Kern had also told the department that Turner was willing to take care
of the interests of those who might hire him for ten dollars per person
and was informed that he could tell the freedmen that they might hire
Turner if they preferred him to the attorneys of the Nation, except for
those on the authenticated roll, who needed no attorney. When he went
to the Indian Territory, Kern told the freedmen that Turner was willing
to take their cases but that they could hire whom they liked.[36]

Among the attorneys present at Hayden during the first week of
the commission's work was R. P. deGraffenreid. About the second or
third day of the session, Turner had told Kern that he was ill and over-
worked and asked if he could hire deGraffenreid to assist him. Kern
claimed that his only interest was to see that the freedmen were properly

represented and that although he barely knew deGraffenreid, he had agreed that Turner might hire him if he was competent. DeGraffenreid relieved Turner but in a day or two fell ill himself, and Kern saw him no more until he appeared at Fort Gibson ten days later. There, Turner was still ailing and, since he was not a trained lawyer, "felt embarrassed somewhat in his work" and asked that deGraffenreid be allowed to assist him further. Kern had no objections. DeGraffenreid worked for a few days, and at the end of his service Turner had no cash with which to pay him. Kern, as a friend, had loaned Turner the money. Kern insisted that in his work he had been impartial in dealing with both Cherokees and freedmen. Because he would not be dictated to by the Cherokees, he had incurred their wrath, he said; this was part of the "game that has been played by the Cherokees for the last 50 years whenever they have found they could not use a person."[37]

Turner filed an affidavit swearing to the same facts regarding deGraffenreid as Kern had presented. And when Clifton reported, he substantiated the stories. DeGraffenreid had become so ill that he had to stay in a freedman's tent for several days before he could return to Muskogee. Clifton was aware that Kern had paid deGraffenreid for Turner. The affidavits of complaint that Mayes had filed were from people who had little reason to like Kern or Turner. One was from Robert L. Owen of Muskogee, whose brother, William, Kern was currently protesting against as a possible appointee as paymaster of the freedman fund. Another was from Dew M. Wisdom, who had represented William and Joseph Brown during the time they had opposed the election of Moses Whitmire as trustee for the freedmen. Still another was from Albert Taylor, who later charged that fraud had been perpetrated in the passage of the compromise bill. In concluding his report, Clifton said that J. Milton Turner was not as familiar with the facts and names of his clients' witnesses as he should have been, suggesting therefore that he could not have been in any collusion with them as to what facts he wanted the witnesses to present. Finally, Clifton charged that the chief's brother, Wiley Mayes, a sheriff, and some of his deputies were more annoying than any other class of people at Chelsea by sitting in or near the enrollment camp late at night, shooting their pistols.[38]

The assistant attorney general for the Interior Department decided that the evidence was not sufficient to support the charges against Kern. The matter rested for a while, but as the freedmen payment progressed in 1897, it became apparent that the Clifton roll was blatantly erroneous in some cases. Toward the end of the year, Kern found himself once more accused of fraud and irresponsibility during the enrollment. Part of the impetus for the new charges came from the Cherokee investigating committee created by the National Council. E. F. Cunningham, an attorney from St. Louis, swore that he had been hired by J. Milton Turner to attend the payment of the Indian Territory and to collect money due Turner on individual contracts with freedmen. Cunningham got James M. Keys, one of the Cherokee attorneys, to help him because Keys knew the freedmen. According to Cunningham, on many occasions Keys told the freedmen that if they did not pay the contracts, he would see that they were taken from the roll, that he knew they had no right to be on the roll, and that their evidence was perjury. Keys allegedly told him that between one thousand and twelve hundred persons on the rolls were imposters from Arkansas, the Creek and Choctaw nations, Kansas, and Texas. Cunningham believed that Keys knew about the imposters when he was representing the Cherokees before the Clifton commission and that by an honest performance of his duty, Keys could have prevented their admittance to the rolls. Kern suggested that Cunningham try to obtain a large fee from the Cherokees and, with Keys's assistance, purge the rolls.[39]

With Cunningham's statement were filed the statements of Sam Shephard of Cooweescoowee District and Cornelia Hill and Sarah Martin of Sequoyah, who swore that at Fort Gibson they paid J. Milton Turner varying sums on contracts they had made with him in 1896 to get them on the Clifton roll. It was their belief, they said, that they would not otherwise have been placed on the roll, and they claimed to know many other freedmen who had paid money to be listed on the roll but who had never been on any previous roll.

Another impetus for the new charges against Kern came from the Delawares. In early December 1897 R. C. Adams and John Bullette presented a petition to the Dawes Commission at Muskogee, alleging that the number of freedmen had been swelled by the Clifton commission by the inclusion of more than a thousand fraudulent names, thereby reducing by the amount of their per-capita payments the national moneys to be shared by all classes. The Delawares therefore filed a formal protest against the Clifton roll. The protest was published in local and regional newspapers, and Adams continued his attack on the validity of the roll by stirring the political air of the time and dragging out the old charge against Kern in the deGraffenreid affair. It was at that point that Inspector McConnell came to the Indian Territory with instructions to investigate the enrollment. Adams filed with him a number of documents referring to the contracts that Turner had made with the freedmen as their attorney during the enrollment and to his collecting money during the payment. Cunningham filed papers implicating Kern in a number of the 1,865 claims yet uncollected under contracts made by Turner.[41] If the documents given McConnell were authentic, there is no doubt that Kern had something to do with the contracts after they were made. It was Adams's contention, of course, that he had been involved in their making.

During his investigation, McConnell took many statements alleging that fraud had occurred during the enrollment. The most damaging testimony came from Louis T. Brown, a freedman who had been hired by Turner in the summer of 1896 to help him get claimants placed on the Clifton roll. Brown testified that when the Clifton commission came to Hayden, Kern called a meeting of the freedmen at a store. He explained the object of the commission and told the freedmen that after the roll and payment were made, they would need an attorney to look after their individual interests when lands were eventually allotted in severalty. Kern proposed to represent them at five dollars per capita. He had contracts printed and distributed by L. A. Bell of Wagoner, Wash French and Allen Lynch of Vinita, and John A. Rose, Henry C. Hayden, and Harry Still of Hayden, who were to get twenty-five cents for each name they collected. Brown claimed that Bell forged three thousand names, which he copied from the Wallace roll. Brown gave McConnell a contract signed by Simon Meigs promising to pay Turner fifty dollars for getting him, his wife, and their three children enrolled by the Clifton commission.[42]

Brown testified that Turner accompanied the commission to all parts of the Nation. At Hayden, Fort Gibson, Tahlequah, Sallisaw, Vinita, and Chelsea, he set up office in a room adjoining the commission's or in a tent adjacent to or facing the office. Brown's duties included talking to claimants, taking their statements, and making up their cases for presentation. Turner then presented the cases to the commission. Also hired in preparing cases were George F. Nave, L. A. Bell, L. W. Cooper, Ellen Buckner, and Emma Hudson. Turner charged ten dollars for getting a person's name on the roll. During the enrollment, Brown alleged, Kern often asked him to go over the accounts of fees made out to Turner and discussed with him the number of cases that seemed good. Turner told Brown more than once that half of the proceeds of the contracts belonged to Kern and that Kern should therefore have access to the accounts at any time. During the Dickson payment at Fort Gibson, Kern wrote to Turner for five hundred dollars as his part in order to complete the construction of a building in St. Louis. Turner therefore had Brown total the accounts, deduct expenses, and calculate what amount was to be divided. Brown wrote two checks drawn on the National Bank of Commerce of St. Louis, they were signed by Turner, and Brown sent them to Kern. [43]

Others testified that Turner had some control over the decisions admitting people to the roll. Daniel Alberty, who claimed to have been a slave of Moses Alberty of Going Snake District, failed to be admitted. He had gone to Turner to secure representation before the commission, but Turner had insulted him. Alberty then employed J. P. Bledsoe of Chouteau. Turner allegedly told Alberty and others that they would not get their names enrolled because they did not hire him. Alberty was convinced that he was refused admission because he would not hire Turner. Frank Vann testified that he was not on the authenticated roll of 1880 because he was away at school at the time. Therefore he went before the Clifton commission for enrollment. Kern told him that he must hire an attorney if he expected to be admitted. He went to a building nearby where Turner had his office and signed a contract, agreeing to pay ten dollars for each of the four members of his family. Their names appeared on the Clifton roll. Vann intimated that his success was due to having Turner as his attorney. [44]

Whether contrived or not, glaring errors in the roll were revealed by the testimony McConnell took. It was generally charged that over a thousand fraudulent names had been placed on the roll. J. T. Cunningham had served the Nation during the enrollment by obtaining witnesses to appear before the commission. He believed that many freedmen's enrollment was based on perjured testimony and charged that the commission accepted the testimony of persons who were known to be professional witnesses and rejected testimony by some of the best Cherokee citizens. He cited the example of Ann B. Shelton, "a lady of unblemished character" and a teacher at the Cherokee Orphan Asylum who had testified concerning the identity of a claimant. Her testimony was contradicted by Wallace's old friend Luster Foreman, who, Cunningham said, was a "noted whiskey-peddler," then in jail at Muskogee.[45]

Daniel Vann testified that George Vann of Sequoyah District was on the roll and had drawn money. Daniel claimed that a white man had come to him in 1896 and offered him $250 to swear that George was his brother and, through his evidence, get George on the Clifton roll. Daniel did have a brother named George, but he had been killed during the war. He refused to give the false testimony. Henry Covel, an interpreter for the executive office, testified that Bryant Hester, his wife, and six children appeared on the Clifton roll but that they had moved to Tahlequah from Texas in 1894. Covel said that they had never been recognized as citizens and did not descend from slaves or free persons of the Cherokee Nation. Fred and Sophia Schrimscher testified that Anderson Bean and his wife were ex-slaves of an Arkansan and had come to the Cherokee Nation about 1888. They were never citizens of the Nation, yet they drew per-capita money. W. S. Agnew testified that Mattie Gales, an ex-slave of Judge Brown of Sequoyah District, had gone to Fort Scott, Kansas, during the war and had come to Muskogee about 1883. She moved from there to the Cherokee Nation in 1890 and was enrolled by the Clifton commission. DeWitt Wilson testified that at the end of the war, Allen Wilson and his family were in the Choctaw Nation with their master, DeWitt's father. Allen Wilson and family did not return to the Cherokee Nation until December 1867, and the Cherokees had never recognized them as citizens. Yet they had appeared on the Clifton roll and had drawn money. Chief Mayes testified that he had gone before the commission to give evidence concerning Wash, Dave, and George Nave, who did not return to the Nation until 1868. Mayes was certain about the date because they had come from Fort Scott, Kansas, and made a crop on the farm of his mother-in-law. Yet they appeared on the Clifton roll and had drawn money.[46]

One of the most obvious failings of the Clifton roll was the omission of the names of many freedmen and free persons who had appeared on the authenticated roll of 1880 and therefore should have appeared on the Clifton roll. M. O. Ghormley, an attorney from Tahlequah, submitted a list of 109 names of such persons who had retained him, and he claimed to know of many more. James M. Keys, one of the attorneys for the Cherokees, at the suggestion of Dickson and Inspector James McLaughlin, took over 180 names of those who appeared on the authenticated roll and who came to Fort Gibson for payment but found that their names had been left off the Clifton roll. There were many instances in which some members of families appeared on the roll while others did not. For example, Nancy Tiner's husband and two children were enrolled, but she and two other children were not. Two of Daniel Vann's children were enrolled, yet he, his wife, and one other child were not. Three of Clara Vann's children were enrolled, yet she and two other children were not. Cynthia Thomas's father, mother, brother, and sisters were enrolled, but she was not. Finally, several complained that their children born between 1880 and May 3, 1894, had been left off the roll.[47]

McConnell offered various explanations of the condition of the roll. Ellen Lynch of Fort Gibson stated that Turner had boarded with her family during the payment made by Treasurer D. W. Lipe in 1897. She said that she heard Turner tell Isaac Smith that Kern had left off many names that had at first been enrolled. Kern supposedly scratched them off indiscriminately to reduce the number of freedmen after receiving several thousand dollars from W. P. Thompson, the Cherokee on the commission. That was Turner's explanation, said Mrs. Lynch, for the absence of the names of so many who were known to be justly entitled to enrollment.[48]

Thompson blamed the condition of the rolls on the method of taking and evaluating evidence presented before the commission. Clifton and Kern had interpreted the term *claimant* to mean that those whose names appeared on the authenticated roll and their descendants need not file a written application for enrollment. When Clifton and Kern decided that all of the testimony would be taken and the decisions deferred until all testimony was written up, Thompson protested and wanted to resign but was dissuaded by the principal chief. George Brown, hired by Kern, took the testimony in shorthand and took the notes to St. Louis where they were written up in Kern's office. When the commission met in St. Louis on November 25, 1896, only part of the notes had been transcribed, and Brown was obliged to read the testimony from his notes. The work was hurried. Thus, Thompson said, the work was not given the care that it would have been given if the commission had passed on the cases at the time the testimony was taken. He was surprised that the names of so many people on the 1880 roll had been omitted, and he would not have signed it had he known. He thought that someone had later stricken the names from the roll.[49]

Robert F. Thompson, a clerk in the Office of Indian Affairs, laid part of the blame on the department for not investigating the roll more closely. The secretary submitted the roll to the Office of Indian Affairs for report on December 21, 1896. On January 16, 1897, it was returned by Commissioner Browning without review since the report was unanimous and signed by all three commissioners. Nevertheless he had referred it to Thompson, who had drafted the instructions by which the commission had worked, for clerical examination and report. Before he could give the matter even a cursory examination, Kern had expressed a strong desire that the matter be reported to the secretary at once so that a disbursing officer could be named and the payment begun. Calls frequently came from the department to expedite the matter; so pressing were the requests that Thompson and another clerk worked on the rolls until late at night. Thus the examination was too hurried to be satisfactory. The rolls were, as the commissioner's report had said, "as nearly accurate as it was possible for this office to make them within the limited time given for their examination."[50]

Inspector McConnell also took evidence concerning the activities of Turner, Kern, and others at the payments made to the freedmen. At the time of the first payment there were charges that Turner had laid out lots near the pay house and had rented them for five dollars a day to "fakers, gamblers, cider stands," with the object of fleecing the freedmen. The weather was bad, and the people had nothing to eat except what Turner had to sell at exorbitant prices. George Vann, a freedman, stated that at the second payment made by Lipe at Chelsea, Lipe paid in one room, and Turner and his clerks and collectors occupied the adjoining room. At the door of the office stood one of Turner's people who asked the freedmen if they had seen Louis Brown, who would make them promise to pay Turner as soon as they were paid. After Lipe made the payment of $53.60, the freedmen were conducted one or two at a time into Turner's office where $10 was demanded of them in return for being placed on the roll. Some were then conducted to Kern, who collected another $5 on the ground that it was necessary for them to employ an attorney to secure their allotments of land at some future time. Vann saw a large number pay Kern and overheard him say that he had got most of them on the roll. Among those he saw pay Kern were Boson Merril, Berry Ward, Reuben Johnson, Sam Whitmire, Ellis Webber, Peter Hudson, Esquire Ward, and Ben Ward of Ruby, Israel Johnson of Tulsa,

Esquire Sanders of Illinois Station, and Rose Allen, Columbus Landris, and Lander Bean of Vinita. Vann testified that Kern had made a speech at Chelsea, telling the freedmen that they needed someone to defend them in getting their allotments. Harrison Foreman of Catoosa, a police guard at the payment, swore to the truth of George Vann's statement.[51]

J. C. Dannenberg testified concerning Kern's and Turner's activities at Tahlequah. Dannenberg was the deputy marshal for the Northern District of the Indian Territory in December 1897, but he had been auditor of the Nation at the time of the payment and had assisted Lipe in making it. He stated that at Tahlequah, Turner procured an office next to the pay office where he and Brown followed the procedure Vann described. Dannenberg said that during the times they were not paying, he went into Turner's office. The freedmen would sometimes say they did not sign a contract and refused to pay. Some were found to be on the authenticated roll of 1880 and were allowed to go unmolested. Dannenberg believed that Turner collected about $10,000 from the freedmen. At Chelsea, there was a large tent erected by the man who had rented a lot on the pay ground. In one corner of the tent Kern had an office. When the freedmen were paid, they were ushered into his office where he collected five dollars to represent them in securing allotments. Dannenberg believed that Kern must have collected a large sum because he often came to the pay room for change for large bills.[52]

Louis T. Brown testified that at the Lipe payments, the clerks and officers of the payment cooperated with Turner by refusing to pay the freedmen until they had agreed to pay Turner. Brown kept Turner's accounts. At the Dickson payments, Turner collected about $4,000 and at the Lipe payment about $7,500. Finally George Nave, a freedman and a schoolteacher from Chouteau, testified that he had observed Kern collecting fees from the freedmen during the payments. However, Nave's testimony dealt more with the activities of others. He claimed that at Fort Gibson he saw armed men seize freedmen after they had received their checks and take them into a room where collectors representing the trader Severs were sitting. He saw two white men forcibly search Rufus Mackey and Elijah Coody of Braggs in an effort to collect for Severs. If a freedman refused to pay, Nave claimed he was put in jail at Muskogee. Among those jailed for failing to pay were Rabbit Sanders of Fort Gibson and Rufus Mackey. Sanders, who had given his check to

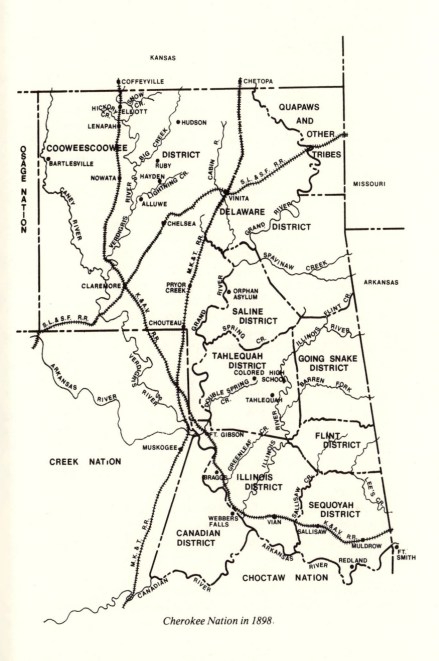

Cherokee Nation in 1898.

Hannah Mayfield of Muskogee, was kept in jail until the check was produced and Severs was paid.[53]

As chief spokesman for the Cherokees, S. H. Mayes told McConnell that the compromise had been a failure. It rid the Cherokees of the hated Wallace roll; that was all they had wanted. They had thought they were agreeing to an enrollment of only those on the authenticated roll and their descendants who were alive on May 3, 1894. Had they known, he said, that the whole matter of citizenship would be reopened, they would not have compromised. He called the making of the Clifton roll "a disgraceful farce."[54] In his final report in January 1898, McConnell agreed: "In brief, the entire transaction of the enrollment of the Cherokee Freedmen and the free colored persons together with the appropriation of the money by the Cherokee Council for the purpose of equalizing the payments was a disgraceful affair." He believed that the roll should be set aside and recommended that proceedings be instituted against Kern for receiving a share of the attorney's fees paid by the applicants while he was a member of the enrolling committee. McConnell recommended proceedings against J. Milton Turner for bribing a government official.[55]

As McConnell drew his investigation to a close, Kern became concerned, charging that McConnell was obtaining affidavits "on unusual terms." Kern laid the blame for his troubles on R. C. Adams and the enmity of the Cherokees—an enmity acquired during his seven years of work for the freedmen. He met with Secretary C. N. Bliss early in 1898 and promised him a written statement: Bliss agreed not to take any action until Kern had had time to review McConnell's report. Kern filed his answer to the charges against him on February 2, 1898. He denied having an interest in Turner's contracts while he was sitting as a commissioner. He denied that he had ever consulted Louis Brown about the fees. He cast doubt on Brown's character by pointing out Brown's recent indictment and pending trial for rape. He also denied having altered the evidence of the rolls. Kern claimed that Whitmire's contract had been fully discussed with Whitmire before the signing. The money was appropriated before he became a commissioner. Therefore there was no conflict of interest as far as his being retained by the freedmen to represent them before the Dawes Commission; he claimed that they came to him voluntarily. Kern claimed that he then told the freedmen that he would look after their interests after the commission was through if a request was signed by a large enough number to pay for his services. It was true that contracts were made, but Kern said that he did not look at them until after the payment had started. He employed three or four freedmen to explain to other freedmen that he would represent them if they wished but that they might hire anyone they chose. At Chelsea, he obtained only four hundred contracts out of the forty-five hundred freedmen. Finally, Kern defended the roll he had helped to make, charging that the number of fraudulent names on it was exaggerated.[56]

The degree of fraud surrounding the freedman compromise and the Clifton commission's work may never be known. The often entangled facts are as hard to sort out now as they were then by investigators who were sent from outside the Cherokee Nation. While evidence suggests that many who pretended to be the freedmen's friends were simply opportunists, the facts were not clear enough for charges to be filed. However, the effect of all of the charges and rumors was the same as if fraud had been proved. The Cherokee people began to lose faith in their national leaders. During the remaining days of the Cherokee Nation, Cherokee politicians often stung their political opponents by recalling the events surrounding the freedman compromise. Another roll that the Cherokees refused to recognize as valid had been produced. By the time McConnell filed his report, the Dawes Commission had begun considering procedures to be followed in making still another roll of the Cherokee freedmen.

NOTES

1. Hoke Smith to Commissioner of Indian Affairs, February 13, 1896, National Archives Microfilm Publications, *Microcopy M606* (Letters Sent by the Secretary of the Interior)-87, 452; 31 *Court of Claims,* 148; W. A. Richardson to Daniel M. Browning, February 18, 1896, in National Archives Record Group 48 (Records of the Department of the Interior, Office of the Secretary), Indian Territory Division, *Chickasaw Freedmen,* box 393 (60b), 15257-96; Browning to Secretary of the Interior, February 20, 1896, National Archives Record Group 75 (Records of the Bureau of Indian Affairs), *Letters Received,* 8545-1927 Cherokee Nation 175.2, pt. 4. The Chickasaw freedmen file, hereafter cited as *Freedmen File,* was apparently mislabeled, for most of the documents it contains relate to the Cherokees.

2. Commission of R. H. Kern, William P. Thompson, and William
Clifton, March 23, 1896, and Secretary of the Interior to Clifton, March
27, 1896, *Letters Received,* 1138-96, 11319-96, 11320-96, 11530-96;
Samuel Smith to S. H. Mayes, April 2, 1896, J. M. Keys and W. W. Hast-
ings to Mayes, August 19, 1896, and Browning to Clifton, Kern, and
Thompson, February 20, 1896, Indian Archives Division, Oklahoma
Historical Society, *Cherokee–Freedmen (Tahlequah).*

3. Browning to Clifton, Kern, and Thompson, February 20, 1896.

4. Ibid. The commission hired Harry Still, Fred Martin, and Frank
Pack, all freedmen, as bailiffs and George Brown of St. Louis as stenographer. "Cash Report of Irregular Employees," July 31, 1896, and
D. R. Francis to Commissioner, October 22, 1896, *Letters Received,*
41292-96, 40738-96.

5. *Report of the Secretary of the Interior for the Fiscal Year Ended
June 30, 1896* (Washington, D.C.: Government Printing Office, 1897),
54; W. H. Sims to Clifton, May 11, 1896, *Microcopy M606-88;* 425; Keys
and Hastings to Mayes, August 19, 1896, *Cherokee–Freedmen (Tahlequah);*
Browning to Clifton, May 16, 1896, *Letters Received,* 8545-1927 Cherokee Nation 175.2, pt. 4.

6. Clifton to Browning, May 14, 1896, Clifton and Kern to Browning,
May 23, 1896, and Kern to Browning, June 8, 1896, *Letters Received,*
8545-1927 Cherokee Nation 175.2, pt. 2, 19924-96, 21806-96; Thomas
P. Smith to Clifton, May 19, 1896, and Browning to Kern, February 20,
1897, Browning to Secretary of the Interior, June 2, 1896, Browning to
Clifton and Kern, June 5, 1896, and Browning to Clifton, June 13, 1896,
Letters Received, 8545-1927 Cherokee Nation 175.2, pt. 4; *Indian Chief-
tain,* April 30, 1896.

7. Commissioner to Secretary of the Interior, June 3, 1896, *Letters
Received,* 20762-96; Hoke Smith to Commissioner, June 3, 1896, *Microcopy M606-89,* 4; Kern to Browning, July 11, 1896, and William A. Little to Secretary of the Interior, September 10, 1896, *Letters Received,*
38017-96.

8. Kern to Browning, July 11, 1896, Hoke Smith to Commissioner,
July 21, 1896, *Letters Received,* 27800-96; Browning to Secretary of
the Interior, July 15, 1896, and Browning to Clifton, July 22, 1896,
Letters Received, 8545-1927 Cherokee Nation 175.2, pt. 4 and pt. 2,
respectively.

9. Clifton to Browning, July 28, 1896, and Kern to Browning, August
17, 1896, *Letters Received,* 31766-96, 28813-96; Keys and Hastings to
Mayes, August 9, 1896, *Cherokee–Freedmen (Tahlequah);* Clifton to
Browning, July 18, 1896, *Letters Received,* 8545-1927 Cherokee Nation

175.2, pt. 2, 27701-96; Hoke Smith to Commissioner, July 30, 1896, *Microcopy M606*-89, 241.

10. Kern to Commissioner, September 8, 1896, Francis to Commissioner, September 16, 1896, and Kern to Browning, September 14, 1896, William H. Mills to Commissioner, October 7, 1896, Francis to Commissioner, October 23, 1896, Clifton to Browning, October 28, 1896, and Kern to Commissioner, November 7, 9, 10, December 2, 13, 1896, January 8, 1897, *Letters Received,* 34774-96, 35765-96, 35474-96, 38470-96, 40739-96, 41812-96, 42675-96, 42768-96, 43088-96, 45541-96, 46796-96, 783-97; Kern to Browning, October 1, 1896, and Kern to Commissioner, October 13, 1896, *Letters Received,* 8545-1927 Cherokee Nation 175.2, pt. 2, 37775-96, 39483-96; Browning to Kern, November 9, December 7, 1896, *Letters Received,* 8545-1927 Cherokee Nation 172.2, pt. 4 and pt. 2, respectively; *Report, 1896,* 55.

11. Clifton et al. to Secretary of the Interior, December 9, 1896, *Letters Received,* 8545-1927 Cherokee Nation 175.2, pt. 5, 4393-96; Browning to Secretary of the Interior, September 29, 1896, in pt. 2 of the same file; and Browning to Secretary of the Interior, January 16, 1897, and Browning to Kern, January 19, 1897, in pt. 4.

12. Thomas P. Smith to T. M. Reynolds, April 30, 1896, National Archives Record Group 75, *Letters Sent,* Finance Volume 169: 280A; Robert L. Owen to Hoke Smith, June 25, 1896, Kern to Browning, June 27, 1896, William Owen to Browning, July 20, 1896, William Owen to Secretary of the Interior, August 24, 1896, Kern to Browning, December 30, 1896, and January 25, 1897, *Letters Received,* 24521-96, 24402-96, 28039-96, 32790-96, 93-97, 3697-97.

13. Peggy Mackey and others to Browning, February 2, 1897, John Tyner and others to Browning, February 2, 1897, E. Porter and C. W. Turner to Browning, February 4, 1897, Lewis Tucker and others to Browning, February 8, 1897, Joseph B. Doe to Secretary of the Interior, February 13, 1897, and E. N. Ratcliff to Secretary of the Interior, February 13, 1897, *Letters Received,* 5208-97, 5054-97, 5056-97, 5497-97, 7723-97; Francis to Secretary of War, February 9, 1897, *Microcopy M606*-90, 478.

14. Browning to Dickson, February 10, 1897, *Letters Received,* 8545-1927 Cherokee Nation 175.2, pt. 4; Francis to Secretary of the Treasury, February 17, 1897, *Microcopy M606*-91, 39; *Indian Chieftain,* June 17, 1897; *Fort Smith Elevator,* March 5, 1897.

15. Dickson to Commissioner, March 10, 1897, and Francis to Dickson, March 3, 1897, *Letters Received,* 9317-97, 8791-97; Cornelius N. Bliss to Secretary of War, March 13, 1897, Bliss to Attorney General,

March 30, 1897, and Thomas Ryan to Attorney General, April 20, 1897, *Microcopy M606*-91, 148, 230, 328; *Indian Chieftain,* June 17, 24, 1897.

16. Bliss to Commissioner, May 4, 6, 1897, Bliss to Frank Armstrong, May 4, 1897, and Bliss to Secretary of War, May 6, 1897, *Microcopy M606*-91, 382, 386, 389, 391; *Indian Chieftain,* June 17, 1897.

17. Dickson to Commissioner, March 2, 1897, and W. M. Springer to Browning, April 1, 1897, *Letters Received,* 8753-97, 12556-97; Bliss to Armstrong, May 4, 1897, *Microcopy M606*-91, 386; *Indian Chieftain,* June 17, 1897; Bliss to S. B. Dawes, May 27, 1897, *Microcopy M606*-92, 14.

18. Bliss to Commissioner, May 22, 1897, *Microcopy M606*-91, 462; Thomas P. Smith to Dew M. Wisdom, June 3, 1897, *Letters Received,* 8545-1927 Cherokee Nation 175.2, pt. 4; *Indian Chieftain,* June 24, 1897; James McLaughlin to Secretary of the Interior, June 24, 1897, *Letters Received,* 25559-97; Thomas P. Smith to Wisdom, June 30, 1897, *Letters Sent,* Finance Volume 180: 105B.

19. D. W. Lipe to Thomas Smith, June 19, 1897, and William H. Hudson to Bliss, July 7, 1897, *Letters Received,* 24827-97, 28307-97; Wisdom to Commissioner, July 19, 1897, *Letters Received,* 8545-1927 Cherokee Nation 175.2, pt. 2, 30014-97; statement of J. C. Dannenberg, December 29, 1897, and statement of Cherokee Strip Fund, December 28, 1897, *Freedmen File,* 4868-00, exhibits A and G[2].

20. Receipt, August 15, 1896, and statement of Moses Whitmire, January 3, 1898, *Freedmen File,* 518-00, exhibits A[2] and B[2].

21. Statement of Allen Lynch, January 5, 1898, and contract and statement of Whitmire, August 13, 1896, *Freedmen File,* 518-00, exhibits C[2] and A[2]; W. J. McConnell to Secretary of the Interior, January 24, 1898, Freedmen File, 4868-00, enclosure 24.

22. *Indian Chieftain,* July 8, 1897; statement of Frank J. Boudinot, June 18, December 1, 20, 1897, *Freedmen File,* 4868-00, exhibits E, F, W.

23. Statement of Boudinot, June 18, 1897, December 1, 20, 1897, *Freedmen File,* 4868-00, exhibits E, F, W.

24. Statements of Addie Boudinot, July 19, December 29, 1897, *Freedmen File,* 4868-00, exhibit E and enclosure 33.

25. Statements of G. W. Benge, October 28, November 3, 1897, *Freedmen File,* 4868-00, enclosure 48 and exhibit E[1].

26. McConnell to Secretary of the Interior, January 24, 1898, and statement of Connell Rogers, December 21, 1897, *Freedmen File,* 4868-00, enclosure 24, exhibit D[2], and enclosure 34; *Indian Chieftain,* December 2, 1897.

27. Statement of Charles O. Frye, December 3, 1897, statement of R. L. Fite, December 2, 1897, statements of Albert A. Taylor, December 2, 29, 1897, statement of J. S. Stapler, December 2, 1897, statement of DeWitt Wilson, December 1, 1897, and statement of Lipe, November 29, 1897, *Freedmen File,* exhibits E, L, and N, enclosure 36, and exhibits M, J, and G.

28. Committee report, December 4, 1897, Joint Resolution No. 12, December 4, 1897, McConnell to Secretary of the Interior, January 24, 1898, and reply to joint resolution, December 28, 1897, *Freedmen File,* 4868-00, enclosure 41, exhibit E^3, enclosure 24, and exhibit F^2.

29. Kern to Mayes, December 13, 1897, *Cherokee–Freedmen (Tahlequah); Indian Chieftain,* December 16, 1897.

30. *Indian Chieftain,* December 23, 1897.

31. Lipe to McConnell, December 28, 1897, statement of Jesse B. Raymond, December 27, 1897, McConnell to Secretary of the Interior, January 24, 1898, statement of John P. Welch, December 29, 1897, statement of Daniel Gritts, December 29, 1897, statement of Mayes, December 28, 1897, statement of C. J. Harris, December 30, 1897, *Freedmen File,* 4868-00, exhibits G^2 and H^2, enclosures 24, 38, 35, and 37 and exhibit T^1.

32. McConnell to Secretary of the Interior, January 24, 1898, *Freedmen File,* 4868-00, enclosure 24.

33. "In re Cherokee Freedmen's Roll. Statement of R. H. Kern," *Freedmen File,* 248-99.

34. Kern to Secretary of the Interior, n.d., Wells H. Blodgett to Secretary of the Interior, January 22, 1898, and agreement with J. E. Campbell, n.d., *Letters Received,* 8545-1927 Cherokee Nation 175.2, pt. 5; "In re Cherokee Freedmen's Roll." Wells H. Blodgett, who had withdrawn from the case after the first compromise proposition, supported Kern's statements regarding the early negotiations with Campbell.

35. Mayes to Grover Cleveland, July 18, 1896, *Letters Received,* 8545-1927 Cherokee Nation 175.2, pt. 5; Hoke Smith to Clifton, July 24, 1896, *Microcopy M606*-89, 219.

36. Kern to Secretary of the Interior, August 1, 1896, *Letters Received,* 8545-1927 Cherokee Nation 175.2, pt. 5.

37. Ibid.

38. Affidavit of J. Milton Turner, in Kern to Secretary of the Interior, August 1, 1896, *Letters Received,* 8545-1927 Cherokee Nation 175.2, pt. 5; Turner to Secretary of the Interior, April 18, 1901, in "In re Cherokee Freedmen's Roll"; Clifton to Hoke Smith, August 1,

1896, National Archives Record Group 48, Indian Division, *Special File 29,* Dawes Commission, Box 740.

39. Francis to Kern, September 29, 1897, *Letters Received,* 8545-1927 Cherokee Nation 175.2, pt. 5; statement of E. F. Cunningham, December 1, 1897, *Freedmen File,* 4868-00, exhibit E[1].

40. Statements of Sam Shephard, Cornelia Hill, and Sarah Martin, August 16, 1897, in *Letters Received,* 8545-1927 Cherokee Nation 175.2, pt. 5.

41. Lee Norwood to M. A. Hanna, December 14, 1897, Norwood to Bliss, December 14, 1897, Norwood to the President, December 15, 1897, and R. C. Adams to Secretary of the Interior, December 27, 1897, *Letters Received,* 199-98, 53740-97, 54680-97; various agreements, *Freedmen File,* 4868-00, exhibit BB.

42. Statement of Louis T. Brown, December 28, 1897, *Freedmen File,* 4868-00, exhibit L.

43. Statement of Brown, December 27, 1897, *Freedmen File,* 4868-00, enclosure 102.

44. Statement of Daniel Alberty, December 27, 1897, and statement of Frank Vann, n.d., *Freedmen File,* 4868-00, exhibits K and G.

45. Statement of Cunningham, December 28, 1897, *Freedmen File,* 4868-00, exhibit H[1]; *Indian Chieftain,* December 23, 1897.

46. Statement of Daniel Vann, December 24, 1897, statement of Henry Covel, n.d., statement of Fred and Sophia Schrimscher, January 1, 1898, statement of W. S. Agnew, December 29, 1897, statement of Wilson, December 29, 1897, and statement of Mayes, December 28, 1897, *Freedmen File,* 4868-00, exhibits W, N, Q, D[1], W[1], and E.

47. Statement of M. O. Ghormley, December 29, 1897, and statement of Keys, December 29, 1897, *Freedmen File,* 4868-00, exhibits Y and T. Some individual cases of omissions are related in statement of William Alberty, December 22, 1897, exhibit W; statements of George Vann, December 17, 1897, exhibits J[1] and N[1]; statement of Harrison Foreman, December 27, 1897, exhibit Z. Cases of partial listing of families appear in statement of Nancy Tiner, December 22, 1897, exhibit V; statement of Daniel Vann, December 24, 1897, exhibit W; statement of Clara Vann, December 27, 1897, exhibit G; statement of Cynthia Thomas, December 28, 1897, exhibit P[1]. Cases of the omission of children born after 1880 appear in statement of June Mackey, December 22, 1897, exhibit H; statement of Sarah Thompson, December 22, 1897, exhibit K; and statement of George F. Nave, December 27, 1897, exhibit M[1].

48. Statement of Ellen Lynch, January 1, 1898, *Freedmen File,* 4868-00, exhibit R.

49. Statement of Thompson, December 29, 1897, *Letters Received,* 8545-1927 Cherokee Nation 175.2, pt. 5.

50. Robert F. Thompson to A. C. Tonner, January 18, 1898, *Freedmen File,* 4868-00, exhibit EE.

51. Fred Strout to Cleveland, February 19, 1897, *Special File 29,* Dawes Commission, box 740; statement of George Vann, December 29, 1897, *Freedmen File,* 4868-00, exhibit X.

52. Statement of Dannenberg, December 29, 1897, *Freedmen File,* 4868-00, exhibit A.

53. Statement of Brown, December 27, 1897, and statement of George Nave, December 27, 1897, *Freedmen File,* 4868-00, enclosure 102 and exhibit L^1.

54. Statement of Mayes, January 1, 1898, *Freedmen File,* 4868-00, exhibit S.

55. McConnell to Secretary of the Interior, January 24, 1898, *Freedmen File,* 4868-00, enclosure 24.

56. Kern to R. C. Kerens, January 17, 18, 1898, and Kern to Commissioner of Indian Affairs, February 2, 1898, *Freedmen File,* 4868-00, enclosures 22 and 2; Kern to Secretary of the Interior, May 27, 1896, *Letters Received,* 20371-96; Browning to Kern, June 10, 1896, *Letters Received,* 8545-1927 Cherokee Nation 175.2, pt. 4, contains Kern's early correspondence regarding his representing the freedmen before the Dawes Commission.

chapter 9

THE DAWES
COMMISSION

By the time the payments authorized by the freedman's compromise were completed, the Cherokee Nation was rapidly approaching dissolution. In every Congress after 1870, there had been efforts to establish a territorial government in the Indian Territory, to dissolve the Indian nations, and to open their surplus lands to non-Indian settlement. The opening of the unassigned lands in 1889 and the subsequent formation of the Oklahoma Territory had momentarily satisfied the American demand for more free land. However, other pressures upon the Cherokees and other tribes had developed. Economic development of the West had made it necessary to solve the "Indian problem"; hence for twenty years after the Civil War, there had been a great interest on the part of reformers and others in assimilating the Indians into American society. Lawmakers thought that they had found a way to effect that end in the General Allotment Act of 1887, commonly called the Dawes Act.[1] The act gave the President discretionary powers to make the reservation Indians give up their common title to the land and take allotments of land in severalty. After each Indian had received his allotment, the government, with tribal consent, could sell the surplus lands to non-Indian settlers. Because of the nature of their title to the land, some tribes were excepted. Of those in the Indian Territory, the Cherokees, Creeks, Chickasaws, Choctaws, Seminoles, Osages, Kaws, Quapaws, and Confederated Peorias did not come under the Dawes Act.[2] In 1893 Congress turned its attention toward the Cherokees and other Civilized Tribes; its object was to dissolve the tribal title to the lands and to carry out its allotment policy. An appropriations act of March 3 provided for the establishment of a commission to negotiate with the Cherokees,

Choctaws, Chickasaws, Creeks, and Seminoles for the extinguishment of their tribal title, by cession, allotment, or any other method mutually agreed upon. The ultimate goal was formation of a state or states of the Union embracing the lands of the Indian Territory. Known as the Dawes Commission, it originally consisted of Henry L. Dawes, Meredith H. Kidd, and Archibald S. McKennon.[3] Its work had a profound effect on the history of not only the Cherokees but the Cherokee freedmen as well. As had so often been the case, the freedmen had little to say concerning their future; once more, their destiny became a central issue of debate between Washington bureaucrats and Cherokee politicians. The result of the debate, however, was the freedmen's sharing with the Cherokees in the final division of the national lands and funds.

When the commissioners arrived in the Indian Territory in 1893, they immediately ran into difficulties. The Indians stubbornly refused to cede any land. They were willing, however, to discuss allotment if the land were divided equally among them and if the Indians could be protected from swindlers. Thus, in the name of the United States, the commission offered to give each allottee enough land for a good home, the land to be inalienable for twenty-five years or longer, if agreeable; to remove from the allotments all persons who did not have written authority to be there; to reserve town sites and coal and minerals discovered before allotment for disposal by terms of a special agreement; and finally to settle all claims against the United States and make a per-capita division of all tribal funds, except school funds. The Cherokees complained that many names on the Wallace roll should not be there, and many freedmen claimed that their names should be added. Chief C. J. Harris suggested that the Cherokees might be willing to submit the disputes to the Dawes Commission but that it might take the addition of a Cherokee to the commission to win the people's acceptance of decisions. The Dawes Commission then offered to establish such a board consisting of two of their members and a Cherokee.[4]

To make offers was as far as the Dawes Commission got in the early negotiations. The Cherokees refused to discuss any agreement until the government fully executed the Cherokee Outlet sale agreement of December 19, 1891, in which the United States promised to remove as intruders all persons who were not considered citizens of the Nation and who were there without legal permits. The exception was the freedmen who were in the Nation under the ninth article of the Treaty of 1866. After the agents had ceased issuing prima facie certificates to citizenship claimants on

August 11, 1886, no further action regarding intruders had taken place until August 21, 1888, when the secretary of the interior recognized a decision by Cherokee authorities against a citizenship claimant as fixing the claimant's status. However, because many claimants had apparently been induced to enter the Nation in good faith, believing they had rights, and in view of the former policy of issuing prima facie certificates, the secretary had directed that those rejected should be given a reasonable time and opportunity to dispose of the property they could not remove. In September rejected claimants were notified that they had six months to dispose of their improvements to Cherokee citizens, but the Cherokees refused to buy the improvements, hoping to take them over at the end of six months. Thus in 1889 the secretary extended indefinitely the time given the intruders to sell their improvements and remove.[5]

The Cherokees harassed those they considered intruders, began ejection proceedings against them, and put their improvements up for sale. Some who had received the per-capita payment subsequent to the Wallace roll had their improvements sold. J. Milton Turner sought the aid of the commissioner of Indian affairs in their behalf but was told to have them appeal to the agent. In 1891 trouble erupted in Cooweescoowee District when the public officials tried to sell freedman improvements. Some Cherokees simply moved in and took over other freedmen's improvements. In 1892 John Mason, an adopted white citizen, moved onto the improvements of Maryland Beck, who had occupied his farm near Vinita for twenty-five years. A Cherokee, Albert Morris, moved onto the improvements of Henry Thornton and Moses Ross near Hudson. All of these men had been enrolled by Wallace and had received per-capita payments, but the Cherokees, not recognizing that roll, considered them intruders. In Saline District, similar trouble erupted between Cherokee citizens and Jess Vann, Dan Henry, Tom Mayfield, Charley Mayfield, and other freedmen.[6]

The act that had created the Dawes Commission also provided for the appraisement of intruders' improvements, work that was undertaken in the summer of 1893, apparently because the Dawes Commission believed that the intruder issue was a major obstacle to their negotiations. A commission, including a Cherokee, Clem V. Rogers, was to make a list of intruders and to appraise the improvements they had occupied before August 11, 1886, which the Nation would purchase. Those who had taken occupancy after that date would not be paid. A Cherokee census of 1893 formed the Cherokees' basis of judgment regarding intruders. In 1892 they had submitted a list of 5,273 people whom they considered intruders. Although U. S. officials doubted the fairness of this list, it and others the Cherokees had submitted from time to time as a result of their census were used by the commission. Chief Harris tried but failed to include some freedmen whose names appeared on the Wallace roll. Without those names, the final list contained 2,858 heads of families, representing an estimated 8,526 persons. Only 385 of the heads of families submitted claims for compensation before the appraisers.[7] The rest were apparently new arrivals in the territory.

The freedmen were concerned over the Cherokees' actions, for they felt that the names of some who claimed citizenship would be listed as intruders. As their attorney, R. H. Kern had asked Secretary Hoke Smith to prevent their removal until the freedmen's case, then pending, came before the court of claims. Of the seventy freedmen listed in the reports of appraisement, nearly half were denied reimbursements for the improvements they occupied. Many claimed to have citizenship; some were married to freedwomen; some, who had been in the Nation for many years, were denied payment because they had moved to new locations in the Nation after August 11, 1886. In view of Kern's appeal, Commissioner D. M. Browning refused to consider individual cases until the court of claims rendered a decision.[8]

Besides the seventy freedman cases, the appraising board submitted to the commissioner of Indian affairs the names of ninety-four freedmen who claimed rights in the Nation under the ninth article of the Treaty of 1866. These were subsequently found to be on either the authenticated Cherokee roll or the Wallace roll. When the commissioner's staff examined the work of the appraisers, they found that some listed as intruders were indeed married to Cherokee freedwomen on one of the rolls and insisted that the removal of their families would violate those families' rights. Thus the secretary suspended the cases of all freedmen listed as intruders until the status of the families of those persons could be decided. By an act of March 2, 1895, Congress delayed removal of any of the intruders until January 1, 1896. By that time, other measures had been introduced to delay the removals further, and the department took no steps while they were pending. Nevertheless the Cherokees had evicted some freedmen whose names appeared on the Wallace roll.[9]

The Dawes Commission's hopes that attention to the intruder problem would make the Cherokees more inclined toward negotiation had failed. Angered at the Indians' resistance, the commissioners urged Congress to dissolve the tribes without the Indians' consent. Between 1893 and 1896, their annual reports, their appearances before congressional committees, and their public statements presented what they purported to be a realistic picture of affairs in the Indian Territory but which, in fact, reflected the arguments of land-hungry white citizens and politicians. They denounced the alleged exploitation of full-blood Indians by the mixed bloods who held political power in the nations. They told how white intruders suffered inconveniences, stressed the great number of violent crimes in the territory, and emphasized the lack of development of its natural resources.[10] Under weltering fire of public opinion, the Indian nations were doomed, yet the Indians steadfastly refused to negotiate.

As a result Congress took further steps against them. In 1895 it authorized a survey of the lands of the Five Civilized Tribes. Then on June 10, 1896, it authorized the Dawes Commission to hear and determine the applications of all persons, including freedmen, who might apply for citizenship in the Indian nations and to enroll the citizens. The act confirmed the existing rolls of the several tribes, and the commission was charged with correcting the rolls by adding those whose names were omitted by fraud or wrong. Their roll was to be considered correct. Any tribe or person who did not agree with the decision of the tribal authorities or the Dawes Commission had sixty days to appeal to the U. S. district court. Finally the act declared it the duty of the United States to establish a government in the Indian Territory to "rectify the many inequalities and discriminations now existing in said Territory, and afford needful protection to the lives and property of all citizens and residents thereof."[11]

The commissioners invited the Cherokees to negotiate the matter of citizenship with them. They set up headquarters in Vinita and published the rules of procedure. All claimants to citizenship would apply in writing and present evidence in affidavits, a copy of which would be submitted to the chief. He was given thirty days to inform the commission of the Cherokees' decision on the application. As soon as it became known that the Dawes Commission would enroll the freedmen, inquiries came to the Indian Office from R. H. Kern (then engaged with Clifton in making their roll) and others concerning appointment as attorney to represent the freedmen before the commission. Always the opportunist,

Kern wanted the secretary of the interior to withhold five dollars from each freedman's payment under the Kern-Clifton roll to pay lawyers' fees for representing the freedmen before the Dawes Commission.[12]

On June 7, 1897, Congress made further inroads on the Indians' resolve by giving the U. S. courts exclusive jurisdiction over all civil and criminal cases arising in the territory after January 1, 1898, if the tribes did not make agreements with the Dawes Commission. The laws of Arkansas and of the United States were extended to all residents in the territory, irrespective of race. The act also clarified the act of June 10, 1896, by construing "rolls of citizenship" to mean the last authenticated rolls approved by the councils of the tribes, the descendants of those on the rolls, and those later added by the councils, the courts, or the Dawes Commission under the act of 1896. All other names were open to investigation by the commission. Anyone whose name was stricken by the commission had the right to appeal to the U. S. courts. Finally no acts passed by the national councils of the tribes were valid unless approved by the President of the United States.[13]

The Cherokees viewed the act as an obstacle to agreement, for it broke former assurances by the commission that the Cherokees could continue their government until allotment. Instead the act struck down nearly one-half of the Cherokee government. The Cherokees insisted on their "immemorial right of self-government," which had been recognized by the Treaty of 1835. The only reason that they had negotiated with the commission was not that they wanted to hold lands in severalty but that they knew that the popular voice would secure the opening of the Indian Territory to non-Indian settlement. They wanted "to avoid some of the bad results of a 'division in severalty' and to connect with any new title some of the advantages of a title in common." Under the Cherokee system, all citizens were assured as much property as they could improve, but under allotment in severalty, the Cherokees predicted a monopoly of real estate among the Cherokees similar to that among the whites. They felt that they were "required by superior power to choose between parting forever with this Government of their fathers, which they think is so deserving of respect on its own merits, and parting with whatever other rights and privileges which are equally theirs" as the Dawes Commission and the Congress might request. To make an agreement under the present conditions of duress would be to concede the authority of the United States to abolish their government at will.[14]

In early October 1897 it appeared that the Dawes Commission, busy to that time with other matters, was about to begin work on the Cherokee freedman rolls. Kern asked to represent the freedmen before the commission, for he believed that he was more familiar than anyone else with the facts related to litigation and roll making in behalf of the freedmen. His request was granted in early November. The commission wanted to use the evidence taken by the Kern-Clifton commission, but they found that after the roll had been approved, the evidence, which had been stored, was stolen and never recovered. Freedmen who had failed to get their names on former rolls tried through attorneys and personal appeals to put their cases before the Dawes Commission, apparently realizing that this would probably be their last chance. Letters came from as far away as Pocatello, Idaho, and one freedman at Muskogee offered to pay the secretary of the interior twenty-five dollars for each of his family members to be placed on the rolls.[15]

Meanwhile the freedmen of the Naiton were divided into factions, apparently as a result of the controversy over lawyers' fees in the freedman's compromise. In January 1898 Moses Whitmire and George W. Lane went to Washington as representatives of the freedmen. Some, however, did not recognize them, and the executive committee of the freedmen called a convention to elect a new delegation. They organized the Cherokee Freedmen Protective Association and elected Richard Foreman as trustee in Whitmire's place. However the Indian Office refused to recognize Foreman as trustee since no litigation was pending on behalf of the freedmen and the legal status of trustee had ceased when the freedmen had won their case before the court of claims in 1896.[16]

The Cherokees hoped to have the Kern-Clifton roll set aside, under the belief that the Dawes Commission could make a correct roll of the freedmen. They estimated that the former commission had allowed a thousand names to be placed on the roll by fraud perpetrated through the rule of allowing one freedman to testify for another. Many from Texas and Arkansas, they charged, had got on the rolls by that method. Inspector William J. McConnell had received large amounts of testimony to that effect during his investigation of the Clifton commission's work and the subsequent payments. In Washington the Cherokee delegation took the charges to Capitol Hill in the spring of 1898, adding that some well-known black Cherokee citizens had been left off the Kern-Clifton roll. The delegation recognized that it would be difficult to recover the large sum of money disbursed under the Kern-Clifton roll, but they stressed the importance of a corrected roll in the event of subsequent disbursements of funds or division of lands.[17]

By that time, all of the tribes except the Cherokees had agreed to negotiate with the Dawes Commission, had appointed delegations, and had drawn up agreements. The Seminoles had ratified theirs, but the others were apparently doomed to failure. Thus Congress took the matter in hand, and on June 28, 1898, passed a bill commonly known as the Curtis act, which ended tribal tenure without the Indians' consent and provided for allotment of lands in severalty. Section 21 of the act confirmed the Cherokee authenticated roll of 1880 as the basis for the enrollment of the Cherokees, with the exception of the freedmen. The Dawes Commission was charged with making a new roll of freedmen in strict compliance with the decree of the court of claims of February 3, 1896. During the deliberation on the Curtis bill, an amendment that would have confirmed the Kern-Clifton roll as the basis of the new roll had failed.[18] Its failure was a victory for the Cherokees if anything in the Curtis act could be called a victory.

On the other hand, rejection of the Kern-Clifton roll boded ill for some of the freedmen. All manifested a strong interest in the upcoming work of the Dawes Commission. Some hired lawyers, who fired questions at the commissioners. Would those who had been enrolled previously be required to appear again? If so, could they do it immediately? Could they select their allotments of land immediately? How many acres would they be allotted? Parents were concerned about getting their children enrolled and having allotments assigned them to ensure their posterity. Opportunists also came out in force. One man reported to be traveling around the Cherokee Nation claimed to have authority from the United States to prosecute the cases of the freedmen whose names appeared on older rolls but not on the Kern-Clifton roll. He was allegedly charging 35 percent of the payments retrieved.[19]

Since the Curtis act abolished their institutions, the Cherokees realized that they must negotiate as favorable an agreement as possible. In late December 1898 the Dawes Commission met with a Cherokee commission. Kern appeared before them and appealed for fairness regarding the freedmen, insisting on their share of any funds paid and property to be divided. The Cherokees wanted to limit the freedmen to allotments of forty acres, "regardless of its character, location or value, including present residences and improvements," and to bar the freedmen from participating in the per-capita distribution of funds. Kern argued that that was not enough. The Cherokees pointed out that the Choctaw agreement had provided for only forty acres for each freedman, yet the Choctaw allotments, per capita, would be larger than those of the Cherokees. The Cherokee commissioners were not united in their view. One mixed-blood member felt that the Treaty of 1866 had to be upheld and the freedmen granted rights of native Cherokees, while a full-blood member argued that the freedmen enjoyed only political rights. The Dawes Commission urged allotments of eighty acres to each citizen and an equalization of allotments, afterward, with land and money.[20]

Concerned at the prospect of receiving allotments of only forty acres, some freedmen called a meeting in early January 1899 at Goose Neck Bend and elected W. H. Vann to submit specific written questions concerning the freedmen to the Dawes Commission: Would not the forty-acre provision violate the Treaty of 1866? Was an agreement containing such a provision likely to be made? Would a delegate from the freedmen be heard, or would their interests be properly cared for by the Dawes Commission? As negotiations proceeded, the freedmen continued to call on Kern, who promised the commission to use his influence to help obtain the ratification of any agreement that was fair to the freedmen. Early in 1899, as a compromise, the two commissions finally agreed not to discriminate against the freedmen in the allotment of land. Kern asked Moses Whitmire to use his influence in favor of the agreement when it came up for ratification by the Cherokee voters. Anxious concerning what the agreement meant to them, the freedmen once more showered the Dawes Commission with questions and made plans for a convention in June to discuss the tactics by which they could protect their interests. They asked the secretary of the interior to write a letter to the freedmen at large to be read at the convention and to indicate what action they should take.[21]

Cherokee opinion split concerning the proposed agreement. Wolfe Coon and George Sanders, members of the Cherokee commission, had refused to sign it. They argued that in signing the Treaty of 1866 and in amending the Cherokee constitution, the Cherokees had guaranteed the freedmen their civil rights but had not intended to give the freedmen right to Cherokee land or to national assets. Sanders and Coon refused to accept the freedmen as equals in property rights with the original owners of the soil.[22] In early 1899 the agreement was ratified by the Cherokees by a majority of about two thousand votes, but it failed ratification by Congress.

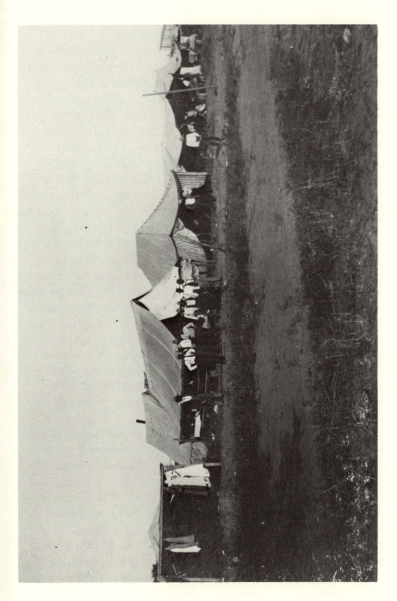

Freedman camp at Fort Gibson during enrollment before the Dawes Commission. Courtesy of the Oklahoma Historical Society.

The question of freedman allotments became a political issue in the
Cherokee elections of 1899. Chief S. H. Mayes was once more accused
of collusion with Kern in the freedman compromise of 1896. He denied
it in the newspapers, insisting that he had been the one who had brought
charges of corruption against Kern in the summer of 1896. The Downing
party dropped Mayes and selected T. M. Buffington as its candidate for
chief. The full bloods, who had generally voted against ratifying the
agreement, chose Wolfe Coon to head the National ticket. The Downing
party candidates won the election. The National party partisans later
charged that the Downing party advocates had at first publicized the
original idea of excluding the intermarried whites and limiting the freedmen to allotments of forty acres as if that would be the final agreement.
The Downing party commissioners had taken credit for the final agreement, the Nationals charged, to get the freedmen's and adopted whites'
votes in ratifying the agreement. There were three thousand such votes,
more than the margin by which it carried. Once it failed in Congress,
the Downings made the agreement part of their platform to ensure the
black and white votes in the summer elections. According to the Nationals,
the black vote was insignificant in six of the nine legislative districts, and
the white vote controlled elections in the others. They further charged
that to ensure winning the election, the Downings had resorted to buying votes, permitting unqualified voters to vote, posting armed men at
polling places, giving whiskey away, and causing fights. One man was
killed near a polling place in Tahlequah District, an election judge was
stabbed in Sequoyah District, and another man was stabbed at a voting
place in Delaware District.[23]

The Nationals wanted to contest the election but claimed that they
could get no cooperation from the Downing men in office to perform
the acts necessary to get the evidence before the National Council.
Since there were no national courts any more, they could not force
them to act. They therefore appealed to the secretary of the interior
to step in. The Downing men had charged the full bloods with being
against progress, while the Nationals claimed that the Downing men
wanted to retain power simply to get rich at the expense of the people.
Frank J. Boudinot, attorney for the full-blood Cherokees, asked the
government to take charge of all Cherokee affairs and treat the property as a private estate to be settled. Some Cherokees feared an outbreak of violence at the meeting of the National Council and appealed

to the government to abolish tribal government altogether and appoint a business committee to handle the Cherokees' affairs.[24]

While controversy over the election raged in the fall of 1899, the Dawes Commission began preparations to make a roll of the Cherokee freedmen under the requirements of the Curtis Act, but the commissioners disagreed concerning what the act had authorized them to do. Chairman Tams Bixby believed that they were empowered to enroll all persons whose names appeared on the authorized roll of 1880 and all others who claimed Cherokee citizenship under the ninth article of the Treaty of 1866. Members A. S. McKennon and T. B. Needles, however, believed that it was their duty to enroll only the freedmen whose names appeared on the roll of 1880 and their descendants born after that date and living on May 3, 1894. Commissioner W. A. Jones believed that since the Kern-Clifton roll had been made under the direction of the department and had been approved, all freedmen whose names appeared on it were entitled to enrollment as Cherokee citizens and that their right could not be questioned by the Cherokee Nation or the Dawes Commission on any ground except fraud. Those freedmen and their descendants who did not appear on the Kern-Clifton roll but could prove their rights under the ninth article of the Treaty of 1866 should be enrolled.[25]

Secretary Ethan A. Hitchcock did not agree. If Congress had intended for the Dawes Commission to use the Kern-Clifton roll, he said, Congress would have made it plain. Instead it had called for a new roll in compliance with the court of claims decision in the Moses Whitmire case, which established the roll of 1880 as a basis for deciding who was to receive a per-capita payment. The enrolling commissioners were permitted to consult other rolls for information, but the right of any person to be enrolled depended upon the appearance of his name or that of his ancestor on the authenticated roll of 1880. Dissatisfied with this construction of the law, Bixby argued that the government had made two rolls already. Had the commissions carried out their trust, no new legislation would have been needed, and it would have been necessary only to add the names of children and to strike the names of the dead. The framers of the new legislation, Bixby argued, must have known the history of litigation between the Cherokee Nation and the freedmen, and had they intended only those on the Cherokee roll to be enrolled, the language of the act would have said so. In Bixby's view, justice demanded that all freedmen claiming a share in the Cherokee Nation have a fair and impartial hearing. Failure to give it would result in endless lawsuits and make final settlement of Cherokee affairs almost impossible. To prevent the Dawes Commission roll from joining the Wallace roll and the Kern-Clifton roll, nothing should be left undone to establish a record that would stand against just criticism, no matter what its source. Apparently persuaded by such arguments, in May 1900 Secretary Hitchcock changed his mind and interpreted the law to authorize the Dawes Commission to make a roll that included the names of all Cherokee blacks who had been liberated or had formerly been free blacks in the Cherokee Nation and had returned to the Nation within six months after the Treaty of 1866. Yet a few days later an appropriation bill reasserted that the commission had authority to receive applications of only those freedmen and their descendants who had been recognized as citizens of one of the Five Civilized Tribes.[26]

In the spring of 1900, the Dawes Commission advertised appointments for enrolling the Cherokees. Freedmen seeking to have their names put on the rolls flocked to the enrollment sites. Those on Big Creek met at Hudson, elected Nelson Grubbs to represent them with the Dawes Commission and sent six questions that they wanted answered: Would the commission hear an attorney in behalf of the freedmen? Which roll would be the basis for determining Cherokee freedman citizenship? Would the freedmen be able to use blacks as witnesses for them, and if so, how many would be allowed and who would pay them? Would one freedman be able to witness for another? Would their representative be allowed to sit with the commission during the taking of testimony? And was there any hope for freedmen whose names did not appear on any freedman rolls?[27] The questions indicated that all of the rumors and false starts concerning enrollment of the freedmen had left the blacks uninformed about their affairs.

The Cherokees felt relieved that the Kern-Clifton roll had been excluded as a base and that the Dawes Commission was to start over because they believed that the names of twenty-six hundred freedmen and their descendants could be dropped from the rolls. They believed that if the commissioners were as careful about accurate evidence concerning the freedmen as they were concerning the Indians, hundreds would be eliminated.[28]

Enrollment sessions had been scheduled at Muldrow, Fort Gibson, Pryor Creek, Vinita, Welch, Bartlesville, Nowata, Oolagah, Claremore, Catoosa, Chelsea, and Tahlequah. But because of the great number of Cherokees who appeared at the sessions and because of the great number of contested cases among the freedmen, the Dawes Commission once more decided to put off enrollment of the freedmen until the spring of 1901 and proceed with that of the Indians. They notified the freedmen to watch the papers for announcement of appointments in the spring. Meanwhile the National Council of 1900 provided for the appointment of three Cherokee attorneys to represent the Nation at all enrollment sessions, to protest against the enrollment of all freedmen they believed were not entitled to rights, and to subpoena witnesses on behalf of the Nation. When, in February 1901, the Dawes Commission announced the dates for the freedman enrollment, the Cherokees still felt assured that many names could be purged from the rolls and sought to appoint attorneys who had unbesmirched private and public records or who had not been involved in representing freedmen. Chief T. M. Buffington filed a formal protest against the involvement of Robert H. Kern, whom the Cherokees held most responsible for the fraud concerning the Kern-Clifton roll. But it was difficult to find people who had not been touched in some way by freedman affairs during the few preceding years. When Buffington appointed L. B. Bell as principal attorney for the Nation, some Cherokees criticized Bell because of statements he had allegedly made years earlier as a member of council: that for so much money and ginger, he could secure the passage of citizenship cases. Said one newspaper, "With Hooly Bell for the Cherokees and Bob Kern for the freedmen the average citizen will not be much surprised if another batch of Kansas negroes are admitted to citizenship."[29] The Cherokees also appointed J. S. Davenport and W. W. Hastings, whose name had been mentioned during the scandals concerning the Clifton commission's work.

Since 1898 the Cherokees had been operating under the provisions of the Curtis Act because no acceptable agreement had been reached. On March 1, 1901, Congress ratified an agreement that the Cherokee delegation in Washington had made with the United States in April 1900. However, when the agreement was submitted to the Cherokee voters on April 29, 1901, it was defeated.[30] It was charged that influential Cherokee citizens had worked to defeat ratification because of their interests in large tracts of land. There were others who wanted all Cherokee children born after April 1, 1900, to be enrolled and to receive allotments, for which the agreement did not provide.

On March 3, 1901, Congress passed an act that made the rolls taken by the Dawes Commission final when they were approved by the secre-

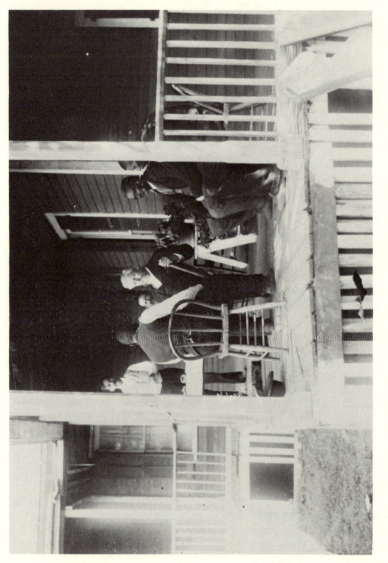

Dawes Commission enrolling Cherokee freedmen. Courtesy of the Oklahoma Historical Society.

tary of the interior. If the secretary and the tribes could not agree upon
a date for closing the rolls, the secretary was to set the date. The act also
made acts of the Cherokee and Creek councils subject to approval by the
President of the United States.[31]

The Dawes Commission began enrolling the freedmen on April 1, and
the work went well at first. Most of those appearing at the first sessions
were on the authenticated roll of 1880. Those who were not residing in
the Cherokee Nation on June 28, 1898, the date of the Curtis Act, were
placed on a doubtful list. Cherokee attorneys Bell, Hastings, and Davenport gathered official records concerning the denial of citizenship to
certain intermarried blacks and sought out witnesses to assist in identify-
ing the freedmen who had rights in the Nation. The freedmen were represented by the firm of Mellette and Smith of Vinita, who had succeeded
Robert H. Kern, but some people sought the aid of local attorneys in
the towns where the enrollment was taking place, while others employed
J. P. Bledsoe, J. R. Sequitchie, A. S. McRea, and L. T. Brown as agents.
The freedmen showed up with large forces of witnesses, some of whom
the Cherokees accused of being professional witnesses. Harry Still, Crap
Lynch, L. D. Daniels, Allen Lynch, Moses Hardrick, Moses Riley, Sheep
Jim Alberty, Nelson Murrell, and others allegedly had testified in from
two hundred to four hundred cases. Such men, the Cherokees charged,
gave perjured testimony, coming before the commission day after day,
"with their pockets full of bribes and their mouths full of lies." One
editor in the Nation wrote, "With this enrollment closes, perhaps, the
darkest chapter in the history of a most unfortunate and beleaguered
people. Let the curtain fall just as soon as possible."[32]

If the Cherokee Nation protested the enrollment of a freedman, his
name was put on a doubtful roll and his case laid aside to be considered
later. Supplemental and rebuttal testimony for and against the numerous
contested claimants was so great that it quickly became impractical to
hear it all, so the commission decided to put off hearing further testimony until the fall of 1901. By July 1 there were 3,150 freedmen on
regular cards, 2,428 on doubtful cards, and 285 on rejected cards. Shortly
thereafter the commissioners left the field and went to Muskogee to com-
pile their work. By that time, they had taken over forty thousand pages
of typewritten testimony and expected to take at least that much more
before the first of September, when the commissioners would again begin
taking rebuttal testimony in the doubtful cases.[33]

Soon after the freedman enrollment had begun, Chief Buffington learned that A. S. McKennon, in disagreement with Chairman Tams Bixby, interpreted the law to confirm the roll of 1880 as the basis for the enrollment. He appealed for a change in instructions to the Dawes Commission, arguing that the instructions then in effect only tempted many poor blacks who had no chance of enrollment to apply anyway and opened the door to perjury and fraud. When, by mid-May, the department had not acted on the chief's request, counsel for the Cherokees complained that the Cherokees were spending thousands of dollars defending against claimants not on the roll of 1880 and asked for prompt action. Failing on that front, the Cherokees turned to another. In August 1901 attorneys John Thomas and William T. Hutchings, acting for the Cherokee Nation, served notice on the Dawes Commission that Bell, Hastings, Davenport, and Buffington would file suit against the commission in the U. S. court at Muskogee, asking Judge Joseph A. Gill to enjoin the commission from hearing the application and from enrolling Ann Tucker, Pollie Boyd, Fannie Vann, Jonas Brown, John Porter, Dempsy Wright, Nancy Ross, Adeline Hampton, Alexander Claggett, Martha Gales, Isaac Chism, and their descendants and to enjoin it from hearing applications or enrolling any other black or freedman claiming citizenship in the Cherokee Nation born prior to 1880 but not appearing on the roll of 1880. Some freedmen whose applications had been heard appeared on the Wallace roll and others on no roll at all. The Cherokees hoped that a ruling in their favor would be the first step in striking the names of all freedmen from the tribal rolls. While they expected to win the cases named in the suit, they planned to file another to attack the rights of the freedmen as a body to any interest in the national estate if the present suit did not accomplish it.[34]

To the Cherokees' disappointment, the court adjourned without rendering a decision on the injunction. And the Dawes Commission, which believed the ruling would go in their favor, continued enrolling freedmen and hearing doubtful cases, holding sessions in September at Fort Gibson and in October at Vinita. Once again the Cherokees attacked their work, charging perjury of witnesses. According to the Cherokee press, blacks came by train from the states to testify concerning the residency of many of the freedmen who had resided outside the Nation since 1866. In the election of 1867, there had been fewer than a hundred votes cast in Cooweescoowee District, the press charged, but if one could believe the testi-

mony before the Dawes Commission, there had been several hundred
freedmen voters in the district at the time.[35]

In late October Judge Gill rendered a decision in favor of the Cherokees. He said that the law of May 31, 1900, clearly authorized the Dawes
Commission to hear only the cases of those listed on the roll of 1880. The
Cherokees' complaint, Gill said, demonstrated sufficient facts to support
allegations that the commission had gone beyond its authority, and he
therefore issued a temporary order to restrain it from proceeding other
than the law directed. The decision did one thing: it opened the courts
of the United States to the Cherokee Nation, through which it could sue
to restrain illegal actions by the Dawes Commission, a statutory body
having certain statutory duties. As they continued to hear cases during
the next few months, the Dawes commissioners made memoranda of
the applications of such freedmen that came within the provisions of
Judge Gill's opinion.[36]

The secretary ordered the commission to close applications for freedmen on July 1, 1902. In order to complete the enrollment, in early
March the commission notified all those listed as doubtful that it would
continue hearing such cases until May 31. After that the cases would
be considered complete, and the commission would begin to render its
decisions.[37]

On July 1, 1902, the Cherokees made another agreement with the
United States. Ratified by the people on August 7, the agreement provided for closing the rolls on September 1, 1902, the rolls to be made in
strict compliance with the Curtis Act. The Dawes Commission was authorized to receive applications during September and October for the enrollment of infants who had been born to enrolled citizens before September 1, 1902. All applications were to cease on October 31. No allotment
of land or other tribal property was to be made to any person or the
heirs of any person whose name was on the roll but who died before
September 1. As soon as practicable after the approval of each citizen's
enrollment by the secretary of the interior, the citizen was to receive an
allotment of land equal in value to 110 acres of the average allottable lands
of the Cherokee Nation. When the citizen selected his allotment, he was
to designate as a homestead a tract equal in value to forty acres of the
average allottable lands; the homestead would be nontaxable and inalienable during the lifetime of the allottee, not to exceed twenty-one

years from the date of the allotment certificate. The allottee's remaining land was inalienable for five years from the date of the allotment certificate. No lien for debt could be placed on the homestead, and the other lands could be incumbered in no way for five years after ratification of the act.[38]

Besides the usual problems of enrollment, there had also been the difficult problem of obtaining affidavits to ascertain the births and deaths that had occurred since enrollment began. In the fiscal year ending June 30, 1902, the commission received affidavits concerning 115 freedman births: 64 listed on regular cards, 49 on doubtful, and 2 on rejected. The total freedmen applications heard to that date included 3,271 on regular cards, 2,883 on doubtful, and 375 on rejected; 98 cases had been suspended by temporary injunctions. A few applications were taken between July 1 and September 1. The Cherokee attorneys had exhausted the funds appropriated by the council for procuring witnesses but felt satisfied that they had obtained the evidence necessary to prosecute the cases still pending. On December 5, 1902, the Dawes Commission sent the commissioner of Indian affairs a schedule containing the first 1,006 freedman names, which were approved by the secretary of the interior on December 23.[39]

For the most part, enrollment was finished. Now it was time for recriminations. The Keetoowah Society of full bloods met in convention in late November 1902 to plan legal action to deny the right of adopted whites and freedmen to participate in the division of lands and moneys of the Nation. The full bloods, who were the mainstay of the National party, dragged out the freedman's compromise of 1896 once more and asked ex-Chief S. H. Mayes to explain his role in it, for it was rumored that Mayes and W. W. Hastings, who had been serving as one of the Cherokee attorneys, had an arrangement whereby one or the other of them would get the nomination of the Downing party in 1903. Mayes came forth with his usual denial of complicity, saying that if he had known what the document would cost the Cherokees, he never would have signed it. His supporters believed that he had cleared himself and had pointed the finger at the real culprits, who deserved to be consumed forever by "the fires of hell." He claimed to have been duped by his advisers, but there still remained the question in many Cherokees' minds of who the robbers of the national treasury were and why they were permitted to commit the act under his administration. The report of the investigation of fraud by Indian Inspector William J. McConnell

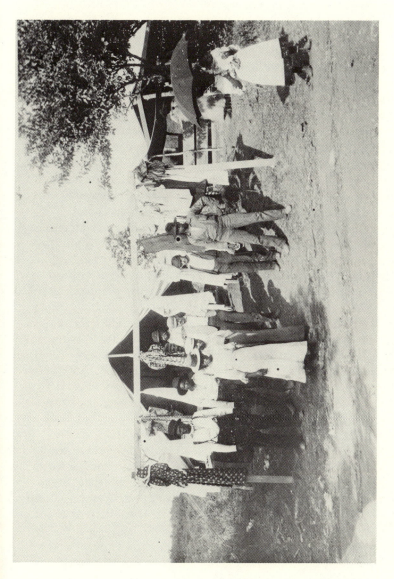

Freedman "store" at Fort Gibson during enrollment. Courtesy of the Oklahoma Historical Society.

was published by Mayes's enemies, who called his explanation "a puny
effort to shift the responsibility onto some one else." Mayes, more than
anyone else, they said, had been in a position to guard the interests of
the Cherokees and should have the decency in 1903 "to keep his mouth
shut." They called Robert Kern "the king bee robber around whom the
little Cherokee bees hovered to get their share of the stolen 'honey'" and
predicted denials similar to Mayes's from all who were involved. As the
Downing nominating convention approached in the spring of 1903, newspapers reprinted McConnell's report in which he called the handling of
the Kern-Clifton enrollment and the Cherokee appropriation of money
to equalize payment to the freedmen "a disgraceful affair." He concluded,
"Men high in the councils of the Cherokee Nation, as well as others trusted
by the Cherokee freedmen and free colored persons, have grossly and out-
rageously betrayed the confidence of their too confiding people."[40]

When the Downing party held its nominating convention at Tahlequah
in early June, it ignored the people who had been involved in the freedman's compromise and nominated W. C. Rogers for chief and D. M.
Faulkner for assistant chief. But the National party sympathizers did not
cease criticism on the issue of the compromise. They published statements
of Frank J. Boudinot and of Mrs. E. C. Boudinot in which they incrimi-
nated Mayes and other Downing party officials. One editor charged that
had the Curtis bill been delayed five years, there would not have been anything left for the Cherokees to divide; it was the Downing party politicians
whose signatures appeared on the acts that had reduced the Nation. Those
same men now backed Rogers for chief, and their money would elect and
control him. Rogers, the editor said, was reputed to be an honest man. On
the other hand, Levi Cookson, the National nominee for chief, was known
to be one.[41]

A speech by Cookson in 1902 had left little doubt where he stood: "For
myself, when the citizenship roll is finally and forever closed, and even the
Secretary of the Interior is unable to add to it, when the status of the
Freedmen is settled by the courts and finally disposed of, when a decision
has been rendered in regard to the claims of the Delawares, and an accounting had with the government as to the amount of money justly due us
from the United States, then, and not until then, shall I cease opposing
allotment. My opposition is founded on the principles of eternal justice
to all men irrespective of race or color, and sober reflection will convince
anyone that all I ask of the United States government is fair and reasonable.

. . . Again our white friends should have a little patience with us. There is
something pathetic in the extinction, the blotting out from the earth of a
nation."[42] After all of the accusations and counteraccusations, Rogers won
the election in August 1903 by 145 votes, as did a majority of Downing candidates for election to the National Council, committed, among other things,
to an equal division of lands among the bona fide citizens of the Nation
and to a course of action that would not prolong the settlement of national
affairs.

While the months of election-year rhetoric had passed, the outstanding
cases of enrollment had been pursued. The Cherokees had succeeded in obtaining temporary injunctions against the Dawes Commission, preventing
it from enrolling freedmen in many cases on the ground that the commission was authorized to determine only those freedmen on the roll of
1880 and was not authorized to hear any other cases. Early in 1903, some
of the affected freedmen felt that Mellette and Smith had been dragging
their feet in getting the injunction lifted, and a group headed by Samuel
Webber and G. W. Lynch sought new council in St. Louis. In actuality,
however, Mellette had been working hard to get the matter resolved. The
Cherokees, though, were dragging their feet because they had been dissatisfied that the injunction was only temporary rather than final. However, in August 1903, Judge Charles Raymond of the Western District
of the Indian Territory rendered a decision that cleared the way for enrolling those against whom injunctions had been obtained. According
to the judge, the directive of the court of claims in the Whitmire case,
in compliance with which the Dawes Commission members were to
operate, was aimed at finding which freedmen were on the roll of 1880
in order to make a per-capita payment. The Dawes Commission, on the
other hand, had engaged in enrolling the freedmen for the purpose of
dividing the property of the Cherokee Nation and he felt that they should
operate under the ninth article of the Treaty of 1866. He therefore dissolved the injunction and dismissed the suit of Chief T. M. Buffington
and others against Tams Bixby and the Dawes Commission. Thus the
enrollment continued, and by late October, there were 3,320 freedmen
on regular cards, 3,108 still on doubtful cards, 381 on rejected cards, and
115 injunction cases on no Cherokee roll, a total of 6,924 freedmen.[43]

An appropriations act of April 21, 1904, provided for the dissolution
of the Dawes Commission on July 1, 1905, and, more significantly, removed all restrictions on the alienation of lands of all allottees of the

Five Civilized Tribes who were not of Indian blood, with the exception of minors' lands and the homestead allotments of all classes of citizens. The act freed 313,500 acres for sales in the Cherokee Nation. The freedmen were free to sell their surplus land as soon as they obtained title to it. By the fall of 1904, land speculators were making arrangements with the freedmen to buy their land when it became available.[44]

Throughout 1904 the Dawes Commission continued taking testimony and making decisions on pending enrollment cases. The Cherokees charged that because of a "herd" of standing witnesses, it was impossible for the commissioners to decide whom to believe. The commissioners were not familiar with the topography and listened to Calvin Goins tell how, before the war, large steamboats plied the waters of Lee's Creek, a shallow mountain stream, carrying race horses to a plantation with a brick house and stable and to a fine brick hotel in the mountainous areas of the sparsely populated Sequoyah District. James Alberty testified that in 1866 he had seen an applicant crossing a ferry across the Arkansas on his way to Muskogee to get tobacco, although there was no town of Muskogee until the early 1870s. Other witnesses did not know the names of streams near where they claimed to have lived or the type of houses their masters had lived in. They did not know when they were born, when they were married, or when their children were born, but they could swear definitely that they returned to the Nation in 1866. The Cherokees charged that the freedmen had formed a secret organization through which they furnished witnesses for freedmen and intimidated witnesses for the Cherokees. On June 30, 1904, there were still 3,188 cases pending. Most of those remaining by the end of the year presented difficult questions to decide. On November 22, in the case of Lemuel Welcome, the secretary of the interior held that a freedman could not confer citizenship by marriage. In view of that decision, the Dawes Commission disposed of 151 applicants to rights by intermarriage. During the next few months, the Cherokees gathered evidence in the territory and in Kansas and elsewhere to fight the enrollment of the remaining doubtful freedmen.[45]

On July 1, 1905, the Dawes Commission ceased to exist. At that time the secretary of the interior had approved the enrollment of 3,923 freedmen and denied it to 1,204; 1,055 cases were pending before the department, and 776 cases were pending before the commission.[46] The work of completing these cases fell to Tams Bixby, whose title was commissioner to the Five Civilized Tribes.

According to a provision of the Curtis Act, the governments of the Five Civilized Tribes were to end on March 4, 1906. As the date drew near, it became apparent that all affairs of the nations would not be completed. A bill to provide for the final disposition of tribal affairs was introduced in Congress, but when it became apparent that the bill would not pass in time, Congress passed a joint resolution that extended the tribal governments until March 4, 1907.[47]

A congressional act of April 26, 1906, extended the time of application for enrollment in the Five Civilized Tribes to December 1, 1905. Bixby was to consider all applications made before that time. For ninety days after the approval of the act, applications were to be received for enrollment of children who were minors living on March 4, 1906, and whose parents had been enrolled as members of the tribes or had applications for enrollment pending at the time of approval of the act. Provision was made for those who failed to receive land because it was all allotted; they were to receive from the tribal funds an amount equal to twice the value of the amount of land deficient. The date for closing the rolls was set as March 4, 1907, after which no applications would be considered. The act defined the Cherokee freedman roll as a list of "only such persons of African descent, either free colored or the slaves of Cherokee citizens and their descendants, who were actual personal bona fide residents of the Cherokee Nation August eleventh, eighteen hundred and sixty-six, or who actually returned and established such residence in the Cherokee Nation on or before February eleventh, eighteen hundred and sixty-seven." That provision, however, did not prevent the enrollment of any person who had made application to the Dawes Commission or its successor and had been adjudged entitled to enrollment by the secretary. The act provided for the continuation of the tribal government under limited conditions until tribal affairs were closed.[48] This important piece of legislation cleared the way for making the final rolls and finally settling the affairs of the Cherokee Nation.

In November 1906 a Senate select committee went to the Indian Territory to investigate conditions in relation to the act of April 26. The interviewers took testimony from J. B. Wilson, a freedman from Lenapah who asked the senators to intervene in behalf of the estimated two thousand freedmen who had been enrolled by Wallace and the Clifton commissions but had been rejected by the Dawes Commission. D. H. Wilson, an attorney from Vinita, presented a petition from these freedmen and expressed the complaints of citizen freedmen whose names had appeared on the Cherokee authenticated roll of 1880 but not on the Wallace or Clifton roll and had been denied their per-capita payments. The committee heard from other noncitizen blacks, but their main concern regarding the freedmen of the Indian Territory was whether further restrictions should be removed from sales of their allotments. On the basis of testimony received, the committee recommended, among other things, that restrictions be removed from even the homestead allotments of the freedmen and intermarried whites. It is apparent from the testimony that the Indian leaders, governmental officials, and whites who hoped to be involved in the economic development of the territory felt little moral responsibility for protecting the freedmen.[49] Unfortunately for the freedmen, in 1908 Congress followed the committee's recommendation. By that time, allotment was completed, and the freedmen had become citizens of the new state of Oklahoma.

By July 1, 1906, practically all of the land of value in the Cherokee Nation had been allotted or chosen as tentative selections by undetermined applicants for enrollment. Citizens stood ready to take allotments as a result of enrollment of minor citizens under the act of April 26, but they waited for the disposition of claimants whose tentative selections included good land. On March 4, 1907, the citizenship cases closed. Four hundred claimants as Cherokees by blood and freedmen and about fifteen hundred intermarried claimants were rejected, throwing a considerable area open to allotment. The Department of the Interior directed tentative selections to be made for the minors, but no absolute rights were recognized, for on March 1, 1907, Congress had authorized the filing of a suit before the court of claims to determine their right to participate in the allotment of land. By June 30, 1907, 4,208 Cherokee freedmen had received allotments totaling 409,500.26 acres, and the 749 freedman minors had tentative allotments. About half of the enrolled citizens of the Cherokee Nation had had homestead and surplus allotment deeds prepared, but very few deeds for Cherokee freedmen had been recorded and delivered.[50]

By the time the rolls closed, there had been 53,724 applications for enrollment in the Cherokee tribe. When the decisions were finally made, there were 41,798 enrolled citizens of the Cherokee Nation, 4,924 of them freedmen. As the roll was adjusted through corrections and by an act of Congress in 1914, there were 41,835 citizens, of whom 4,919 were freedmen.[51]

The work of enrolling the freedmen and making allotments had been tedious, and it had been accompanied by contested allotments and appeals for rehearings. Mistakes were made, and home places of some were allotted to others. Land speculators had flocked to the Indian Territory to prey on the ignorant. By the time the rolls were closed, some allottees had already fallen victim to graft and fraud and, through bad business deals, had lost what they had gained through dissolution of the Cherokee Nation.

After the work of the Dawes Commission was over, there were many freedmen who had lived in the Cherokee Nation for decades and whose names had appeared on either the Wallace roll or the Kern-Clifton roll, or both, but whom the commission had refused to enroll, for the most part because they had returned to the Nation too late. Their struggle for rights to share in the Cherokee national assets continued past Oklahoma statehood. These freedmen had nearly succeeded in 1905 and 1906 in getting a rehearing of their cases on the basis of their previous enrollment. They had the test case of Mary A. Riley and her descendants brought before the secretary in June of 1905. Assistant U. S. attorney General Frank L. Campbell ruled that it was within the power of the secretary to order a rehearing. In October it was reported that the secretary would investigate the entire matter of the Kern-Clifton roll. The Cherokees wondered why the roll, which they considered inaccurate, had not been investigated years earlier. They were now distrustful of the investigation, supporting it only if the government's intention was to purge it of fraudulent names, not to leave them or add more.[52] However, the act of April 26, 1906, had defined the freedmen eligible for enrollment as those who had returned within the time set by the Treaty of 1866. If a freedman had been listed on both the Wallace roll and the Kern-Clifton roll and could not show that he had returned in time, he was not eligible for enrollment by the Dawes Commission.

In the summer of 1907, the excluded freedmen asked the secretary to suspend the process of removing them from their homes and improvements until the court of claims rendered a decision in a suit filed by Moses Whitmire, trustee for the freedmen. The secretary's office requested the names of the people and information about their holdings, the filings for allotment thereon by enrolled citizens, the percentage of the freedmen still in possession of the lands, and the extent to which the enrolled citizens would be deprived of their allotments if the removal of unsuccessful claimants was discontinued.[53] Meanwhile litigation was slowed down by the death of Whitmire.

The freedmen appointed Jacob B. Wilson of Lenapah to replace Whitmire and to institute proceedings to prevent discriminatic 1 in allotments and per-capita distributions of Cherokee national fun ls. On May 6, 1908, Wilson filed a supplemental petition in the court of claims in behalf of the estimated twelve hundred excluded freedmen. On March 29, 1909, the court confirmed Wilson's appointment, decided that it had the power to inquire whether its judgment had been executed in the case of the Kern-Clifton roll, and found that the injunction placed on the United States and the Cherokee Nation by its decree of 1896 had been violated by the Dawes Commission. This decision opened the door for about fourteen hundred freedman applicants to prove that they were unjustly rejected by the Dawes Commission and were therefore entitled to allotments. Their success would, in effect, reopen the Cherokee rolls. The government sought but failed to have the decision set aside.[54]

On June 29, 1909, the superintendent of the Union Agency was instructed, pending adjudication of the case, that the unallotted lands occupied and claimed by the freedmen whose case was pending should be withheld from sale until he received further instructions. The freedmen were not to be disturbed in their occupancy of the land, provided the occupied lands did not exceed in value the amount to which they would be entitled to receive as their allotments if they were enrolled. In most cases, the land originally occupied by many of the rejected freedmen had been allotted to others and patents had been issued. That land had passed beyond the jurisdiction of the department. It could not maintain the freedmen in possession of land from which they had been ejected by state authorities. Because of the large number of people who had claims and because of the delay of the government in removing the claimants from the land, while at the same time denying their right to it, the court of claims reexamined legislation enacted since 1890 and on February 20, 1911, held that any person whose name appeared on the Kern-Clifton roll was entitled to allotment of land and a share in the distribution of funds, even if his name did not appear on the Dawes Commission roll.[55]

The Cherokee Nation and the United States appealed to the Supreme Court, which reversed the lower court's decree on January 29, 1912. It ruled that the Kern-Clifton roll, made by administrative officers, had been superseded by the Dawes Commission roll. The Dawes Commission had the authority and jurisdiction to determine who was to be enrolled. Congress did not accept the Kern-Clifton roll as an authentic identification of the individual freedmen. Its accuracy had been questioned. Had it been reported to the court and its integrity established by the judgment of the court, Congress could not have ignored it. Thus, the Supreme Court reversed the decision of the court of claims with directions to dismiss the supplemental petition.[56]

Many of the freedmen had been permitted to make tentative allotment selections while their cases were pending settlement, and in 1912 some were still in possession of the land they claimed. They had been protected by departmental orders since 1909. Now that the Supreme Court had rendered its decision, protection was removed. The superintendent of the Union Agency was directed to place allottees whose allotments were in the possession of rejected freedmen in possession of their property.[57]

Under a special jurisdictional act of 1924, the Cherokee Nation sought, through the court of claims, to recover the funds paid in 1897 to those whose names had appeared on the Kern-Clifton roll but not on the final roll. In a decision of April 5, 1937, the court held that the Supreme Court had made a distinction between the purposes of the Kern-Clifton roll and the Dawes Commission roll and that the former was a legitimate roll for the distribution of funds.[58]

In 1951 the excluded freedmen filed suit before the Indian Claims Commission, which had been established in 1946 to hear claims of tribes against the United States before that date. In 1952 the United States argued for dismissal on the grounds that the petitioners did not constitute a "tribe, band or other identifiable group of American Indians" and that the claims were individual rather than tribal or group. The Indian Claims Commission denied the request to dismiss on the belief that a hearing was necessary to determine if the claims were individual. The case was decided in 1960 after hearings were held in Tulsa. By that time several similar claims had been heard by the commission, which had held uniformly that they were individual and not group claims, and the commission therefore had no jurisdiction. So it was in the Cherokee freedman case, decided on December 28, 1961. The freedmen appealed to the court of claims, which in 1963 remanded the case to the Indian Claims Commission for further proceedings to consider whether the freedmen, by virtue of having been paid under the Kern-Clifton roll, were not entitled to a share in funds and not in allotments. The Cherokee Nation had won a judgment in 1961 which said that it was entitled to recover $14,789,476.15, less allowable offsets, for the Cherokee Outlet, and Congress appropriated the money. In 1962 Congress authorized the per-capita distribution of the funds, except nearly $1.5 million set aside to pay any offsets. The excluded Cherokee freedmen sought to intervene in the case, but it had already gone out of the commission's jurisdiction. In the process of the Cherokee case, it was found that the case did not cover two million acres, and when the Cherokees filed a separate claim for recovery of payment for that land, the commission invited the freedmen to intervene in the case so that it could rule on their claim. This the freedmen did, and in 1970, the commission dismissed their motion for summary judgment; its decision was affirmed by the court of claims.[59]

Thus, the work of the Dawes Commission had far-reaching social and legal implications. While the hopes of the excluded freedmen had been blasted, most of the freedmen whose names had appeared on the final rolls had looked forward to ownership of their land and to becoming citizens of the United States and the new state of Oklahoma. However, long before Oklahoma became a state on November 16, 1907, there were indications that their lot in their new citizenship status was not to be a happy one. Some began to fear—and subsequent events bore out the fear—that their condition as American citizens would be far worse than it had been as Cherokee citizens.

NOTES

1. A thorough study of Indian policy following the Civil War is Henry E. Fritz, *The Movement for Indian Assimilation, 1860-1890* (Philadelphia: University of Pennsylvania Press, 1963).

2. Lawrence Mills, *Oklahoma Indian Land Laws* (St. Louis: Thomas Law Book Company, 1924), 335-339.

3. United States Commissioner to the Five Civilized Tribes, *Laws, Decisions, and Regulations Affecting the Work of the Commissioner to the Five Civilized Tribes, 1893-1906* (Washington, D.C.: Government Printing Office, 1906), 11-12. Other members of the Dawes Commission included Frank C. Armstrong (1895-1905), Tams Bixby and Thomas B. Needles (1897-1905), Clifton R. Breckenridge (1900-05), and William E. Stanley (1903-04).

4. Report of the Commission to the Five Civilized Tribes, 54th Cong., 1st sess., *Senate Document 182,* 86-87.

5. Ibid.; *Annual Report of the Secretary of the Interior for the Fiscal Year Ended June 30, 1896* (Washington, D.C.: Government Printing Office, 1897), 78-79.

6. G. W. Lynch to John W. Noble, May 2, 1891, Moses Ross to Commissioner of Indian Affairs, August 20, 1891, Maryland Beck to T. J. Morgan, May 17, 1892, Henry Thornton to Noble, May 14, 1892, Leo Bennett to Commissioner, September 7, 1892, and R. V. Belt to Ross, September 20, 1895, National Archives Record Group 75 (Records of the Bureau of Indian Affairs), *Letters Received,* 16188-91, 31139-91, 18748-92, 18379-72, 32961-92, 35226-95; Noble to J. Milton Turner, May 4, 1891, National Archives Microfilm Publications, *Microcopy M606* (Letters Sent by the Secretary of the Interior)-72, 8; *Indian Chieftain,* May 28, 1891; Belt to Thornton, May 23, 1892, and Belt to Bennett, July 5, 1892, National Archives Record Group 75, *Letters Sent,* Land Letter Book 238: 58; and Land Letter Book 240: 189; E. S. Adair to C. J. Harris, June 15, 1892, Indian Archives Division, Oklahoma Historical Society, *Cherokee–Freedmen (Tahlequah).*

7. *Indian Chieftain,* May 4, 1893; Marcus D. Shelby to Harris, July 19, 1893, Indian Archives Division, Oklahoma Historical Society, *Cherokee–Citizenship (Tahlequah);* Shelby to Harris, July 22, 1893, Shelby to D. M. Browning, July 22, 1893, and Acting Secretary to Commissioner, July 28, 1893, *Letters Received,* 28155-93 and enclosures; Thomas P. Smith to Secretary of the Interior, May 27, 1895, *Letters Sent,* Land Letter Book 306: 379; *Annual Report of the Commissioner of Indian Affairs to the Secretary of the Interior* (Washington, D.C.: Government Printing Office, 1893), 79-80.

8. R. H. Kern to Hoke Smith, June 14, 1893, *Letters Received,* 22720-93; National Archives Record Group 75, *Reports on Appraisement of Improvements of Cherokee Intruders, 1893-95;* Browning to Houston West, October 16, 1893, and Browning to Lee J. Norwood, June 19, 1894, *Letters Sent,* Land Letter Book 267: 36, 282: 397.

9. Thomas P. Smith to Secretary of the Interior, May 27, 1895, Browning to Dew M. Wisdom, December 10, 1895, and Smith to Wisdom, October 30, 1895, *Letters Sent,* Land Letter Book 306: 379, 320: 95, 317: 367; Ross to Belt, August 20, 1895, *Letters Received,* 35226-95.

10. Angie Debo, *And Still the Waters Run* (Princeton: Princeton University Press, 1972), 23-24; Loren N. Brown, "The Dawes Commission," *The Chronicles of Oklahoma* 9 (March 1931): 85-86.

11. *Laws and Decisions,* 12-13; Debo, *And Still the Waters Run,* 32; Brown, "Dawes Commission," 88-89.

12. *Annual Report, 1896,* 151-153; Brown, "Dawes Commission," 89-90; Kern to Secretary of the Interior, May 27, 1896, Browning to Kern, June 10, 1896, and Browning to C. Claggett, July 24, 1896, *Letters Received,* 20379-96, 8545-1927 Cherokee Nation 175.2, pt. 4 and pt. 2 respectively.

13. *Laws and Decisions,* 13-14; Brown, "Dawes Commission," 100-101.

14. D. W. Bushyhead et al. to Tams Bixby et al., October 28, 1897, Indian Archives Division, Oklahoma Historical Society, *Dawes Commission—Cherokee.*

15. Kern to Chairman of the Dawes Commission, October 3, 1897, Kern to Dawes Commission, October 27, 1897, abstract of reply, November 3, 1897, Reeves and Tschudy to A. L. Aylesworth, November 6, 1897, Wiley Haynes to Secretary of the Interior, December 4, 1897, and Anthony Crafton, December 7, 1897, *Dawes Commission—Cherokee;* A. C. Tonner to Bixby, October 26, 1897, *Letters Sent,* Land Letter Book 366: 12.

16. W. H. Vann to Cornelius N. Bliss, January 28, 1898, and J. E. W. Nelson to Commissioner, February 2, 1898, *Letters Received,* 6073-98, 6158-98; Tonner to Wisdom, April 29, 1898, *Letters Sent,* Land Letter Book 379: 7.

17. *Indian Chieftain,* December 23, 1897; W. A. Duncan et al. to Secretary of the Interior, March 11, 1898, *Dawes Commission—Cherokee.*

18. Debo, *And Still the Waters Run,* 32-33; *Laws and Decisions,* 20; *Congressional Record,* May 23, 1898, pt. 6, 5582-5583; 46 *Court of Claims* 227.

19. Francis R. Brennan to Bixby, August 11, 1898, Eliza Hardrick to Secretary of the Interior, November 14, 1898, Gus Buffington to Secretary of the Interior, August 15, 1898, and Thomas Ryan to J. George Wright, August 27, 1898, *Dawes Commission—Cherokee.*

20. Proceedings, Joint Session of the United States and Cherokee Commissions, December 21, 1898, *Dawes Commission—Cherokee.*

21. Vann to Dawes Commission, January 2, 1899, Vann's credentials, January 4, 1899, Kern to A. McKennon, December 24, 1898, Kern to Moses Whitmire, January 16, 1899, Kern to Dawes Commission, January 16, 1899, Willie Starr to Henry L. Dawes, January 24, 1899, Louis T. Brown to Dawes Commission, January 28, 1899, and L. A. Hughes to Secretary of the Interior, May 9, 1899, *Dawes Commission—Cherokee.*

22. *Claremore Progress,* January 28, 1899; Frank J. Boudinot to Secretary of the Interior, October 14, 1899, Indian Archives Division, Oklahoma Historical Society, *Cherokee—Elections,* 926-A.

23. *Indian Chieftain,* May 18, 1899; Boudinot to Secretary of the Interior, October 14, 1899, *Cherokee–Elections,* 926-A.

24. Boudinot to Secretary of the Interior, October 14, 1899, and Sam H. Benge to Commissioner, October 21, 1899, *Cherokee–Elections,* 926-A.

25. Tonner to Secretary of the Interior, September 21, 1899, Bixby to Secretary of the Interior, September 12, 1899, and W. A. Jones to Secretary of the Interior, November 3, 1899, National Archives Record Group 48 (Records of the Department of the Interior, Office of the Secretary), Indian Territory Division, *Chickasaw Freedmen,* box 393 (60b), 2729-99, 3226-99; *Indian Chieftain,* October 12, 1899. The Chickasaw freedmen file, hereafter cited as *Freedmen File,* was apparently mislabeled, for most of the documents it contains relate to the Cherokees. Documents cited subsequently are from box 393 unless otherwise indicated.

26. E. A. Hitchcock to Acting Chairman of the Commission to the Five Civilized Tribes, November 23, 1899, *Dawes Commission–Cherokee;* Bixby to Willis Van Devanter, April 7, 21, 1900, *Freedmen File,* 1585-00, 1586-00; Hitchcock to Acting Chairman of the Commission to the Five Civilized Tribes, May 11, 1900, Ryan to Commissioner, May 12, 1900, *Letters Received,* 23584; *Eighth Annual Report of the Commission to the Five Civilized Tribes to the Secretary of the Interior for the Fiscal Year Ended June 30, 1901* (Washington, D.C.: Government Printing Office, 1901), 22-23.

27. *Eighth Annual Report,* 23; *Cherokee Advocate,* June 8, 1900; Elick Freeman to the Dawes Commission, August 3, 1900, *Dawes Commission–Cherokee.*

28. *Cherokee Advocate,* August 11, 1900; *Indian Chieftain,* September 27, 1900.

29. *Eighth Annual Report,* 23; T. B. Needles and C. R. Breckenridge to Dawes Commission, August 6, 1900, *Dawes Commission–Cherokee; Cherokee Advocate,* August 25, 1900; Senate Bill No. 9, November 28, 1900, Indian Archives Division, Oklahoma Historical Society, *Cherokee Volume 311;* Edward M. Dawson to Commissioner, January 5, 1900, *Letters Received,* 1406-01; *Indian Chieftain,* February 7, March 14, 1901: Bixby to T. M. Buffington, March 20, 1901, Buffington to Bixby, March 25, 1901, Bixby to Buffington, April 3, 1901, *Cherokee–Freedmen (Tahlequah); Cherokee Advocate,* April 6, 1901; Bixby to Secretary of the Interior, March 19, 1901, *Freedmen File,* box 392 (60a); *Webbers Falls Monitor,* March 29, 1901. When Kern heard of the renewed accusations against him in making the roll, he wrote and published a lengthy defense of his and J. Milton Turner's actions during the enrollment and

asked that it be filed with Inspector McConnell's report of 1898, which charged Kern with fraud. Kern to Hitchcock, April 23, 1901, Hitchcock to Kern, April 25, 1901, Jones to Secretary of the Interior, July 16, 1901, Hitchcock to Commissioner, July 9, 1901, "In re Cherokee Freedmen's Roll. Statement of R. H. Kern," *Freedmen File.*

30. *Eighth Annual Report,* 9-10; Joseph B. Thoburn and Muriel H. Wright, *Oklahoma: A History of the State and Its People* (New York: Lewis Historical Publishing Company, 1929), 2: 617-618.

31. *Laws and Decisions,* 36; Thoburn and Wright, *Oklahoma,* 2: 618-619.

32. *Indian Chieftain,* April 11, July 4, 1901; L. B. Bell, W. W. Hastings, and J. S. Davenport to J. T. Parks, June 11, 1901, *Cherokee—Freedmen (Tahlequah).*

33. *Indian Chieftain,* July 4, 11, 1901; *Annual Reports of the Department of the Interior for the Fiscal Year Ended June 30, 1902* (Washington, D.C.: Government Printing Office, 1903), 34; *Eighth Annual Report,* 25-26; Needles and Breckenridge to Commission to the Five Civilized Tribes, July 17, 1901, *Dawes Commission—Cherokee.*

34. T. M. Buffington to William M. Springer, April 10, 1901, Springer to Hitchcock, April 15, 1901, Springer to Van Dervanter, April 19, 22, 1901, Springer to Secretary of the Interior, April 20, May 16, 1901, *Freedmen File; Annual Reports, 1902,* 121-123; *Indian Chieftain,* August 15, 22, 29, 1901; *Cherokee Advocate,* August 31, 1901; Needles to Secretary of the Interior, August 16, 1901, W. A. Jones to Secretary of the Interior, August 23, 1901, and Breckenridge to Secretary of the Interior, September 9, 1901, *Freedmen File,* box 392 (60a).

35. *Annual Reports, 1902,* 35; *Indian Chieftain,* September 5, October 3, 17, 1901; Bell, Hastings, and Davenport to Parks, October 4, 1901, *Cherokee—Freedmen (Tahlequah).*

36. Case No. 4424, U. S. Court for the Northern District of the Indian Territory, October 26, 1901, P. C. Knox to Secretary of the Interior, and Jones to Secretary of the Interior, *Freedmen File,* box 392 (60a); Commission to the Five Civilized Tribes to Commissioner, October 29, 1901, *Letters Received,* 61671-01; *Indian Chieftain,* October 31, 1901; *Annual Reports, 1902,* 121-123, 35.

37. *Annual Reports, 1902,* 35; Bixby to Secretary of the Interior, January 31, 1902, National Archives Record Group 48, Indian Territory Division, *General Incoming Correspondence, July 1898-April 1907,* file 2824, box 358 (40a).

38. *Laws and Decisions,* 71-72, 73-74.

39. *Annual Reports, 1902,* 35, 36-37; Bell, Hastings, and Davenport to

Buffington, October 22, 1902, in *Cherokee Advocate,* November 15, 1902; *Cherokee Advocate,* November 1, 1902; *Indian Chieftain,* November 6, 1902; Ryan to Commissioner, December 23, 1902, *Letters Received,* 75641-02. The Dawes Commission filed monthly reports and sent schedules of persons enrolled during the month. The reports are in *General Incoming Correspondence,* (1900 File 3203), Dawes Commission Monthly Reports, boxes 403-405, renumbered 68a-68c, respectively.

40. *Cherokee Advocate,* November 22, 1902; *Sallisaw Star,* November 28, 1902, February 7, 13, 20, May 29, 1903.

41. *Sallisaw Star,* June 5, July 17, 1903; Elzie Ronald Caywood, "The Administration of William C. Rogers, Principal Chief of the Cherokee Nation, 1903-1907," *The Chronicles of Oklahoma* 30 (Spring 1952): 31.

42. *The Daily Chieftain,* September 11, 1903; Caywood, "Administration of Rogers," 31.

43. Tonner to Secretary of the Interior, February 10, March 30, 1903, J. C. McReynolds to Secretary of the Interior, August 31, 1903, and Jones to Secretary of the Interior, December 4, 1903, *Freedmen File,* box 392 (60a); *Indian Journal,* August 28, 1903; *Cherokee Advocate,* August 29, 1903; *Indian Chieftain,* October 22, 1903.

44. *Laws and Decisions,* 81-82; Debo, *And Still the Waters Run,* 89, 114; *Purcell Register,* September 24, 1904.

45. "General Brief on Part of the Cherokee Nation," National Archives Record Group 75, *Central Classified File,* 1909-103416 Cherokee Nation 053, 1904-71708; Frank L. Campbell to Secretary of the Interior, January 31, 1905, and Bixby to J. Blair Schoenfelt, February 9, 1905, *Dawes Commission—Cherokee;* accounts of James M. Keys, February 28, April 19, 1905, *Cherokee—Freedmen (Tahlequah): Report of the Commission to the Five Civilized Tribes to the Secretary of the Interior for the Year Ended June 30, 1905* (Washington, D.C.: Government Printing Office, 1905), 23.

46. *Report of the Commission, 1905,* 26-27.

47. Thoburn and Wright, *Oklahoma,* 2: 622-623.

48. *Laws and Decisions,* 88-89; Thoburn and Wright, *Oklahoma,* 2: 263. The Cherokee property was not finally disposed of until 1914, when on June 30, the tribal government ceased, except for the chief, who remained in office only to sign deeds.

49. 59th Cong., 2d sess., *Senate Report 5013,* pt. 1, v, 205-212, 214-217, 410-419.

50. *Reports of the Department of the Interior for the Fiscal Year Ended June 30, 1907* (Washington, D.C.: Government Printing Office, 1907), 2: 299, 301, 304-305, 317, 321.

51. Ibid., 2: 290-292; Debo, *And Still the Waters Run,* 47.

52. 10 *Indian Claims Commission* 109, in Indian Archives Division, Oklahoma Historical Society, *Section X;* Frank Pierce to Attorney General, May 6, 1911, *Central Classified File,* 5-1 Five Civilized Tribes, Cherokee—Enrollment—Moses Whitmire; *Laws and Decisions,* 183-184; *Cherokee Advocate,* October 28, 1905.

53. C. F. Larrabee to Commissioner to the Five Civilized Tribes, June 27, 1907, *Letters Sent,* Land Letter Book 983: 202; Samuel A. Putnam and Charles Poe to Commissioner of Indian Affairs, July 26, 1907, James Colbert to Commissioner, July 29, 1907, Putnam and Poe to Acting Commissioner, July 31, 1907, and Acting Commissioner to Colbert, August 9, 1907, *Letters Received,* 65262-07, 66720-07, 66371-07; Eufaula *Indian Journal,* July 19, 1907.

54. *Cherokee Nation* v. *Whitmire* 223 *U. S.* 108; Jesse E. Wilson to Attorney General, November 12, 1908, Frank Pierce to Cora Alberty, March 4, 1911, and John Q. Thompson to Secretary of the Interior, June 12, 1911, *Central Classified File,* 5-1 Five Civilized Tribes, Cherokee—Enrollment—Moses Whitmire; 44 *Court of Claims* 253; 46 *Court of Claims* 227; Oklahoma City *Daily Oklahoman,* May 5, 1909.

55. C. F. Hauke to Secretary of the Interior, May 17, 1911, Pierce to Clerk of the Court of Claims, June 19, 1909, and Hastings to Secretary of the Interior, October 19, 1910, *Central Classified File,* 5-1 Five Civilized Tribes, Cherokee—Enrollment—Moses Whitmire; 46 *Court of Claims* 227; 10 *Indian Claims Commission* 109.

56. *Cherokee Nation* v. *Whitmire* 223 *U. S.* 108; 10 *Ind. Cl. Comm.* 109; *Indian Chieftain,* February 2, 1912.

57. 10 *Indian Claims Commission* 109; Samuel Adams to Commissioner to the Five Civilized Tribes, March 1, 1912, *Central Classified File,* 5-1 Five Civilized Tribes, Cherokee—Enrollment—Moses Whitmire.

58. 85 *Court of Claims* 76; 10 *Indian Claims Commission* 109.

59. 10 *Indian Claims Commission* 109; 13 *Indian Claims Commission* 33; Norman A. Ross, ed., *Index to the Decisions of the Indian Claims Commission* (New York: Clearwater Publishing Company, 1973), 67-68.

chapter 10   RETROSPECTION

The closing of the Cherokee tribal rolls marked the end of a forty-year struggle for rights by the Cherokee freedmen. During that time, many blacks who had been associated with the antebellum Cherokee Nation were denied access to the courts, the political system, and the public schools. They cultivated land, but their rights to their improvements were never secure. The freedmen citizens fared somewhat better; they had access to the courts, sat on juries, served as elected officials, had some security in their improvements, and had access to limited school facilities. While most of the freedmen ultimately triumphed in their struggle for a share in the tribal lands and funds, their victory was not one that they could savor. The price they had exacted from the Cherokees was too great.

It may be impossible to estimate finally how much the freedmen's quest for rights contributed to the destruction of the Cherokee Nation, but it was great. To the Cherokees, it represented a constant problem and diverted their attention from other matters at crucial times in Cherokee affairs. During Reconstruction the Cherokees found themselves beset by pressures from an American public bent on developing the West. Railroad companies lobbied for generous land grants, for the establishment of a territorial government in the Indian Territory, and for the opening of surplus Indian lands to non-Indian settlement. To many Americans, the government was too slow in extinguishing the Indian title to the lands, and they became squatters on Cherokee lands. The Cherokees were powerless to remove these intruders, yet the Cherokee courts had no jurisdiction over them. Beset by these powerful, destructive forces from without, the Cherokees were faced as well with the serious domestic problem of the freedmen's status.

Cherokee efforts to deal with the freedmen transformed the domestic matter into a federal issue. To the Cherokees the Treaty of 1866 was clear in its stipulations regarding the freedmen. The Indians no doubt made errors in judgment of individual cases, and they flatly ignored the postwar circumstances that had prevented the freedmen from returning to the Nation within the six-months' limitations of the treaty. U. S. officials, however, were more sympathetic toward the blacks and refused to remove them. Had the Cherokees adopted those who had returned too late during the early years of Reconstruction, the freedmen's status may have remained a domestic issue. Instead, as the intruder problem grew and the freedman issue grew with it, definition of citizenship rights in the Cherokee Nation became a serious point of contention between the Cherokee Nation and the United States.

In order to relieve the pressure on their legislative and judicial systems, the Cherokees created special courts of commission on citizenship, which the United States refused to recognize. While the freedmen campaigned for their rights, with little success, through protests, appeals, memorials, and delegations to the National Council and to Washington, the Cherokee Nation and the United States carried on a legal tug of war that resulted in a sapping of Cherokee national strength and a weakening of Cherokee resolve, yet failed to settle the matter of citizenship rights. What may have been sympathy for the excluded freedmen on the part of individual bureaucrats was transformed into federal policy, usually overt in its objective, aimed at subversion of the autonomy of the Cherokee Nation and dissolution of the tribal status.

Only after the judicial machinery of the U. S. courts and the power of Congress came to their aid in the late 1880s and early 1890s did the freedmen make significant progress toward securing their rights. The Cherokees, maintaining that adoption had given the freedmen the right only to occupy the land and not to have title to it, were once more forced to divert the same kind of time, energy, and money toward thwarting the freedmen that they had spent in attempting to deal with the citizenship problem in the 1870s and 1880s. The freedmen's success in their suits against the Nation was another blow to the Cherokees, who, upon removal to the West, had never thought it possible that they would have to share with any other people the lands that they had bought with the cession of the lands of their fathers. The freedmen's success ultimately cost the Cherokees millions of acres of tribal lands and millions of dollars from the tribal treasury. But that was not all. It raised the specter of the citizenship question once more and resulted in the hated Wallace roll and Kern-Clifton roll.

Throughout this second phase of their struggle, the freedmen once more were pawns. Represented by a trustee, they little understood the legal processes undertaken in their behalf, and they were represented by men whose motives ranged from altruism to opportunism. The freedmen had tried to use political force to secure their rights, but there is little evidence that any executive officers of the Nation had favored them except Lewis Downing, William P. Ross, and Dennis W. Bushyhead. Now, however, they had become a wedge between Cherokee political parties at a time when national unity was important. The unpopularity of the Wallace and Kern-Clifton rolls among the Cherokees, who regarded only their censuses as accurate rolls of the freedmen, resulted in scandal and rumors of fraud in relation to the compilation of the government rolls. The freedman wedge divided the Cherokees and caused a loss of faith in public officials, thereby further weakening the Nation in the face of federal pressures.

Once Congress intervened in behalf of the freedmen, federal policy was aimed not only at defining which freedmen were citizens but also at ensuring that the freedmen received an equitable share of the common property and funds upon dissolution of the Nation. When it fell upon the Dawes Commission to make a new roll in preparation for allotment, the Cherokees once more found it necessary to come forth with time, energy, money, and legal know-how to attempt to prevent the enrollment of freedmen and other persons whom the Cherokees had not recognized as citizens. To the Cherokees, the freedmen's thirty-year investment in the Nation did not weigh as much as the centuries of Indian rights to the land, but their opposition to allotment was futile.

The freedman victory was filled with ironies. In their struggle for rights, the freedmen had helped undermine the Cherokee Nation. Subsequent events would demonstrate that the freedmen's lot in Cherokee society was better than their lot in American society.

American citizenship brought for the freedmen only slight advantages in educational matters. Limited educational facilities for the freedmen had existed in the Cherokee Nation for nearly forty years before Oklahoma statehood. The United States had assumed some control of the educational systems in the Indian Territory under the general provisions of the Curtis Act of 1898. On November 4, 1898, Secretary Cornelius N. Bliss issued regulations, which were amended in 1899, establishing the office of Superintendent of Schools for the Indian Territory, whose duty it was to inspect, organize, and reorganize schools and to make the changes necessary to remedy any defects. In each nation was established the office of school supervisor, charged with visiting and inspecting the schools and reporting statistics concerning teachers and enrollment. The superintendent was authorized to open as many day schools as funds permitted.[1]

The primary schools serving the freedmen were located in areas of the densest freedman population. During the 1890s complaints had frequently come from those who had no schools in their areas. Many on the Wallace roll were not recognized by the Cherokees and were refused school privileges, but the United States had refused to interfere. The government would not go to any expense to educate any member of the tribe. That was up to the Cherokees. During 1892 to 1896 there were fourteen freedman primary schools. In 1900 there were fifteen. Average daily attendance was only 948, yet there were over 2,000 freedman children between six and eighteen years of age. Many freedmen were not within accessible distance of a school, yet there was great interest in education among them. Early in 1900 the Dawes Commission received inquiries from freedmen near Nowata concerning the amount of public land to be allowed for public school purposes. A committee of freedmen selected a tract of forty acres one mile north of the village for the establishment of an industrial school for freedmen and asked how much of the tract could be set aside.[2]

Public schools could be organized only within the limits of incorporated towns. Towns such as Claremore, Fort Gibson, Vinita, and Tahlequah issued bonds for education; all of these towns had freedman schools. All school matters outside incorporated towns were under the supervision of the superintendent of education for the territory. Government officials urged attention to the rural areas and small towns so that when the tribal government ceased, the children in those areas might be provided for.[3]

The Cherokee agreement of 1902 provided that the Cherokee school fund should be used for the education of the children of Cherokee citizens according to Cherokee laws under the direction of a supervisor appointed by the secretary of the interior and an elected Cherokee school board. The necessary funds were to be appropriated by the National Council, but when it failed to do so, the secretary could direct the expenditure of the necessary funds from the Cherokee school funds. In addition to schools maintained from tribal funds, Congress appropriated funds on March 21, 1904, for maintaining, strengthening, and enlarging the tribal schools of the Cherokee and other Indian nations and for educating non-citizen children, particularly in rural areas. A similar appropriation was made on March 3, 1905, but by the 1905-06 school year, the Cherokees maintained only seventeen schools for blacks. The act of April 26, 1906, directed the secretary of the interior to assume control and direction of the tribal schools in the Indian Territory, to prescribe rules and regulations for their operation, and to retain the present system and such tribal educational officers as he chose until a public school system could be established under territorial or state government. These schools were to be operated with tribal funds. Congress also appropriated funds to provide for the education of children of parents of other than Indian blood. The country was rapidly filling up with white tenant farmers, and the new law provided education for their children as well as those of noncitizen freedmen. In the 1906-07 school year, 317 day or neighborhood schools were maintained in the Cherokee Nation, 23 of which were for blacks. The most difficult problem was to build up the schools in the rural areas. Attendance was higher and enrollment was up, the result in part of hiring more trained teachers. Records of the black schools for the first quarter of 1907 show that those were attended by both citizen and noncitizen freedmen, as well as by a few Indians.[4] Upon statehood, maintenance of these schools was assumed by the state of Oklahoma.

Enrollment in the Colored High School increased between 1901 and 1907, when there was a strong emphasis on industrial education. The school was continued until 1910, when it was sold.[5] For many years thereafter, only blacks who lived in towns large enough to maintain high schools for them had an opportunity to pursue an education beyond the elementary grades. Under federal control of the schools, the noncitizen freedmen finally gained access to the educational facilities they had been denied by the Cherokees.

Whatever gains the freedmen made in educational matters were eclipsed by their losses elsewhere. As American citizens, they found themselves faced with a new brand of racial hatred. Prejudice among the Cherokees had grown stronger as the decades passed, and language used in the Cherokee press suggests that by the 1890s the Cherokees' racial attitudes were rapidly approximating those of whites.[6] But there is little evidence that the Cherokees practiced the systematic racial discrimination that the freedmen confronted as new members of a society dominated by whites, who controlled the political offices of the new state.

Racial hatred was a basic issue in the founding of the state of Oklahoma. Delegates were elected from Oklahoma Territory and Indian Territory to attend a state constitutional convention in Guthrie, Oklahoma Territory, in November 1906. The race issue was paramount in the campaign for seats in the convention. The Democrats campaigned for separate schools, coaches, and depots and against mixed marriages and the election of blacks to public office. They favored the insertion of a jim crow provision in the constitution. The Republicans split over the race issue, and the result was the election of ninety-nine Democrats, twelve Republicans, and one Independent. Perhaps the hardest fought issue of the convention was the jim crow provision. Fearing that President Roosevelt would veto a document containing such a provision, southern politicians urged the democrat leaders of the delegates not to insert it and instead to pass a jim crow law in the first legislature of the new state. The Democrats followed the advice. When the first legislature convened on December 2, 1907, a jim crow bill was introduced immediately in both houses, and a law was passed on December 5. It went into effect, attended by racial violence, on February 16, 1908. In subsequent months, laws were passed prohibiting marriages between whites and blacks and segregating public institutions. In 1910 Oklahoma adopted the grandfather clause, which effectively disfranchised the black population of the state.[7]

The Cherokee freedmen were accustomed to segregated education, which had been the policy of the Cherokee Nation. However, they had had the vote and were accustomed to being an important factor in national and local elections. They had had access to the Cherokee court system and had sat on juries. They had held public office. Blacks in the area that had been the former Indian Territory were elected to local offices between the time of statehood and the adoption of the grandfather clause.[8]

Racial prejudice touched the freedmen's lives on all levels. In Vian, for instance, the government surveyor had set aside a plot for a cemetery. The white officials in the town fenced it, locked the gate, and forbade the freedmen to enter. Because allotments were restricted from sale, it was impossible for the freedmen to buy and get title to a plot for a cemetery. They appealed to the secretary of the interior for relief and were told by Indian inspector J. George Wright that the department could take no action, that the freedmen could purchase land from "some Indian citizen who is authorized to sell," and that they should take the matter up with the town authorities.[9]

Racial prejudice made it possible for land speculators to take advantage of the ignorant freedmen and divest them of their allotments. An act in 1904 had provided for removal of restrictions on the sale of the freedmen's surplus allotments but had retained the restrictions on their homestead allotments. Removal of restrictions had been urged by whites and Indians alike. Federal Judge John Thomas of Muskogee, for instance, believed that restrictions were thwarting the economic development of the country. One way to stimulate the economy and get money in circulation was to shake the freedmen loose from their land. "These negroes won't work if they can avoid it and as long as they have one hundred and sixty acres of land, they won't work," Thomas said. Indian leaders such as Creek Chief Pleasant Porter knew that the freedmen's ignorance of legal matters would result in a loss of their land, yet he saw no reason to protect them. After restrictions were removed on the surplus allotments of freedmen and other classes of citizens, agitation continued for the removal of restrictions on their homestead allotments. The Senate select committee that had investigated matters in the Indian Territory in 1906 heard much testimony concerning removal of restrictions and as a result recommended to the Senate that, among other things, restrictions be removed on the surplus allotments of all citizens, except minors, and on the homestead allotments of all citizens who were not of Indian blood, particularly the intermarried whites and the freedmen.[10]

Congress finally enacted legislation on May 27, 1908, removing restrictions from all allotments of not only whites and freedmen but also Indians of less than half blood, removing restrictions on the surplus allotments of Indians of one-half to three-quarters blood, and maintaining restrictions on all allotments of Indians with more than three-quarters blood. Historian Angie Debo has graphically described the means by which land speculators took advantage of the weak and ignorant and divested them of their property through flattery, fraud, and deceit. She has also described the bewilderment and fear with which the unassimilated Indians entered the new society. But, she writes, "The most unfriended were the freedmen, coddled by speculators eager to protect their 'rights' in the division of the tribal property, and regarded by the general populace with hate and envy while they owned their allotments, and with hate and contempt after they lost them."[11]

While allotment was perhaps the freedmen's most triumphant moment, their forty-year struggle ended in, at best, a jaded victory. The struggle was one of several major influences that had weakened the Cherokee Nation and had ultimately led to its dissolution. Unfortunately for the freedmen, they had contributed to the removal of the protection of the Indian nation, in which they had been tolerated and given access to the political and judicial structures as well as to a tax-free use of the land. With the allotment of lands and the destruction of their nation's protection, they were thrust into the Anglo-dominated society at a time when racial hatred was at one of the highest points in America's history.

NOTES

1. W. A. Jones to Secretary of the Interior, December 24, 1900, National Archives Record Group 48 (Records of the Department of the Interior, Office of the Secretary), Indian Territory Division, *General Incoming Correspondence, July 1898-April 1907,* 1898 file no. 169, Cherokee Nation Legislative Acts, box 351 (36a); Angie Debo, *And Still the Waters Run* (Princeton: Princeton University Press, 1972), 66-67; *Rules and Regulations Governing Mineral Leases, the Collection and Disbursement of Revenues, and the Supervision of Schools in the Indian Territory, Under the General Provisions of the Act of Congress Approved June 28, 1898 (30 Statutes, 495)* and *Regulations Concerning Education in the Indian Territory* in National Archives Record Group 48, Indian Territory Division, *Letters Received,* 252-98 Schools.

2. Andrew T. Marty to Interior Department, December 22, 1891, G. W. Vann to Commissioner of Indian Affairs, July 3, 1892, Edward

E. Hale to Commissioner, December 12, 1898, and George F. Nave to Commissioner, January 21, 1901, National Archives Record Group 75 (Records of the Bureau of Indian Affairs), *Letters Received,* 155-92, 24740-92, 47066-93, 51145-01; D. M. Browning to E. R. Rollins, November 24, 1894, National Archives Record Group 75, *Letters Sent,* Land Letter Book 232; "List of Primary Teachers Appointed for the Fall Term of 1893 and Cherokee National School Fund, Term Beginning 10th February, 1897," Indian Archives Division, Oklahoma Historical Society, *Cherokee Schools–Miscellaneous (Tahlequah); Annual Report of the Commissioner of Indian Affairs to the Secretary of the Interior* (Washington, D.C.: Government Printing Office, 1892), 254; *Annual Reports of the Department of the Interior for the Fiscal Year Ended June 30, 1900* (Washington, D.C.: Government Printing Office, 1900), 167, 168; A. Claggett to Dawes Commission, January 13, 1900, Indian Archives Division, Oklahoma Historical Society, *Dawes Commission– Cherokee.*

3. *Annual Reports of the Department of the Interior for the Fiscal Year Ended June 30, 1902* (Washington, D.C.: Government Printing Office, 1903), 2: 233; *Report of the United States Indian Inspector for the Indian Territory to the Secretary of the Interior for the Year Ended June 30, 1906* (Washington, D.C.: Government Printing Office, 1906), 22, 23, 46-47; Benjamin S. Coppoch to Frank C. Churchill, November 16, 1901, *Dawes Commission–Cherokee.*

4. *Annual Reports, 1902,* 240; *Reports of the Department of the Interior for the Fiscal Year Ended June 30, 1907* (Washington, D.C.: Government Printing Office, 1907), 2: 337, 349, 350, 351, 359; Coppoch to John J. Benedict, January 28, 1905, *Dawes Commission–Cherokee; Report of the Inspector, 1906,* 10, 11, 51; National Archives Record Group 75, *Attendance Statistics for Cherokee Day Schools in Indian Territory, 1906.*

5. *Annual Reports, 1902,* 245; *Report of the Inspector, 1906,* 59, 60; *Reports, 1907,* 2: 351, 358; Thomas Ryan to Commissioner to the Five Civilized Tribes, February 4, 1911, Indian Archives Division, Oklahoma Historical Society, *Cherokee Schools–Colored High School (Tahlequah).*

6. See, for example, *Cherokee Advocate,* August 26, 1893, October 17, 1894; 59th Cong., 2d sess., *Senate Report 5013,* pt. 1, 209.

7. *Purcell Register,* September 13, October 18, 1906; "Address by Hon. E. J. Giddings, Oklahoma City, O. T., September 22nd, 1906," Oklahoma Historical Society Library, *Fred S. Barde Collection,* Vertical File, "Negroes"; *Muskogee Cimeter,* September 19, 27, 1906; *Shawnee*

Daily Herald, September 27, October 19, 1906, February 27, December 4, 19, 1907; *Muskogee Times Democrat,* January 10, 16, December 3, 1907; *Journal of the Constitutional Convention of Oklahoma* (Muskogee: Muskogee Printing Co., 1907), 222; *Oklahoma City Weekly Times-Journal,* April 27, 1907; *Journal of the House of Representatives of the First Session of the First Legislature of Oklahoma* (Guthrie: Leader Printing and Manufacturing House, 1908), 12, 14; *Atoka Indian Citizen,* December 26, 1907.

8. See *Lexington Leader,* July 16, 1909, and *Purcell Register,* July 22, 1910.

9. J. F. Taylor to Secretary of the Interior, January 16, 1906, *Dawes Commission—Cherokee.*

10. Debo, *And Still the Waters Run,* 136, 157; 59th Cong., 2d sess., *Senate Report 5013,* pt. 1, v.

11. Debo, *And Still the Waters Run,* chaps. 4, 8, esp. pp. 181-183.

BIBLIOGRAPHY

MANUSCRIPTS

Records of the Bureau of Indian Affairs (National Archives Record
    Group 75)
    Affidavits, 1891-92
    Attendance Statistics for Cherokee Day Schools in Indian Territory,
        1906
    Irregularly Shaped Papers
    Letters Received Relating to Cherokee Citizenship, 1875-89
    Matter Concerning Attorneys' Claims against the Old Settler Chero-
        kees, 1888-95
    Records of the Office of Indian Affairs: Central Classified File, Let-
        ters Received, Letters Sent, Report Books
    Reports on Appraisement of Improvements of Cherokee Intruders,
        1893-95
    Supplementary Census Rolls, 1891-92
Records of the Cherokee Nation (Indian Archives Division, Oklahoma
    Historical Society)
    Cherokee—Citizenship (Tahlequah)
    Cherokee—Elections
    Cherokee—Ejectment (Tahlequah)
    Cherokee—Freedmen (Tahlequah)
    Cherokee—Intruders (Tahlequah)
    Cherokee—Treasurer
    Cherokee Schools—Colored High School (Tahlequah)
    Cherokee Schools—Miscellaneous (Tahlequah)
    Cherokee Volume 248
    Cherokee Volume 311
    Dawes Commission—Cherokee

Records of the Department of the Interior, Office of the Secretary
   (National Archives Record Group 48)
   Indian Division: Special File 29
   Indian Territory Division: Chickasaw Freedmen
   Indian Territory Division: General Incoming Correspondence, July
      1898-April 1907—1898 File 169, 1900 File 3203, 1902 File 2824
   Indian Territory Division: Letters Received
Records of the United States Army Continental Commands, 1821-1920
   (National Archives Record Group 393)
   Fort Gibson: Letters Received, Letters Sent
   Frontier District: 7th Army Corps and Department of Arkansas,
      Letters Received, 1865-66

MICROFILM

Documents Relating to the Negotiation of Ratified and Unratified
      Treaties with Various Indian. Tribes, 1801-1869 (National Archives
      Microfilm Publications, *Microcopy T494*), roll 7
Letters Sent by the Secretary of the Interior (National Archives Micro-
      film Publications, *Microcopy M606*), rolls 13, 20, 44, 64, 66, 68,
      69, 70, 72, 84, 86, 87, 88, 89, 90, 91, 92
Office of Indian Affairs, Letters Received (National Archives Microfilm
      Publications, *Microcopy M234*), rolls 101, 103, 104, 105, 106, 107,
      108, 110, 835, 836, 865, 867, 871, 872, 873, 875
Office of Indian Affairs, Letters Sent (National Archives Microfilm Pub-
      lications, *Microcopy M21*), rolls 79, 98, 110, 116, 118, 120, 125,
      126, 138, 144, 147, 152, 158
Office of Indian Affairs, Report Books (National Archives Microfilm
      Publications, *Microcopy M348*), rolls 15, 26, 27, 28, 32
Records of the Southern Superintendency of Indian Affairs, 1832-1870
      (National Archives Microfilm Publications, *Microcopy M640*), roll 22
Schedules of Federal Population Censuses (National Archives Microfilm
      Publications, *Microcopy M653*), roll 54

FEDERAL DOCUMENTS

United States Congress
   Congressional Record
   Statutes of the United States of America. vols. 26, 27 Washington:
      Government Printing Office, 1890, 1893
   39th Congress, 1st session, *House Executive Document 1*

41th Congress, 2d session, *House Executive Document 1*
41st Congress, 3d session, *House Executive Document 1*
42d Congress, 2d session, *House Executive Document 1*
42d Congress, 3d session, *House Executive Document 1; House Report 98*
43d Congress, 1st session, *House Executive Document 1*
43d Congress, 2d session, *House Executive Document 1*
45th Congress, 3d session, *Senate Report 744*
49th Congress, 1st session, *Senate Executive Document 82; Senate Report 1278*
49th Congress, 2d Session, *House Executive Document 1*
50th Congress, 1st session, *Senate Executive Document 83*
51st Congress, 1st session, *House Executive Document 456*
54th Congress, 1st session, *Senate Document 182*
59th Congress, 2d session, *Senate Report 5013*
United States Court of Claims. *Cases Decided in the Court of Claims of the United States.* Vols. 30, 31, 44, 46, 85. Washington, D.C.: Government Printing Office, 1896, 1910, 1912, 1938.
United States Department of the Interior. *Annual Report of the Commissioner of Indian Affairs to the Secretary of the Interior.* Washington, D.C.: Government Printing Office, 1892.
——. *Annual Report of the Commissioner of Indian Affairs to the Secretary of the Interior.* Washington, D.C.: Government Printing Office, 1893.
——. *Annual Report of the Commissioner of Indian Affairs to the Secretary of the Interior for the Year 1876.* Washington, D.C.: Government Printing Office, 1876.
——. *Annual Report of the Commissioner of Indian Affairs to the Secretary of the Interior for the Year 1887.* Washington, D.C.: Government Printing Office, 1887.
——. *Annual Report of the Commissioner of Indian Affairs to the Secretary of the Interior for the Year 1889.* Washington, D.C.: Government Printing Office, 1889.
——. *Annual Report of the Secretary of the Interior for the Fiscal Year Ended June 30, 1896.* Washington, D.C.: Government Printing Office, 1897.
——. *Annual Reports of the Department of the Interior for the Fiscal Year Ended June 30, 1900.* Washington, D.C.: Government Printing Office, 1900.
——. *Annual Reports of the Department of the Interior for the Fiscal Year Ended June 30, 1902.* Washington, D.C.: Government Printing Office, 1903.
——. *Eighth Annual Report of the Commission to the Five Civilized*

Tribes to the Secretary of the Interior for the Fiscal Year Ended
June 30, 1901. Washington, D.C.: Government Printing Office,
1901.

——. Laws, Decisions, and Regulations Affecting the Work of the Commissioner to the Five Civilized Tribes, 1893-1906. Washington,
D.C.: Government Printing Office, 1906.

——. Report of the Commission to the Five Civilized Tribes to the
Secretary of the Interior for the Year Ended June 30, 1905.
Washington, D.C.: Government Printing Office, 1905.

——. Report of the Secretary of the Interior. Washington, D.C.:
Government Printing Office, 1866.

——. Report of the Secretary of the Interior. Washington, D.C.:
Government Printing Office, 1867.

——. Report of the Secretary of the Interior. Washington, D.C.:
Government Printing Office, 1868.

——. Report of the Secretary of the Interior. Washington, D.C.:
Government Printing Office, 1869.

——. Report of the United States Indian Inspector for the Indian
Territory to the Secretary of the Interior for the Year Ended
June 30, 1906. Washington, D.C.: Government Printing Office,
1906.

——. Reports of the Department of the Interior for the Fiscal Year
Ended June 30, 1907. Washington, D.C.: Government Printing
Office, 1907.

United States Supreme Court. Cases Argued and Decided in the Supreme
Court of the United States. Lawyer's Edition, Book 56. Rochester,
N.Y.: The Lawyers' Co-operative Publishing Company, 1912.

BOOKS

Abel, Annie Heloise. The American Indian Under Reconstruction. Cleveland: Arthur H. Clark Company, 1925.

Bailey, Minnie Thomas. Reconstruction in Indian Territory: A Story of
Avarice, Discrimination, and Opportunism. Port Washington, N.Y.:
Kennikat Press, 1972.

Britton, Wiley. Memoirs of the Rebellion on the Border, 1863. Chicago:
Cushing, Thomas & Co., Publishers, 1882.

Compiled Laws of the Cherokee Nation. Tahlequah, Cherokee Nation:
National Advocate Print, 1881.

Constitution and Laws of the Cherokee Nation. St. Louis: R. & T. A.
Ennis, 1875.

Constitution and Laws of the Cherokee Nation, Published by an Act of *the National Council, 1892.* Parsons, Kan.: Foley R'y Printing Co., 1893.

Debo, Angie. *And Still the Waters Run.* Princeton: Princeton University Press, 1972.

——. *The Rise and Fall of the Choctaw Republic.* Norman: University of Oklahoma Press, 1934.

——. *The Road to Disappearance.* Norman: University of Oklahoma Press, 1941.

Foreman, Grant. *The Five Civilized Tribes.* Norman: University of Oklahoma Press, 1937.

——. ed. *A Traveler in Indian Territory: The Journal of Ethan Allen Hitchcock, Late Major-General in the United States Army.* Cedar Rapids, Iowa: Torch Press, 1930.

Fritz, Henry E. *The Movement for Indian Assimilation, 1860-1890.* Philadelphia: University of Pennsylvania Press, 1963.

Halliburton, R., Jr. *Red over Black: Black Slavery among the Cherokee Indians.* Westport, Conn.: Greenwood Press, 1977.

Hawkins, Benjamin. *Letters of Benjamin Hawkins, 1796-1806.* Collections of the Georgia Historical Society, vol. 9. Savannah: The Morning News, 1916.

Journal of the Constitutional Convention of Oklahoma. Muskogee: Muskogee Printing Co., 1907.

Journal of the House of Representatives of the First Session of the First Legislature of Oklahoma. Guthrie, Okla.: Leader Printing and Manufacturing House, 1908.

Laws and Joint Resolutions of the National Council. Passed and Adopted at the Regular Session of the National Council, 1876, 1877, and Extra Session of 1878. N.p., Printed by Authority of the National Council, 1878.

Laws of the Cherokee Nation: Adopted by the Council at Various Periods. Tahlequah, Cherokee Nation: Cherokee Advocate Office, 1852.

Laws of the Cherokee Nation Passed During the Years 1839-1867. St. Louis: Missouri Democrat Print, 1868.

McReynolds, Edwin C. *The Seminoles.* Norman: University of Oklahoma Press, 1957.

Mills, Lawrence. *Oklahoma Indian Land Laws.* St. Louis: Thomas Law Book Company, 1924.

Porter, Kenneth Wiggins. *The Negro on the American Frontier.* New York: Arno Press and the New York Times, 1971.

Ross, Norman A., ed. *Index to the Decisions of the Indian Claims Commission.* New York: Clearwater Publishing Company, 1973.

Ross, Mrs. William P., comp. *The Life and Times of William P. Ross.* Fort Smith, Ark.: Weldon & Williams, Printer, 1893.

Royce, Charles C. "The Cherokee Nation of Indians," *Fifth Annual Report of the Bureau of Ethnology*. Washington, D.C.: Government Printing Office, 1887.

Thoburn, Joseph B., and Muriel H. Wright. *Oklahoma: A History of the State and Its People*. New York: Lewis Historical Publishing Company, 1929.

Thwaites, Reuben Gold, ed. *Early Western Travels, 1748-1846*. Reprint ed. New York: AMS Press, 1966.

Wardell, Morris L. *A Political History of the Cherokee Nation, 1838-1907*. Norman: University of Oklahoma Press, 1938.

Woodward, Grace Steele. *The Cherokees*. Norman: University of Oklahoma Press, 1963.

NEWSPAPERS

Afro-American Advocate (Coffeyville, Kan.)
Cherokee Advocate (Tahlequah, Cherokee Nation)
Claremore Progress
Daily Oklahoman (Oklahoma City, Oklahoma Territory)
Fort Smith Elevator
Indian Chieftain (Vinita, Cherokee Nation)
Indian Citizen (Atoka, Choctaw Nation)
Indian Journal (Eufaula, Creek Nation)
Indian Journal (Muskogee, Creek Nation)
Langston City Herald
Lexington Leader
Muskogee Phoenix
Muskogee Times Democrat
New York Times
Purcell Register
Sallisaw Star
Shawnee Daily Herald
Webbers Falls Monitor
Weekly Times-Journal (Oklahoma City)

ARTICLES

Ballenger, T. L. "The Colored High School of the Cherokee Nation." *The Chronicles of Oklahoma* 30 (Winter 1952-53): 454-462.

Brown, Loren N. "The Dawes Commission." *The Chronicles of Oklahoma* 9 (March 1931): 71-105.

Caywood, Elzie Ronald. "The Administration of William C. Rogers, Principal Chief of the Cherokee Nation 1903-1907." *The Chronicles of Oklahoma* 30 (Spring 1952): 29-37.

Davis, J. B. "Slavery in the Cherokee Nation." *The Chronicles of Oklahoma* 11 (December 1933): 1056-1072.

Doran, Michael F. "Population Statistics of Nineteenth Century Indian Territory." *The Chronicles of Oklahoma* 53 (Winter 1975-76): 492-515.

Duncan, James W. "Interesting Ante-Bellum Laws of the Cherokees, Now Oklahoma History." *The Chronicles of Oklahoma* 6 (June 1928): 178-180.

Foreman, Carolyn Thomas. "Joseph Absalom Scales." *The Chronicles of Oklahoma* 28 (Winter 1950-51): 418-432.

Halliburton, R., Jr. "Origins of Black Slavery among the Cherokees." *The Chronicles of Oklahoma* 52 (Winter 1974-75): 483-496.

"Journal of the Adjourned Session of First General Council of the Indian Territory." *The Chronicles of Oklahoma* 3 (June 1925): 120-140.

"Journal of the General Council of the Indian Territory." *The Chronicles of Oklahoma* 3 (April 1925): 33-44.

Litton, Gaston L. "The Principal Chiefs of the Cherokee Nation." *The Chronicles of Oklahoma* 15 (September 1937): 253-270.

McLoughlin, William G. "Red Indians, Black Slavery and White Racism: America's Slaveholding Indians." *American Quarterly* 26 (October 1974): 367-385.

Meserve, John Bartlett. "Chief Lewis Downing and Chief Charles Thompson (Oochalata)." *The Chronicles of Oklahoma* 16 (September 1938): 315-325.

Morrison, James D. "The Union Pacific, Southern Branch." *The Chronicles of Oklahoma* 14 (June 1936): 173-188.

"Okmulgee Constitution." *The Chronicles of Oklahoma* 3 (September 1925): 216-228.

Warren, Hannah R. "Reconstruction in the Cherokee Nation." *The Chronicles of Oklahoma* 45 (Winter 1967-68): 180-189.

MISCELLANEOUS

Indian Archives Division, Oklahoma Historical Society. *Section X:* 10 *Indian Claims Commission* 109; 13 *Indian Claims Commission* 33.

Oklahoma Historical Society Library. Fred S. Barde Collection. Vertical file, "Negroes."

INDEX

ABOUT THE AUTHOR

Daniel E. Littlefield, Jr., professor of English at the University of Arkansas at Little Rock, is the author of numerous articles and books, including *Africans and Seminoles* (Greenwood Press, 1977).